The Psychology of Extremism

Katherine V. Aumer

Editor

The Psychology of Extremism

 Springer

Editor
Katherine V. Aumer
University of Hawai'i–West O'ahu
Kapolei, HI, USA

ISBN 978-3-030-59700-9   ISBN 978-3-030-59698-9   (eBook)
https://doi.org/10.1007/978-3-030-59698-9

This Springer imprint is published by the registered company Springer Nature Switzerland AG
The registered company address is: Gewerbestrasse 11, 6330 Cham, Switzerland

Foreword

On a sweltering July day in 2015, I found myself in a bar on the outskirts of Knoxville, Tennessee. The bar was of the divey sort, located next to a freeway with a body shop and a strip club as its closest neighbors. It was early in the day, so the two pool tables in the back of the bar were unused and the jukebox in the corner was quiet. Surrounding me around the shaded tables on the bar's front porch was a menagerie of Nazis, klansmen, Southern secessionists, and garden-variety racist, almost all of them in some way draped in a Confederate flag.

Only a few weeks earlier, the white supremacist Dylann Roof had attacked the Emanuel African Methodist Episcopal Church in Charleston, South Carolina, killing nine people as they worshipped, because, according to Roof, "black people raped white women daily" (Chicago Tribune News Sources, 2016). Radicalized in the online cesspool of white supremacy, the same ecosystem that had already produced Anders Behring Breivik in Norway and would go on to motivate Brenton Tarrant's Christchurch massacre, Robert Bowers' attack on the Tree of Life synagogue in Pittsburgh and many others, Roof came armed with 8 ammunition clips, each capable of carrying 13 rounds. Roof however had loaded them with only 11 rounds because he wanted to fire 88 shots, no more no less. In the numerology obsessed world of white supremacists, eight represents the eighth letter in the alphabet. 88 = HH. "Heil Hitler."

The racists in the bar in Knoxville were there as a response to Roof, or rather as a response to the response. The massacre in Charleston had set off a much needed discussion in America about the widespread use and profoundly racist meaning of the Confederate flag. This in turn had led to talk of tearing down Confederate monuments and the removal of the flag from federal buildings. It was a conversation that was deeply painful for many and cathartic for some. It forced a reckoning of sorts, and although grievously overdue and profoundly lacking in scope, it was a reckoning that compelled American society to explore its racist past and present, as complex, ugly, confusing, and heartrending as it was and still is. To everyone except the crowd in the bar, that is.

"They want to take our heritage," a skinhead with a face full of tattoos said in a measured manner that completely contradicted the message sent by the "Racial

Holy War" tattoo that was adorning his skull. "It's a genocide of white people and white culture." The group had just driven through downtown Knoxville, waving their flags and shouting slogans like "heritage not hate" and "southern pride." According to the main speaker of the rally, national-socialist Matthew Heimbach, the Left and the Social Justice Warriors of the world smeared the Confederate flag with their accusations of racism and bigotry. Slavery had nothing to do with it, according to them. Nor did systemic racism, the specter of Jim Crow and the groundswell of white nativist sentiment that at that moment was about to manifest into the alt-right. In their eyes it was all a ruse, designed to malign them and their ancestors by their enemies. Thus, the past had been sanitized and bleached. Scrubbed of nuance and uncomfortable notions of guilt and enduring culpability. It was easy, neat, and required no painful introspection and evaluation, not on a personal and a societal level. It was a frame of mind that had echoed through history, an ideological bait-and-switch that had informed Jim Crow laws, the rise of the KKK, Richard Nixon's Southern Strategy, and all the way to today's maligning of the Black Lives Matter movement. It was, in a word, simplicity. Blissful and comforting simplicity.

Throughout my near decade-long foray into the world of white supremacy in America, where I embedded myself as a journalist (I should point out that I never concealed my identity, my profession, and my admittedly left-leaning politics) within some of the most racist and extreme groups in the country, I encountered this yearning for simplicity in almost everyone I met. I still see it in the racist and con-spiratorial subcultures that I'm currently researching. Although there are myriad ways to be radicalized, a common factor seems to be the yearning for simplicity and reason in a capricious and befuddling world. A white supremacist's certainty that Jews are secretly controlling the world and working tirelessly toward the eradica-tion of the white race is not so different from a QAnoner's assertion that a Satanic core of Democrats are working to destroy a Messianic Donald Trump. Both these views create significance from happenstance and order from chaos. To put it simply: extremism is a way to make the confusing understandable. At its core, radicalization and the embracing of extremist ideas are a way to carve out a place for the self within a turbulent and complex world. This is of course not unique to extremists. The feeling of helplessness that often comes with living in the modern world can be deeply painful. The knowledge that we live in a society to which we as individuals are, statistically speaking, immaterial, marooned on a world which will spin just as reliably with or without us through a universe that is utterly oblivious and unmoved by our presence, is enough to cast even the strongest of us into bouts of existential malaise. However, the process of radicalization aims to divide a confusing world into easily digestible narratives of victims and oppressors, of struggle and val-iant battle.

The allure of the extremist mindset is that it lifts you out of the passive and into the active. You are no longer a hapless bystander as the world takes place around you. You are a player. One of the most infamous and influential slogans of the white supremacist movement is "We must secure the existence of our people and a future for white children." Conceived in prison by convicted white supremacist David Lane, these 14 words have become a mantra among a vast swath of white racists throughout the world, so ubiquitous that it has been reduced to the shorthand "14 words" or simply "14." These words serve as a useful reminder of the key selling point of extremism: it provides the individual with agency and offers the person a place of power and significance within a greater struggle. This call to action and the promise of a seat at the table are vital, and remarkably similar across disparate extremist movements. Just as ISIS offer its fighters an opportunity to step out of their humdrum existence in a secular society and bring about the prophesized Caliphate (McCants, 2014), white supremacists see themselves as part of a blood-line that reaches back through history and that is locked in an epic struggle for its very survival. Banking on a feeling of dispossession, these movements provide their recruits a new identity and a sense of manifest destiny. Who among us wouldn't want that?

On a muggy evening in Georgia in 2016, I stood among the hulking skinheads of the Confederate Hammerskins, a notoriously violent white supremacist group, and listened to their then leader, Chester Doles, lay out this idea plainly. Holding a hol-lowed-out horn harvested from some unknown bovine creature and filled with tepid Miller Lite, a particularly American spin on a homage to the Norse Vikings, Doles cast each and every person on that field—they were overwhelmingly male—as play-ers in an epic struggle. "We are modern day Vikings," he explained to the heavily tattooed, extensively armed, and precariously drunk crowd. "We are the alpha males of today. We are men with courage and have great pride in our European heritage. We are husbands and fathers. We are protectors and providers of our families. We are proud, white men." He then explained how the Vikings would tie a lock of their wives' or daughters' hair around their weapons before going into battle and that they should do the same, although he advised that they use AR-15s rather than swords and axes.

Looking around I could tell how his words resonated with what appeared to be a crowd of low education and income. He was offering them a choice. When they looked in the mirror they could choose to see a helpless cog in a vast machine, lost to the whims of a capricious system, or they could see a warrior; the culmination of their bloodline and a shaper of their own future. All of them had chosen the latter.

Interestingly, this is a more positive approach to radicalization than what others have pointed to as common methods of individual radicalization. For instance, the National Institute of Justice at the US Justice Department claims that "the radical-ization process often involves embracing a terrorist belief system or narrative that identifies particular others or groups as 'enemies' and justifies engaging in violence against them" (Smith, 2018). While this is no doubt a vital part of the radicalization process, my experience often suggested that it was not the initial step. Rather than creating enemies, the white supremacists I spent time with seemed to base not only their radicalization efforts, but also the continuing maintenance of their networks, on building a positive sense of community. The groups I researched tended to define themselves by who they were, not who they were against. The Hammerskins con-sidered themselves a tribe. The KKK often saw themselves as family and kin. The neo-fascist group Proud Boys call themselves a fraternity. These groups differ vastly in ideology and methods, but they all emphasize forging of internal bonds before fighting an enemy.

Providing new members with a sense of belonging, an ideological family, is imperative in the radicalization process, and both my experiences taking part in the lives of white supremacists and the research bear this out. In fact, a study by the Kanishka Project in Canada, the Arc of Terrorism and Office for Security and Counter-Terrorism research programs in the United Kingdom, and the Department of Homeland Security from 2015 cite feelings of lack of meaning, wanting status, and wanting to belong as key risk factors for radicalizing to violent extremism (National Institute of Justice, 2015). An "us versus them" worldview and the feeling of being under threat are also cited, but it is clear that extremist groups prey on feelings of isolation and lack of self-worth. You don't just go up to someone and start blaming the Jews for the ills of the world. First you make the person feel heard, respected, and valued.

In his book about growing up in rural Appalachia, *Hillbilly Elegy,* the author J.D. Vance writes "There is a lack of agency here—a feeling that you have little control over your life and a willingness to blame everyone but yourself." While this is both a facile and unfair description of the inhabitants of Appalachia, it does point to the sense of impotency and anger that fuels the wave of right-wing populism that has bedeviled democracies all over the world of late. In America in particular, a confounding rise in the mortality rates of white, middle-aged men raises many red flags. A study in the *Proceedings of the National Academy of Sciences* attributed the trend to what they called "despair deaths," which are suicides, drug overdoses, and alcohol-related diseases (Bernstein & Achenbach, 2015). In a report for the *Commonwealth Fund* David Squires and David Blumenthal write "On a range of social and economic indicators, middle-aged whites have been falling behind in the 21st century. They have lower incomes, fewer are employed, and fewer are married" (Khazan, 2016). In her book *The Politics of Resentment*, political scientist Kathy Cramer explains how rural Americans often feel disrespected and tread on by elites who do not understand or care about them. Taken together these paint a picture of an electorate ripe for radicalization, and millions of column inches have been written to explain how this resentment and desperation gave rise to Donald Trump. While it is an unfair oversimplification to blame the presidency of Donald Trump on angry Appalachians, the frustration and anger felt in many parts of America due to deindustrialization, opioid addiction, lack of education, and employment opportunities have provided fertile ground for far-right extremist recruiters. However, it is far from the whole story.

When Caleb Cain dropped out of college after three semesters and moved back to his small Appalachian hometown, he struggled with bouts of depression and loneliness (Roose, 2019). Many of his friends had left town and Cain felt disconnected, both from the friends he had left in college and from the community he had returned to. Seeking a way out of his depression he began watching self-help videos on YouTube. Initially his viewing habits were mostly benign, videos with tips on how to cope with loneliness, but he soon found himself drawn to YouTubers whose ideas on mental health and happiness had a more sinister tone. He discovered Stefan

Molyneux, the self-professed philosopher and at the time hugely popular YouTube personality. Molyneux spent a lot of time talking about masculinity and what it meant to be a man. He danced up to the line of acceptability, but Cain liked that about him. Raised in the era of online gaming, Cain had an affinity for those who pushed boundaries simply for the joy of pushing. Molyneux talked extensively about feminism. He was a men's right advocate and claimed that feminism was socialism and that modern gender roles had been forced onto society by the Left and that it was holding young men back. The more Cain watched the more he agreed with what he saw and the more he agreed the happier the YouTube algorithms were to feed him ever more content. Via Molyneux, Cain was introduced to a host of right-wing influencers, all thriving within the permissive ecosystem of YouTube. He discovered Paul Joseph Watson, a conspiracy monger and alt-right pundit who would later be banned from Facebook for being a "dangerous individual," Lauren Southern, a white nationalist with a huge audience, and Jordan Peterson, a Canadian men's rights activist. None of these were the rabid, foaming-at-the-mouth blow-hards one might associate with white supremacists, rather they presented themselves as rational, tongue-in-cheek iconoclasts who weren't afraid of speaking truth to power. Caleb was enthralled. In an interview with the *New York Times*, Caleb explained that "When I found this stuff, I felt like I was chasing uncomfortable truths. I felt like it was giving me power and respect and authority" (Roose, 2019).

When I first met Caleb a couple of years ago, he explained to me the heady feeling of having your world explained to you, to watch the pieces fall into place and to see, finally, what your role in that world is. In a real sense, his world had been made simple for him. He was not to blame for his troubles; feminists were, socialism and the Left were. I met Caleb when he had made his way out of the morass he had sunk into, and since then he had achieved a clarity that he wanted to share with others. He recognized the factors that had pushed him into his online radicalization. He was honest about having had troubling and deeply offensive beliefs, and assigns blame to both himself and the online snake oil salesmen that litter the internet, waiting to pounce on kids like himself. However, he was most disturbed about the ease with which YouTube had facilitated his descent into political extremism. While the algorithms that decide what video you watch next are vastly complex and ever changing, the programming that governed the site at the time of Caleb's radicalization was primed to encourage users to delve deeper into whatever rabbit hole they currently found themselves. Also, as Becca Lewis at Data & Society revealed in her report Alternative Influence: Broadcasting the Reactionary Right on YouTube, political influencers on YouTube had created an "Alternative Influence Network (AIN)," an alternative media system that adopts the techniques of brand influencers to build audiences and "sell" them political ideology (Lewis, 2018). In her report, Lewis claimed that YouTube had become "the single most important hub by which an extensive network of far-right influencers profit from broadcasting propaganda to young viewers." She also concluded that "YouTube monetizes influence for everyone, regardless of how harmful their belief systems are. The platform, and its parent company, have allowed racist, misogynist, and harassing content to remain online—and in many cases, to generate advertising revenue—as long as it does not explicitly include slurs." Of course, at the time, Caleb and the thousands of other young men, just like him who were tuning into increasingly extreme content provided to them by the world's largest video sharing website, had no idea that their radicalization was incentivized and monetized. They just felt seen and understood for the first time. They had gone through the looking glass. In the parlance of online extremism, Caleb had been redpilled.

In the 1999 movie *The Matrix* the main character Neo is offered a chance to see the world as it really is. A mysterious stranger that seems to understand him in a way nobody else does offers him a choice of two pills: "You take the blue pill—the story ends, you wake up in your bed and believe whatever you want to believe. You take the red pill—you stay in Wonderland and I show you how deep the rabbit-hole goes." Since then "taking the red pill" or "being redpilled" has become shorthand for a political awakening. In the world of modern extremism, radicalization itself has become a meme.

The dawn of online culture has caused a seismic shift in not only the way extremist groups organize and recruit. While historically only a small part of the right-wing extremist movement has belonged to organized groups, the movement itself was dominated by influential individuals and groups. Organizations like Aryan Nations, The Hammerskin Nation, and National Alliance were powerful entities that to a large degree dictated the tone and tenor of the right-wing movement. By contrast, the alt-right was conceived by a fractious coalition of online trolls and racist contrarians and never coalesced into a cohesive movement in anything but the loosest sense of the word. While the extremists of old were forced into making some kind of personalized buy-in—a real mailing address for newsletters or actually showing up to group meetings—the alt-right required no such thing and encouraged a wholly nihilistic way of political engagement. Their vocabulary and frames of reference were heavily influenced by online and gaming culture, and the movement found a vast cache of adherents in the legion of disaffected young men spending their days engaging with the world through the flickering light of a computer screen. Borrowing heavily from popular culture and gaming, the movement developed a nomenclature not just tailor-made to entice the disaffected men who came to it, but also to push them further. Those who had been redpilled often found themselves "blackpilled" meaning that they had moved beyond political awakening and discovered that the world is irredeemably broken. In the world of right-wing extremism, the black pill means realizing that the system will always be rigged against white men. The black pill then becomes a gateway to mass murderers like Anders Breivik, Dylann Roof, Brenton Tarrant, and Robert Bowers. In the bleak and dystopic world of incels, the black pill is the realization that the world has no use for men like them, and that there is no remedy except death, their own or that of others.

The key here is the ease with which a shorthand for radicalization has developed. A new online ecosystem has emerged where for the most part unaffiliated extremists share memes, conspiracy theories, and methods designed to fast-track the radicalization process and facilitate the dehumanization of everyone who does not belong to the movement. It is from this subculture that has risen not only the infamous mass murderers mentioned above but also a new generation of extremists, determined to accelerate the race war that they pine for. However, I would argue that as different the modern right-wing extremist movement is from earlier incarnations, it is still driven by the same fundamental impulses that drove others before it and that drives other violent extremist ideologies: belonging.

In March 2019, before he massacred 50 people in Christchurch, New Zealand, the white supremacist Brenton Tarrant posted his rambling manifesto to the message board site 8chan. The same site was used by Patrick Crucius before he killed 22 people at an El Paso Walmart and so did John Earnest before opening fire inside a synagogue in Poway, California. 8chan had become a breeding ground for violent extremists and a cesspool of murderous fantasies. The website's tagline was "Embrace Infamy," and that was exactly the goal of the men posting their manifestos there. As much as their predecessors and their cohorts in other violent extremist movements, this new generation of white supremacists yearn for meaning and belonging. This iteration of the movement provides a way for them to transcend the fleeting meaninglessness of their lives and step into a pantheon of warriors and martyrs, aided by a steady numbing to the realities of mass violence and the dehumanization of their alleged enemies. As such, this version of the right-wing extremist movement shares many key aspects of Islamic extremism as espoused by ISIS. Much like Chester Doles in George implored his Hammerskin members to take part in a generational struggle, the modern right-wing mass murderers yearn to place themselves within a larger battle. The language and methods are different, but the need to belong and to matter is the same.

There are of course many roads that lead to Rome and people come to violent extremism in a myriad of ways and for different reasons. Some, like many of the KKK members I met, are born into the movement, raised in a generational hatred that can be difficult to get out of. I once attended a KKK funeral with a man who, after having threatened to kill me at least twice, explained to me how he was introduced to the Klan by his father when he was nine back in the 1970s and made to do terrible acts that he didn't want to talk about. "Nobody should make a child do what I had to do," he sobbed loudly while a cross burned behind him. Others seek it out as an escape from loneliness, or as a lark that over time can become deadly serious. Plenty of alt-right extremists have claimed that they joined the movement "for the lulz," internet speak for "as a joke," drawn to the offensive, boundary pushing mayhem of internet message boards. Yet others drop into the rabbit hole out of curiosity, falling for the enticing distortions of YouTube charlatans or bigoted pseudo-scholars, and antisemitic revisionists and eugenicists who preach racism and hatred concealed in garbage science. Then there are those who are filled with violent fantasies, those who care less for politics than for the prospect of mayhem, murder, and power through terror. Although they are relatively few compared to the others, these are the ones who end up in the news: the Tarrants, Breiviks, and Roofs of the world.

Yet as different as their motivations are, there is one factor that is reliably the same with only a few exceptions. The trolls of the alt-right, the mass shooters, the incels, the ISIS warriors, the neo-Nazis, and anti-government militia members are almost always men. It is impossible to underestimate the gender gap in violent extremism. Although there are exceptions to the rule, violent extremist spaces are overwhelmingly masculine. When the FBI compiled a list of active shooters in America between 2010 and 2018 it revealed that only 9 out of 250 shooters were women (FBI, 2019). Islamic extremism is almost exclusively governed by men and although there are many examples of women undertaking operational roles in jihadi organizations—ISIS, Jaish al-Fatah, and Jabhat Fateh al-Sham are all known to use female fighters—it has been reported that these women lack agency within the larger organization (Women in International Security, 2017). The far right, certainly in America, is utterly dominated by men. Women play a key role although they are more often than not reduced to archetypes rather than human beings with interests of their own. There are women in the movement, some of them even have prominent roles and, in the influencer-driven ecosystem of modern online culture, they command large followings. Female superstars of the alt-right like Faith Goldy, Lauren Southern, and Brittany Pettibone have all been vastly influential. Likewise the anti-Islam bigots Pamela Geller and Laura Loomer have both built influential personal brands. However, their impact on the movement has rarely been to empower women, rather to perpetuate harmful gender stereotypes that reduce women and equate progress with decline, or as in the cases of Geller and Loomer, use the term feminism as a cudgel to attack Islam through distortions and generalizations. In an interview on the alt-right podcast Hanging Chads, Faith Goldy explained that "there has been in the past 50, 60 years, an organized campaign to tear down the institutions that provide order outside of government. And that is mainly the family." This campaign's goal, Goldy asserted, is to "deconstruct man and woman as they are intended to be" (Eyes on the Right, 2017, para. 3). Lauren Southern, an alt-right darling and white nationalist, has equated feminism with female supremacy and claimed that it makes victims of men (Southern, 2015). Brittany Sellner (2019), a far-right men's rights activist who is married to white nationalist Martin Sellner, has described feminism as a "war on men," and said that "It comes as no surprise to me at this point that movements such as the men's rights have gained such popularity. Men are tired of being shamed for their inherent qualities such as masculinity and pigeonholed as the perpetrators of all the world's problems." One might argue that at least part of the reason why these women have gained popularity in such a masculine space is because they espouse a particularly reactionary view of gender that resonates with those who feel threatened or disturbed by progressive values and equal rights. These women serve a role as radicalizers because they not only confirm the prejudices about society in general and feminism in particular that the young men who fall into these rabbit holes often hold, but by nature of being women who preach anti-feminism, they give them legitimacy. In a sense, these women only remain influential so long as they are oppressing themselves.

In general, women are ciphers within a far-right movement that is often incredibly hostile to them. The problem of domestic violence in extremist circles could fill many books, and many of the women who have left the movement leave with stories of violence and abuse. This is no doubt the result of a movement that is incredibly violent, rife with alcohol and substance abuse, and overwhelmingly masculine. In terms of the radicalization process however, women serve different purposes to different groups. In the hypermasculine fraternity that is the neo-fascist group Proud Boys, women are banned because they are a distraction to the valuable bonding between men who worship "western culture." To them feminism has softened the Western Man and made him weak. As a tonic, the Proud Boys promise their recruits male companionship. The absence of women is a major selling point.

The incel movement is fueled exclusively by hatred toward women and feminism, no doubt concealing a much greater self-loathing by its members. To them women are evil and calculating, winners of a genetic lottery that has made perennial losers out of them. Far from all incels harbor violent fantasies toward women and only a miniscule fraction act on those fantasies, but incels are behind several brutal mass killings. In their world, failure with women and morbid self-loathing are badges of honor, worn with pride. Their redpilling moment is when they realize that they will never be loved. Their blackpilling moment is when they see that they never stood a chance in the first place.

To white supremacists, women fill several roles. They are a weaker sex that needs to be protected by the barbarian hordes, they are walking wombs to perpetuate the white race, and they are enemies whose fight for equality will no doubt mean the demise of said race. Anti-feminism, the desire for reactionary gender roles, is a powerful recruitment tool to a generation of men that often struggles with figuring out what it means to be a man. This is a moment when the fight for equal rights for women, people of color, and the LGBTQ community has gained acceptance throughout large parts of society. It has exposed deep structural and cultural inequalities and shown us how behavior once accepted and even encouraged is harmful and damaging. Much like how recent events have given us an opportunity to face this country's racist past, we are also grappling with society's misogynistic past and present. Like the former, the latter also provides fertile ground for extremist recruitment. There is significant overlap between the manosphere, the incel movement, and the white supremacist movement. All of them share a profound feeling of victimization and of living in a world they no longer recognize and are no longer welcome in. It is this sense of aggrievement that often leads young men to groups and ideologies where they feel heard and where their anger is validated, a movement that will allow them to look in the mirror without a confused face staring back at them.

At their most basic level, extremist groups offer their members a world that is tidy and neat. They abhor progress as weakness because it creates confusion, and confusion is the antithesis of the extremist ideal: simplicity. The modern world, with its equality and progressive norms, is antithetical to the simpler times for which extremists pine. It is the same yearning found in Donald Trump's slogan "Make America Great Again." While utterly unspecific, as most slogans are, it implies that there was once a better time and that something nefarious and pernicious has eroded our society and taken it away from those better times when things were great. It is pointless, as I have learned through years of painful effort, to point out that this ideal time never existed. There was never a time when women were universally happy in their subservience nor is it true that, as a participant at a Richard Spencer rally in Alabama once told me, "blacks were happy during Jim Crow because they knew where they stood." Yet this hardly matters. Extremism is never about altruism or the greater good. It is not about making society better for everyone so much as it is to make it bearable for yourself. It is an eminently egoistic frame of mind, however much the zealots try to convince us otherwise. The world of the extremist is a zero sum game where the progress of some comes at a cost for others. It is a world where if black lives matter, then white lives matter slightly less, where if women gain rights men lose theirs. It can be an enticingly simple world to live in.

Anti-Defamation League's Center on Extremism   Vegas Tenold,
New York, NY, USA

References

Bernstein, L., & Achenbach, J. (2015, November 2). A group of middle-aged whites in the U.S. is dying at a startling rate. *The Washington Post*. Retrieved from https://www.washingtonpost.com/national/health-science/a-group-of-middle-aged-american-whites-is-dying-at-a-startling-rate/2015/11/02/47a63098-8172-11e5-8ba6-cec48b74b2a7_story.html

Chicago Tribune News Services. (2016, December 10). Dylann Roof's confession, journal details racist motivation for church killings. *Chicago Tribune*. Retrieved from https://www.chicagotribune.com/nation-world/ct-dylann-roof-charleston-shooting-20161209-story.html

Eyes on the Right. (2017, November 25). Faith Goldy preaches the gospel of anti-feminism on alt-right podcast. *Angry White Men*. Retrieved from https://angrywhitemen.org/2017/11/25/faith-goldy-preaches-the-gospel-of-anti-feminism-on-alt-right-podcast/

FBI. (2019, July 3). *2000 to 2018 active shooter incidents*. Retrieved from https://www.fbi.gov/file-repository/active-shooter-incidents-2000-2018.pdf/view

Khazan, O. (2016, January 29). Why are so many middle-aged white Americans dying? *The Atlantic*. Retrieved from https://www.theatlantic.com/health/archive/2016/01/middle-aged-white-americans-left-behind-and-dying-early/433863/

Lewis, R. (2018, September 18). *Alternative influence: Broadcasting the reactionary right on YouTube*. Data & Society. Retrieved from https://datasociety.net/library/alternative-influence/

McCants, W. (2014, November 5). *Islamic state invokes prophecy to justify its claim to caliphate*. Brookings. Retrieved from https://www.brookings.edu/blog/markaz/2014/11/05/islamic-state-invokes-prophecy-to-justify-its-claim-to-caliphate/

National Institute of Justice. (2015, July 28–30). *Radicalization and violent extremism: Lessons learned from Canada, the U.K. and the U.S.* U.S. Department of Justice. Retrieved from https://www.ncjrs.gov/pdffiles1/nij/249947.pdf

Roose, K. (2019, June 8). The making of a YouTube radical. *The New York Times*. Retrieved from https://www.nytimes.com/interactive/2019/06/08/technology/youtube-radical.html

Sellner, B. (2019, October 5). *The War on Men*. [Video File]. YouTube. Retrieved from https://www.youtube.com/watch?v=pBjMuiIQxFg&feature=emb_logo

Smith, A. G. (2018, June). *How radicalization to terrorism occurs in the United States: What research sponsored by the National Institute of Justice tells us*. U.S. Department of Justice. Retrieved from https://www.ncjrs.gov/pdffiles1/nij/250171.pdf

Southern, L. (2015, April 8). *Lauren Southern: Why I am not a Feminist*. [Video File]. YouTube. Retrieved from https://www.youtube.com/watch?time_continue=56&v=vNErQFmOwq0&feature=emb_logo

Women in International Security. (2017, May). *Women in Jihadist Organizations: Victims or Terrorists*. Retrieved from https://wiisglobal.org/wp-content/uploads/2016/07/5th-WIIS-Policy-Brief-v3-5-26-17.pdf

Preface

Extremist ideologies and violence wax and wane over time. Between 2015 and 2019, the Institute for Economics and Peace has noted a 320% increase in far-right terrorism in Western Europe, North America, and Oceania (Institute for Economics and Peace, 2019). Although terrorism and extremism can be an extension of any ideology, the rise in far-right extremism in the U.S. is especially concerning. The U.S. covers a broad geographical area populated by people from a variety of ethnic and racial backgrounds, and it is estimated that Whites will be a minority of the U.S. population by 2045 (Fey, 2018). Far-right extremism can be associated with broad ideologies rooted in the ongoing politics of a given geographical area. However, the common thread throughout most far-right extremism is nationalism, authoritarianism, nativism, and racism (Institute for Economics and Peace, 2019). The recent rise in far-right extremism, especially in the U.S., may have far reaching consequences not only to the growing diverse population of those within the U.S., but to those in other democratic nations.

This book was initially written and compiled before the 2020 U.S. presidential election. Since that time, much has occurred. This preface both acknowledges the rapidly changing events happening in the U.S. and provides readers with a guide to the chapters in this book and their respective application to these events. One particular event occurred on January, 6, 2021. Hours after President Donald Trump told his supporters that "…if you don't fight like hell, you're not going to have a country anymore," the U.S. Capitol with senators, representatives, and the vice president in it was attacked (Savage, 2021). Afterwards, some characterized this attack as a protest (Brown, 2021). However, the brandishing of weapons, breaking of windows, violence, placing of pipe bombs, and subsequent deaths suggest that the term "protest" may not be the most accurate or appropriate description of events. Although the investigation of the attack on the U.S. Capitol is ongoing, this event seems to have had some coordinated planning by far-right extremist groups such as the Proud Boys (Feuer, 2021). U.S. senators, representatives, and the vice president had to be evacuated to safe hiding places to protect them against threats to their lives. While this all happened, the president of the U.S. watched the chaos unfold at the U.S. Capitol from the White House free of fear from harm or danger (Parker, Darsey, & Rucker, 2021). It is unclear what he was thinking while news of violence from his supporters crept his way. His Tweets at the time suggest that maybe he didn't want the police to be harmed; however he expressed no concern for the senators, representatives, or the vice president (Sherman, 2021). The mayhem that ensued left 5 dead, many wounded (at least 140 police officers), and many in the nation shocked and disgusted (Healy, 2021; Jackman, 2021). Investigators are still discovering what happened that day. Among the hoard of insurgents that descended upon the U.S. Capitol were members of far-right extremist groups who brandished White supremacy logos and insignias while taking selfies during the attack and posting them on social media (Neilson & McFall-Johnsen, 2021). By their side were a number of current and former members of the military, CEOs of companies, business owners, bartenders, construction workers, advertising consultants, and even a gold medal Olympian (Hanna, Polantz, & Cohen, 2021; Valentino-DeVries et al., 2021). This seeming diversity among Trump's supporters only calls more attention to their averageness. These attackers came from various strata in society and were pulled together by a shared belief that they were defending the work of their president and a shared desire to be part of his significance (Barry, McIntire, & Rosenberg, 2021).

Research suggests that the desire to achieve significance is one of the key factors leading to extremism (e.g., Kruglanski et al., 2014). In Chaps. 3 (by Seyle and Besaw) and 4 (by Aumer and Erickson) of this book, the complex relationship between seeking significance, identity, and emotions in extremism is discussed. Many seek significance among their peers and recognition by their societies as worthy heros. The rhetoric and myth of victimization becomes a part of politics and fuels the absurdity in the arguments. However, in the moment of any drama, whether it be called a protest, fight, battle, or attack, the absurdity of the situation is not recognized as such, but instead takes on the guise of righteous indignation. The battle needs enemies, an "other," a target. People's ability to become divided over both significant and insignificant differences can stem from genuine issues and injustice. Nevertheless, some of this division also stems from a more superficial root of group identification. Identity becomes an anchor for values, emotions, and actions. Identification with a group can have an overwhelming grip on perceptions and feelings (Silverstein & Flamenbaum, 1989). While playing out one's identity, one's role in a group, a benign action by a fellow group member may be seen in a very different light that evokes much more dangerous emotions if done by someone perceived to be an enemy. These emotions, both positive and negative, can lead to quixotic paths. Love, which can be so unifying, may divide when it is invested in nationalistic and conspiratorial theories. Hate, which can be so damaging, may create bonds between those who find themselves targeting the same foe. There is no doubt that many of those in the U.S. Capitol attack on January 6, 2021, were attempting to play out their roles—a natural extension of their identity—with the calamity and error of their behavior obfuscated by their loyalty to a party and a president.

Only a small minority of the 74 million people who voted for U.S. President Donald Trump in 2020 sought to attend the U.S. Capitol attack. But some supporters of Trump who did not attend and judged it to be a terrible event responded by blaming Antifa for it (Herndon, 2021). Antifa is an anti-fascist movement composed of highly decentralized autonomous groups of people that aims to end right-wing extremism through either nonviolent or violent means (LaFree, 2018). Although investigations are ongoing, many sources have indicated that the photos of the event used by some to claim Antifa participation are not supported (Staff, 2021). Others sought to excuse the attack by comparing it with violence seen at retail stores during protests over the police killing of George Floyd. This false equivalence between the nation's capital and its retail stores brings to light how Trump's supporters may equate their government and democracy as places of merchandise. Accordingly, many who have since been charged with crimes for their roles in the attack have attempted, as if at a retail store, to purchase clemency and pardons from Trump (Schmidt & Vogel, 2021). The inability to see the extreme nature of the U.S. Capitol attack, to see its perniciousness and severe consequences for democracy, speaks to the viewpoint that many far-right-wing extremists have asserted about the U.S. for decades: The U.S. is theirs, and as the owners, they can define and defend it as they see fit. Historically, unity in the U.S. has not come by dismantling White supremacy but by fortifying, ignoring, or rebranding it (Chait, 2021).

Recently, elements of the White supremacist movement have adopted the QAnon conspiracy theory. The QAnon conspiracy theory holds that many Democrats and Hollywood stars are secretly a cabal of Satan worshipers who are leading an underground child sex trafficking ring (Roose, 2021). As ridiculous as the QAnon conspiracy sounds, it is not an unfamiliar political strategy. Historically, dehumanization and fantasy have been employed to annihilate targets who were seen as threats to power (Parramore, 2021). Women were accused of being servants of the Devil during the Salem Witch Trials. Blacks and the mentally ill were judged to be inferior and even subhuman by eugenicists during the European and U.S. eugenics movement. Jews were depicted as aliens in Nazi school curriculum. The evocation of fantasy and the use of dehumanization to target, attack, and expel enemies are not unusual in human history (Romano, 2020). The use of reframing and the setting of extremist psychology within the narratives that extremists use are examined in Chap. 2 of this book by Roseman, Rudolph, Steele, and Katz. The QAnon conspiracy, the conservative rhetoric, and the fight to maintain White supremacy are likely to be an ongoing battle in the U.S., and understanding the narratives and psychology that help maintain their hold will become more important in determining how to overcome its spiral toward increasing violence and chaos.

When conflict is witnessed, it can be convenient to step away and distance oneself from the impending damage and strife. However, for many in the U.S., the attack on the U.S. Capitol has extended into their personal relationships. Families and marriages have fallen apart because of these extreme ideological shifts in society. After the attack, some who saw their mothers, fathers, friends, or significant others posting selfies on social media that were taken while attacking the U.S. Capitol found themselves reporting their loved ones to authorities (Paul, 2021). These battles of extremism are not just being played out on a global stage, but also within private spheres. In Chap. 5, Hatfield and Rapson discuss useful ways to handle confrontations, ranging from the benign to the more disquieting, which can happen when discussing politics with family members. These kinds of conversations and subsequent relational upheavals due to differences in political beliefs and ideologies have long been a part of the history in the U.S., as is the idea that the racism professed by many far-right extremists is merely an alternative viewpoint and that anger expressed over racial injustice is an overreaction. Much of the rhetoric and ideology espoused in the relational spheres stems from a larger structural group. Whether individuals experience or witness extremism in their personal relationships, it is important to identify and investigate the systematic support and proliferation of these ideologies to make informed policies to prevent and de-radicalize. Conor Seyle and Clayton Besaw (in Chap. 3) provide insights and evidence-based procedures that can help individuals, organizations, and governmental institutions de-radicalize by considering the psychological group needs of individuals who seek membership in extremist groups, including White power extremists.

White supremacy and White privilege are sometimes challenged by conservatives because they threaten the conveniences and privileges of being White. The changing racial and ethnic landscape of the U.S., and its impact on the identity and feelings of those who are White and of far-right extremists, is discussed in Chap. 4 by Aumer and Erickson. Fieder, Schahbasi, and Huber touch upon the origins of these tribalistic attitudes in Chap. 6. All of the chapters in this volume provide insight into how any of us can be vulnerable to the appeal of extremism. Self-reflection and empathy can help us avoid being drawn in by nationalistic and polarizing rhetoric. Contact with communities that bolster division has become easier with the internet and availability of social media. This book provides a foundation upon which more research regarding the powerful influences of emotions, identity, and relationships can grow and help prevent further damage. The storming of the U.S. Capitol on January 6, 2021, will not be the last attack on democracy or on the growing diversity of the U.S. The U.S. Capitol attack exemplifies the power of populism coupled with the ease of mass gatherings facilitated by the use of social media. Counterterrorism experts have warned that violent extremism has become "part of the cultural mainstream" and could pose a threat for "10–20 years" (Johnson, 2021). While some may have seen the U.S. Capitol attack as a protest, still others characterize it as a failed coup (Graham, 2021). Experts acknowledge that coup events have declined over the past several decades. However the coup events and attempts that are occurring seem to be increasingly targeting democratic states (Besaw et al., 2019). For many, the U.S. Capitol attack is a reminder of the fragility and vulnerability of democratic processes, everywhere. Extremism and violence are likely to remain a part of our human history, but with continued dedication to understanding the psychology of extremism, we may find better ways to avoid future harm and our own self-destruction.

Kapolei, HI, USA   Katherine Aumer

References

Barry, D., McIntire, M., & Rosenberg, M. (2021, January 9). 'Our president wants us here': The mob that stormed the Capitol. *The New York Times*. Retrieved from https://www.nytimes.com/2021/01/09/us/capitol-rioters.html?smid=em-share

Besaw, C., Frank, M., Keels, E., Benson, J., Filitz, J., & Powell, J. (2019, April). *Annual risk of coup report. One earth future*. Retrieved February 6, 2021, from https://www.oefresearch.org/sites/default/files/documents/publications/Risk_of_Coup_Report_2019.pdf

Brown, S. (2021, January 13). Trump calls for 'no violence' as more armed protests reportedly planned for US, state capitols. *CNET*. Retrieved from https://www.cnet.com/news/more-armed-protests-planned-for-us-state-capitols-fbi-and-police-reportedly-warn/

Chait, J. (2021, January 21). Why are conservatives so angry Biden denounced white supremacy? *New York Magazine Intelligencer*. Retrieved from https://nymag.com/intelligencer/2021/01/why-are-conservatives-angry-biden-denounced-white-supremacy.html

Feuer, A. (2021, February 5). Did the proud boys help coordinate the Capitol riot? Yes, U.S. suggests. *The New York Times*. Retrieved from https://www.nytimes.com/2021/02/05/nyregion/proud-boys-capitol-riot-conspiracy.html

Fey, W. H. (2018, March 14). *The US will become 'minority white' in 2045, census projects*. Retrieved February 6, 2021, from https://www.brookings.edu/blog/the-avenue/2018/03/14/the-us-will-become-minority-white-in-2045-census-projects/

Graham, D. A. (2021, January 6). This is a coup. *The Atlantic*. Retrieved from https://www.theatlantic.com/ideas/archive/2021/01/attempted-coup/617570/

Hanna, J., Polantz, K., & Cohen, M. (2021, January 15). Key arrests so far from the Capitol riot. *CNN*. Retrieved from https://www.cnn.com/2021/01/13/politics/notable-arrests-capitol/index.html

Healy, J. (2021, January 11). These are the 5 people who died in the Capitol riot. *The New York Times*. Retrieved from https://www.nytimes.com/2021/01/11/us/who-died-in-capitol-building-attack.html

Herndon, A. W. (2021, January 17). How republicans are warping reality around the Capitol attack. *The New York Times*. Retrieved from https://www.nytimes.com/2021/01/17/us/politics/Capitol-conspiracy-theories-blm-antifa.html?auth=login-google

Institute for Economics and Peace. (2019, November). *Global Terrorism Index 2019: Measuring the impact of terrorism*. Retrieved February 6, 2021, from https://www.economicsandpeace.org/wp-content/uploads/2020/08/GTI-2019web.pdf

Jackman, T. (2021, January 27). Police union says 140 officers injured in Capitol riot. *The Washington Post*. Retrieved from https://www.washingtonpost.com/local/public-safety/police-union-says-140-officers-injured-in-capitol-riot/2021/01/27/60743642-60e2-11eb-9430-e7c77b5b0297_story.html

Johnson, K. (2021, February 4). Domestic extremism has become 'mainstream,' could threaten American life for 20 years. *U.S.A. Today*. Retrieved from https://www.usatoday.com/story/news/politics/2021/02/04/domestic-terrorism-could-pose-terrifying-threat-next-20-years/4387600001/

Kruglanski, A. W., Gelfand, M. J., Bélanger, J. J., Sheveland, A., Hetiarachchi, M., & Gunaratna, R. (2014). The psychology of radicalization and deradicalization: How significance quest impacts violent extremism. *Political Psychology, 35*, 69–93.

LaFree, G. (2018). Is Antifa a terrorist group? *Society, 55*, 248–252.

Neilson, S., & McFall-Johnsen, M. (2021, January 6). Several groups of extremists stormed the Capitol on Wednesday. Here are some of the most notable individuals, symbols, and groups. *Business Insider*. Retrieved from https://www.businessinsider.com/hate-symbols-and-extremist-groups-at-the-us-capitol-siege-2021-1

Parker, A., Darsey, J., & Rucker, P. (2021, January 11). Six hours of paralysis: Inside Trump's failure to act after a mob stormed the Capitol. *The Washington Post*. Retrieved from https://www.washingtonpost.com/politics/trump-mob-failure/2021/01/11/36a46e2e-542e-11eb-a817-e5e7f8a406d6_story.html

Parramore, L. S. (2021, January 11). Like QAnon's Capitol rioters, the Nashville bomber's lizard people theory is deadly serious. *NBC News*. Retrieved from https://www.nbcnews.com/think/opinion/qanon-s-capitol-rioters-nashville-bomber-s-lizard-people-theory-ncna1253819

Paul, K. (2021, January 17). 'I had no qualms': The people turning in loved ones for the Capitol attack. *The Guardian*. Retrieved from https://www.theguardian.com/us-news/2021/jan/17/capitol-attack-reporting-family-internet-sleuths-qanon

Romano, A. (2020, November 18). Conspiracy theories, explained. *Vox*. Retrieved from https://www.vox.com/21558524/conspiracy-theories-2020-qanon-covid-conspiracies-why

Roose, K. (2021, January 29). What is QAnon, the viral pro-Trump conspiracy theory? *The New York Times*. Retrieved from https://www.nytimes.com/article/what-is-qanon.html

Savage, C. (2021, January 10). Incitement to riot? What Trump told supporters before mob stormed Capitol. *The New York Times*. Retrieved from https://www.nytimes.com/2021/01/10/us/trump-speech-riot.html

Schmidt, M. S., & Vogel, K. P. (2021, January 17). Prospect of pardons in final days fuels market to buy access to Trump. *The New York Times*. Retrieved from https://www.nytimes.com/2021/01/17/us/politics/trump-pardons.html

Sherman, A. (2021, January 11). A timeline of what Trump said before Jan. 6 Capitol riot. *Politifact*. Retrieved from https://www.politifact.com/article/2021/jan/11/timeline-what-trump-said-jan-6-capitol-riot/

Silverstein, B., & Flamenbaum, C. (1989). Biases in the perception and cognition of the actions of enemies. *Journal of Social Issues*, *45*(2), 51–72.

Staff, R. (2021, January 9). Fact check: Men who stormed Capitol identified by Reuters are not undercover Antifa as posts claim. *Reuters*. Retrieved from https://www.reuters.com/article/uk-factcheck-capitol-mob-antifa-undercov/fact-check-men-who-stormed-capitol-identified-by-reuters-are-not-undercover-antifa-as-posts-claim-idUSKBN29E0QO

Valentino-DeVries, J., Ashford, G., Lu, D., Lutz, E., Matthews, A. L., & Yourish, K. (2021, February 4). Arrested in Capitol riot: Organized militants and a horde of radicals. *The New York Times*. Retrieved from https://www.nytimes.com/interactive/2021/02/04/us/capitol-arrests.html

Contents

Introduction

Katherine V. Aumer

Currently, the U.S. is faced with extremism almost everywhere. The death of George Floyd by police chokehold has given rise to protests nationwide that have formed fault lines within communities and even divided families. The COVID-19 pandemic, a health crisis that can impact and harm anyone, has nevertheless become political and divisive. The racism in the US is bold and shocking. The conspiracy theories about and moral indignation against COVID-19 is fervent and unrelenting. Racism and conspiracy theories are now well documented on various social media platforms and news outlets. Throughout the discord, the term "extremism" has been bandied by both the right and left wing parties. The psychology of this extremism is the focus of this book. Although we do not assume or assert that extremism is impossible for people with left-leaning ideologies, most of the evidence and research concerning extremism that is used in this book stems from right-leaning ideologies. Extremism is not ideologically specific and although the current crises in the U.S. may seem abrupt, societal extremism has been a part of all cultures throughout history. This book is interdisciplinary, with researchers from a variety of disciplines reviewing the motivations of those who exhibit extremist behavior and the social and emotional contributions that enable and foster extremist groups.

Extremism has been discussed and defined in a variety of ways. Most groups including the FBI (2020) and the International Center for the Study of Violent Extremism (ICSVE, 2020) focus on violent extremism and terrorism. The Southern Poverty Law (SPLC, 2020) Anti-Defamation League (ADL, 2020) monitors over 1600 extremist and hate groups. For a variety of organizations, including the ones above, the discussion of extremism is often discussed in tandem with hate, terrorism, and violence. In the following chapters, we do not specify any one extremist organization or group nor do we examine any one specific ideology. Instead, the chapters in this book examine the universal aspects of extremism: elicitors, support-

K. V. Aumer (✉)
University of Hawai'i–West O'ahu, Kapolei, HI, USA
e-mail: kaumer@hawaii.edu

© Springer Nature Switzerland AG 2020
K. V. Aumer (ed.), *The Psychology of Extremism*,
https://doi.org/10.1007/978-3-030-59698-9_1

ing mechanisms, and methods to abate extremism. Although many researchers and organizations may define extremism differently, in this book all the authors have written their chapters with the definition that extremism is a psychological state, where a person aligns their identity with a group that is absolute in their moral agenda. Many examples of certain extremist groups and specific ideologies will be used to help illustrate points made in these chapters, but these examples should not be considered exhaustive.

This book can be used as a supplement for any upper-division undergraduate or graduate course with either the whole book being assigned or specific chapters being used weekly. The purpose of this book is to provide a variety of frameworks for which extremism can be investigated while also considering the assortment of situations in which one can encounter extremism.

A foreword by Vegas Tenold, an award-winning journalist and author of *Everything You Love Will Burn: Inside the Rebirth of White Nationalism in America* who works with the Anti-Defamation League, provides context for the following chapters. His first-hand experience interviewing people who belong to extremist groups and who has covered various extremist rallies and events provides a backdrop for the psychological theories and studies presented in these chapters. This foreword presents an image of extremism as providing a kind of comforting and simple narrative that many men in the U.S. currently crave.

"A Tale of Two Outcomes: Understanding and Countering Extremist Narratives" by Roseman, Rudolph, Steele, and Katz provides readers with a very narrative theory on the development of extremism. They identify five components: identificational, behavioral, normative, explanatory, and evaluative that are often embedded in narratives by those espousing extremist ideology. Although this chapter covers a variety of examples of extremism, Roseman and colleagues specifically utilize examples of rhetoric, policy, and behavior of Donald Trump to help exemplify the five components and their consequences. Their theory helps provide a concrete framework in which future research can be used to study and predict outcomes of extremism.

Seyle and Besaw's chapter: "Identity, Extremism, and (De)radicalization" focuses specifically on the social psychology of extremism emphasizing the role of identity-based mechanisms that contribute to the recruitment into and formulation of extremist groups. Seyle and Besaw provide a thorough background and application of their theory which is strongly rooted in research on identity. They conclude their chapter with evidence-based recommendations on how extremist groups can be weakened and members can be (de)radicalized.

Aumer and Erickson in their chapter "The Use of Love and Hate in Extremist Groups" utilize both social psychology and findings in emotions science to better understand the role of love and hate in extremist groups. Beginning with a discussion of the latest findings of love and hate they conclude with a theory on how both emotions (love and hate) can be utilized to help recruit, maintain, and justify identification with extremist groups. This chapter provides insights into how love and hate can be used to help those who feel disenfranchised with their circumstances, find solace and friendship in extremist groups.

Hatfield and Rapson's chapter: "Political Identities, Emotions, and Relationships," focuses specifically on the extremism commonly encountered with family members and friends. They review literature from both social and clinical psychology to provide ways in which family members can confront, discuss, and examine one's encounters with family members who may have extremist ideologies. This chapter is useful for both academics and laypersons who want to better understand how to navigate the more common day-to-day encounters one may have with ideologically mismatched relationships.

"Homogamy and Tribalism: How Finding a Match can Lead to Social Disruption," by Fieder, Schahbasi, and Huber approaches the origins of extremism from an evolutionary psychology framework. The argument that educational homogamy can lead to extremist out-group behavior provides a foundation for future research and exploration. Unlike the other chapters, much of the research in this chapter draws upon evolutionary psychology and how tribalism and homogamy can lead to more extremist behaviors.

Together these chapters provide insight into the psychological characteristics of extremist behaviors from a variety of disciplines. After reading this book, laypersons, students, researchers, and practitioners will have a better understanding of the motivation and emotion of individuals who exhibit extremist behaviors as well as the situational variables that contribute to recruitment and maintenance of extremism. All of these chapters provide evidence and advance theory concerning the reduction of extremism, both at the individual and social level. We specifically avoid moral judgment concerning extremism. However we do recognize in both the foreword and these chapters that extremism is and can be powerful and dangerous. Extremism, especially violent extremism, is something that societies throughout history have had to endure and manage. The research reported in this volume clarifies the meaning of extremism and helps to advance the understanding of extremism and methods to reduce its negative costs and violent consequences.

References

ADL. (2020, July 3). *Anti-Defamation League*. Retrieved from https://www.adl. org/?Artistdetail=1017

FBI. (2020, July 3). *What is violent extremism?* Retrieved from https://www.fbi.gov/cve508/ teen-website/what-is-violent-extremism

ICSVE. (2020, July 3). *International Center for the study of violent extremism*. Retrieved from https://www.icsve.org/

SPLC. (2020, July 3). *Southern poverty law center*. Retrieved from https://www.splcenter.org/ issues/hate-and-extremism

A Tale of Two Outcomes: Understanding and Countering Extremist Narratives

Ira J. Roseman, Ben Rudolph, Amanda K. Steele, and Steven Katz

This chapter considers conceptualizations of extremism; discusses a variety of processes that can lead to extreme beliefs and extremist actions; explains how extreme beliefs and behaviors are often embedded within narratives that are grounded in strong motives and amplified by particular intense emotions (using narratives employed by Donald Trump as an example); and concludes by offering suggestions for countering extremist views.

1 Conceptualizations of Extreme Beliefs and Extremist Actions

According to the American Heritage Dictionary (n.d.-a), the first meaning of the word *extreme* is "Most remote in any direction; outermost or farthest." It derives from the Latin *extrēmus*, the superlative of *exterus* which means outward. By this definition, extreme beliefs are those quite different from the norm; the more different, the more extreme they are. Consistent with this definition, Schmid (2014) maintains that a movement can only be defined as extremist by contrast to some non-extreme reference point. For example, Van Hiel and Mervielde (2003) operationalized extremism by an individual's distance from the median value on left–right ideology and political party position agreement scales. Note that if extremity is deviation from the norm in any direction, one might be, for example, extremely (quite unusually) conservative, egalitarian, or pacifistic.

An *extremist* is "a person who advocates or resorts to measures beyond the norm, especially in politics" (American Heritage Dictionary, n.d.-b). So extremism can be also defined in terms of nonnormative behaviors (or goals), as well as, or instead of,

I. J. Roseman (✉) · B. Rudolph · A. K. Steele · S. Katz
Department of Psychology, Rutgers University, Camden, NJ, USA
e-mail: ira.roseman@rutgers.edu

© Springer Nature Switzerland AG 2020
K. V. Aumer (ed.), *The Psychology of Extremism*,
https://doi.org/10.1007/978-3-030-59698-9_2

beliefs (Borum, 2011). Behaviorally, one might be, for example, extremely (very unusually) religious, permissive, or fashionable.

Extremism may be studied on the individual, group, and societal levels (cf. Berger, 2019), and from context-dependent or context-independent perspectives. Individuals may be compared to population norms, groups to typical group behaviors, and societies to other societies, contemporary or historical. From a context-independent perspective, New England Puritan prohibitions on theater, secular music and dance, and common games (Daniels, 1993), as well as the Salem witch trials, can be regarded as extreme, even if they were endorsed by most group members, as might naturism as advocated by members of the Lebensreform movement in Germany (Williams, 2007).

However, in the political domain, scholars who study extremists or extremism typically have a prototype with particular content in mind (even if not all agree on what that content is). As discussed by Backes (2010), an intellectual tradition going back to Aristotle (that great advocate of moderation) conceptualizes political extremism as antithetical to the ideal of the constitutional state, which is pluralistic (regarding differing views as legitimate), oriented toward the common good, governed by laws (to which all, including rulers, must adhere), and characterized by popular self-determination (e.g., democratic). In contrast, political extremists are monistic (intolerant of opposition or even dissent), oriented toward particular interests (e.g., their own or those of their group), unregulated by laws or limits on the exercise of power, and autocratic. According to this conception, Soviet-style communism (in which there are no institutional controls on the power of the state), South African apartheid (in which established institutions served the interests of whites over blacks), and Nazism (in which there were no limits on state power and the state pursued the interests of one ethnonational group over others) are varieties of extremism (Backes, 2010, p. 185).

Contemporary prototypical conceptions of political extremism include willingness to engage in unlawful, undemocratic, or violent behavior to achieve political goals (Berger, 2018; Schmid, 2013). According to Berger, antagonism to outgroups is also a defining feature. Midlarsky (2011) defines political extremism as the seeking of power by a group (typically opposed to existing authorities), which limits individual freedom and engages in mass murder of actual and potential opponents. Schmid (2014) views religious extremists (e.g., Islamists) as close-minded dogmatists who believe in the absolute supremacy of their view and, if circumstances are favorable, are willing to impose it using authoritarian and potentially violent means.

Here we will proceed from the broad conceptualization of extremism as belief and/or behavior that is very different from the norm, and also incorporate prototypical conceptions of condoning, endorsing, or taking extralegal or violent actions. Extremists include those who advocate, endorse, or excuse highly counter-normative behaviors, as well as those enacting them. We will use, as concrete examples, specific norm-violating beliefs and extreme behaviors of American President Donald Trump. When we drafted this chapter in July of 2020, we wrote: "It may be difficult for some to accept that an elected American president is a political extremist. Trump has not directly ordered killings of civilians or seized power in a coup. However, as we will see, many of Trump's public statements and actions fall within conceptualizations of extremism. These include statements that endorse or condone violence, his actual initiation of violent actions, and conduct contrary to American constitutional democracy and American laws." In mid-January 2021, it appears that Trump's unlawful attempts to remain in power after he was defeated in 2020 have shown that his words and deeds before and after the 2016 election (discussed in this chapter) were part of an unparalleled extremist pattern.

Followers of extremist leaders may also be regarded as extremists, especially if they give the leaders unqualified or unwavering support. This accords with conceptualizations of extremism in terms of belief rigidity (resistance to argument or evidence) or single-mindedness (in which one goal or value is pursued above and regardless of all other considerations; Schmid, 2013). Given these criteria, we will also examine factors leading to strong support for Trump and his norm-violating actions among his ardent supporters.

2　Pathways to Extremism

A majority of scholars who have examined the determinants of extreme behaviors (e.g., terrorist attacks) maintain that there is no single profile or etiology of an extremist (e.g., Bakker, 2006; Hafez & Mullins, 2015; Horgan, 2003). For example, McCauley and Moskalenko (2008) describe 12 mechanisms of political radicalization at the level of the individual (e.g., personal victimization), group (e.g., cohesion in response to threat), and mass public (e.g., reacting to the death of martyrs killed by police). In this section, grouping across specific mechanisms, we will briefly outline four general ways in which individuals might arrive at extreme beliefs or behaviors.

2.1　The Cognitive Route

Like other beliefs and attitudes, extremist beliefs can be learned via socialization, from one's family of origin (e.g., Miklikowska, 2017), peers (e.g., van Zalk, Kerr, van Zalk, & Stattin, 2013), the internet and social media (e.g., Hassan et al., 2018), and educational (e.g., Siddique, 2009) and religious (e.g., Ahmed & Bashirov, 2020) institutions. However, many authors caution that neither learning nor socialization are unidirectional processes in which an individual passively absorbs presented or observed ideas. Instead ideas are evaluated, selectively pursued (Pauwels & Schils, 2016), and differentially adopted. This process can be influenced by interpersonal relationships (e.g., Sageman, 2004) and group affiliations (Neumann & Rogers, 2007), as well as life experiences such as personal crises (Wiktorowicz, 2005), deprivations and injustices (e.g., Moghaddam, 2005), and encounters with authorities (e.g., della Porta, 2018). These are given relevance and importance in terms of individual motives, needs, desires, and concerns (see discussion of the motivational route below). However, in each case the cognitive content of the beliefs, and whether such content is accepted, rejected, or modified, either defines what is extreme or is central to understanding, organizing, and guiding extreme actions.

Several of the processes that Abelson (1995) discusses as producing the extremification of attitudes rely on cognitive mechanisms. These include (1) polarization produced when, in group discussion, more of the arguments voiced favor the position held by the majority, shifting the group's attitude further in that direction (Burnstein & Vinokur, 1977)—a type of informational social influence (Deutsch & Gerard, 1955); (2) similar polarization occurring when individuals think about their own attitudes, and generate previously unconsidered arguments in support of their position (Tesser, Martin, & Mendolia, 1995); and (3) polarization occurring when prior beliefs bias the perception and evaluation of subsequent information (e.g., Nickerson, 1998) so that belief-consistent information is accepted and inconsistent information challenged or minimized.

2.2   The Motivational Route

As noted in the previous section, beliefs may be adopted and maintained because they serve functions for an individual (Katz, 1960), and this may be especially likely for beliefs that are extreme in the sense of being resistant to counter-argument and disconfirming evidence (Roseman, 1994). Motives, needs, and goals are also likely influential in extreme behaviors, insofar as deviance requires support to survive pressure and rejection from majorities who adhere to mainstream norms (e.g., Schachter, 1951). Other costs of adopting extreme beliefs and enacting extreme behaviors may include giving up comforts and pleasures of conventional lifestyles (such as sexual relationships or consuming alcohol) and, in the case of violent extremism, risking or sacrificing one's life (Bélanger, Caouette, Sharvit, & Dugas, 2014).

A wide variety of motivations can anchor extreme belief and action. These include self-interest (Howe & Krosnick, 2017); self-esteem or self-respect (Fiske, 2010); meaning (Frankl, 2000); personal significance (Kruglanski et al., 2014); reduction of uncertainty (Hogg, 2014) or of threats to individual or group identity (Seyle & Besaw, 2021); maintenance of group dominance (Piazza, 2017); redress of or revenge for grievances (McCauley & Moskalenko, 2008; van den Bos, 2020), immortality or heavenly reward (Stern, 2003); and, especially in the context of groups, belongingness (Bjørgo, 2011; Borum, 2014), acceptance (Federal Bureau of Investigation, 2006), and approval/honor/status (Venhaus, 2010). In some cases, individuals who take actions or positions more extreme than other group members may be admired as more dedicated or committed to the group or its goals (Abelson, 1995).

2.3   The Emotional Route

The field of psychology has alternated over time in viewing motivation (e.g., Cofer & Appley, 1964; Hull, 1943; Murray, 1938) or emotion (e.g., Izard, 1991; Plutchik, 1980; Tomkins, 1970) as primary energizers of behavior. Now it is widely recognized that both are needed to adequately understand influences on cognition and action (e.g., Reeve, 2018). The two constructs may play different roles as determinants. For example, Frijda (1986) proposed that the action tendencies and readinesses of emotions have priority (*"control precedence"*), intruding into thoughts and interrupting other behaviors (cf. Cannon's 1932 emergency theory of emotions). Drawing on this work, as well as that of Tomkins (1970), Roseman (2013) proposed that motivational processes tend to govern behavior in response to relatively less important, less imminent, or slower changes in motive-relevant events, whereas emotions become increasingly preemptive as motive-relevant events are more important, imminent, and rapid. These views suggest that emotions may be particularly influential in initiating and maintaining beliefs and behaviors that seem imperative and are resistant to evidence and argument.

   A number of theorists and researchers have proposed that emotions are important influences on extreme beliefs and behaviors. According to Midlarsky (2011), fear (of return to a subordinate position) was a causal factor in Chechen terrorism after a Russian invasion in 1999; anger (in response to a failed coup viewed as an injustice) was operative in the killing of half a million Communists by the Indonesian military and its allies in 1965; and shame (about perceived humiliation) contributed to the rise of Nazism after Germany's defeat in World War I and the signing of the Versailles Treaty). Aumer and Erickson (2021) propose that members of extremist groups tend to share hatred toward members of an outgroup who are seen as a threat, and that this shared hatred serves social cohesion and protective functions. Rip, Vallerand, and Lafrenière (2012) found feelings of hatred to be an antecedent of a sample of devout Muslims endorsing actions such as "severe punishment" and "preparation for a holy war" after being shown Pope Benedict's 2006 comments in Regensburg that disparaged Islam. Hope (e.g., for an ideal society) may be a crucial motivator and sustainer of extremist campaigns (Schmid, 2013).

2.4   The Behavioral Route

People may also exhibit extreme beliefs or behaviors partly due to individual differences in response propensities or in countervailing influences, such as impulse control. For example, individuals may differ in propensity for impulsive violence due to low levels of serotonin (reviewed in Manchia et al., 2020) or high levels of monoamine oxidase A, which breaks down serotonin (McDermott, Tingley, Cowden, Frazzetto, & Johnson, 2009). These may only be operative in combination with adverse childhood experiences (Reif et al., 2007) or current aggression-eliciting events (e.g., provocation, oppression, political conflict; Hatemi & McDermott, 2012). A path analysis of survey data by Brandstätter and Opp (2014) found that the behavior-relevant personality variables of high openness to experience and low agreeableness predicted self-reported political protest activity. In these instances, individual differences related to behavior may make some individuals more prone to taking extreme actions, especially if those actions are provoked and/or incentivized by current environmental conditions.

Behaviors may also influence beliefs and additional behaviors through processes related to cognitive dissonance (Festinger, 1957). McCauley and Moskalenko (2008) note that having first engaged in a nonviolent task for a terrorist group may lead to justifying that behavior and becoming more willing to engage in violent actions such as using a gun or bomb.

3 Integrating Accounts of the Psychology of Extremism within Extremist Narratives

3.1 Five Belief Components

Each of the influences on extreme belief and behavior may operate with some degree of independence. However, as noted earlier they may also have combined and interactive effects. Our narrative theory includes components corresponding to the behavioral, cognitive, motivational, and emotional influences on extreme belief and action, and adds components recognizing the effects of norms (e.g., Pilecki, 2015) and identity-related processes (Seyle & Besaw, 2021). Here, as promised, we illustrate this theory using examples of extreme beliefs and behaviors of President Donald Trump and Americans who strongly endorse them. Salient examples are shown in Fig. 1.

In these narratives, the *evaluative* component encompasses motivational influences that reinforce or incentivize beliefs and behaviors. According to the theory, strongly held beliefs typically serve some function(s) for a person, making an important difference in a person's life. Thus the evaluative component is represented in terms of alternative motive-relevant outcomes differing significantly in desirability. For example, in his 2016 acceptance speech at the Republican convention in Cleveland, Trump (2016) described the alternative outcomes at stake in his run for the presidency to include vulnerability to attack vs. safety, and low wages and lost jobs vs. prosperity. As shown in Fig. 1, Trump contrasted the existing state and trajectory of the U.S. with the starkly different destination to which he said his election would lead—he would make America safe, rich, and great again.

The more important the outcomes that are believed to be at stake, and the greater the disparity between them, the stronger the incentive to maintain the belief system, and the more extreme the actions that can be warranted by the beliefs. Indeed, extremist belief systems tend to involve a claim that the ingroup's survival or freedom is at

Identificational component	Behavioral component	Normative component	Explanatory component	Evaluative component
Donald Trump (Affection)	Restricts illegal immigration	Illegal is wrong		Our country ours again (Hope)
"I am your voice"	Cuts regulations and taxes	Regs, taxes excessive	Made billions in business	America rich again
Says what he thinks	Cracks down on crime			America safe again
Forgotten Americans	Vote for Trump		Crowds at rallies cheer	America great again
White			Fox News hosts approve	We are respected (Pride)
Virtuous (e.g., work hard)		We deserve respect		America proud again

Making America Great Again

The Road to Disaster

Illegal immigrants	Take our jobs (Anger)			Lost jobs, lower wages (Shame)
Mexicans, drug dealers	Commit crimes		Murders in Chicago	Innocents killed
Islamic radicals	Commit terrorist acts (Hatred)		Benghazi disaster (Fear)	Vulnerable to attack
Elites	Make huge profits	Shouldn't control us		
Crooked Hillary (Contempt)	Lies, enriches herself	They are biased	Condemned on Fox News	
Special interests	Keep rigged system in place	Undemocratic		Rich donors benefit
Dishonest media	Lie, conceal the truth		Crowds at rallies jeer	

Fig. 1 Belief components and emotions in Donald Trump's 2016 nomination acceptance speech narrative (from Roseman, Steele, & Goodvin, 2019b)

risk (Berger, 2018). For example, Hirschberger, Ein-Dor, Leidner, & Saguy (2016) note that concerns about physical survival (mortality salience) were found to increase Iranians' support for suicide bombings targeting Americans (Pyszczynski et al., 2006), Israelis' support for a preemptive nuclear attack against Iran (Hirschberger, Pyszczynski, & Ein-Dor, 2009), and conservative Americans' support for military actions to combat terrorism (Pyszczynski et al., 2006). Hirschberger et al. (2016) propose an expanded conception of existential threat beyond an *individual's* death, to include a *group's* physical annihilation, and its *symbolic* annihilation (e.g., obliteration of its identity or way of life) as well as concerns about past victimization. An example of symbolic identity threat was when white nationalists in Charlottesville in 2017 chanted "Jew will not replace us" (Spencer & Stolberg, 2017).

The *behavioral* component contains actions that can influence which of the contrasting outcomes will occur. If there are no actions by which important outcomes can be influenced, then low efficacy, helplessness, hopelessness, and depression may inhibit strong belief and instrumental action (e.g., Bandura, 1997; Baumeister, 1991; Ruiter, Kessels, Peters, & Kok, 2014; van Zomeren, Spears, Fischer, & Leach, 2004). Extremist ideologies prototypically advocate actions such as using violence to achieve group goals, defying legal authority, and punishing deviants (Schmid, 2013). Particular extreme actions may be differentially appealing to different groups and individuals, depending on such factors as genetic predispositions (McDermott & Hatemi, 2017), personality (e.g., Bettencourt, Talley, Benjamin, & Valentine,

2006), socialization (Keniston, 1968), learning history (Altemeyer, 1981), and group and cultural norms (e.g., Nisbett & Cohen, 1996; Staub, 1989).

In Trump's, 2016 campaign narrative, weak authorities had allowed and would (if they continued in power) allow illegal and criminal immigrants to take Americans' jobs and kill innocent citizens. In contrast, Trump would "restore law and order" by building a wall to halt illegal border crossings and cracking down on crime, and would cut regulations and taxes. According to our theory, support for a belief system's narrative is increased by approving and endorsing its recommended actions.

The *identificational* component names individuals and groups who take the actions and experience the outcomes specified in the belief system, along with the salient motives and attributes that explain their actions. "Crooked" Hillary Clinton ("puppet" of selfish special interests) and President Obama (who put her in charge of America's foreign policy) were the politicians whose actions and failures to act allowed terrorists and illegal immigrants with criminal records to threaten and harm Americans (Trump, 2016). Rich, successful Trump, who has "no tolerance for government incompetence...no sympathy for leaders who fail their citizens" would fight for "the forgotten men and women of our country" who work hard but have been "neglected, ignored, and abandoned." "I am your voice" he said, and "I alone can fix it."

In claiming to fight for hard-working yet forgotten men and women against a corrupt elite, Trump propounds a populist worldview (Mudde & Rovira Kaltwasser, 2012). In also targeting Islamic radicals and illegal immigrants, portrayed as threatening the safety and economic security of Americans, it is a species of *right-wing* populism (Betz, 1994; Pelinka, 2013).The identities offered seem to have been especially effective in connecting with whites without college degrees who scored high on measures of racism and hostile sexism (Schaffner, MacWilliams, & Nteta, 2018). Such voters may have seen their economic and social status threatened by the loss of manufacturing jobs due to globalization, social policies designed to reduce racial and gender discrimination, and demographic trends, including immigration, that would soon result in a "majority minority" American population (Bobo, 2017). Those who saw themselves as working hard while immigrants and ethnic minorities cut into line in front of them and deprived them of the share of the American dream that they had earned (Hochschild, 2016) were thus invited into Trump's narrative, where they were recognized (Lamont, Park, & Ayala-Hurtado, 2017) and put "first," and thus restored to a pre-eminent or dominant position. Reicher, Haslam, and Rath (2019) discuss how Trump portrayed foreigners and self-interested American politicians as obstacles to the existence and expression of American identity—in the same way that Islamic radicals depict Jews and Christians.

Strongly held beliefs often also have a *normative* component, which makes claims about the moral qualities of the actors, actions, and outcomes included in the narrative (Garrett & Bankert, 2018). Extremists typically see themselves as particularly virtuous (e.g., as having been victimized or treated unjustly), and their enemies as unethical or evil (Reicher, Haslam, & Rath, 2008; Sedgwick, 2007). They also see the outcomes that they seek as legitimate and good, and their beliefs and actions as absolutely right (justified in themselves or as necessary for the outcomes they deserve; Moghaddam, 2005). According to Bandura (1990, p. 163) "People do not ordinarily engage in reprehensible conduct until they have justified to themselves the morality of their actions."

In Trump's 2016 campaign narrative, his opponents have bad motives (politicians put their interests, and those of their rich donors, above those of the country); take actions which are immoral in themselves (e.g., *illegal* immigration and other crimes are wrong because they are unlawful) and because they lead to outcomes that are unfair (e.g., hardworking Americans lose their jobs) or reprehensible (e.g., America is vulnerable to terrorist attack, and innocent citizens are murdered by criminals). Worthy purposes are used to justify questionable or unethical actions such as separating young children from their mothers at the southern U.S. border (to deter illegal immigration; American Immigration Council, n.d.) and torturing of detainees (to obtain information about possible terrorist attacks; Weaver & Ackerman, 2017).

Finally, to attract adherents, it is proposed that a belief system must be compatible with their ideas about the way the world works (see Wiktorowicz, 2005, on "frame alignment"). Thus ideologies have an *explanatory* component, containing principles, arguments, examples, and metaphors which demonstrate that the system of beliefs is true. It is especially important that the identified actors have the capacity to take the specified actions (and would indeed do so), and that those actions would in fact lead to the envisioned outcomes. For example, according to Wiktorowicz (2005), recruitment into the Islamic jihadist organization al-Muhajiroun was aided by Omar Bakri Mohammed's use of religious evidence from the Qur'an and Islamic practices. Hafez and Mullins (2015) observe that violent Islamic extremists reframe suicide bombings as the acts of martyrs defending the faith, rather than as suicide (which is proscribed in Islam). McCauley and Moskalenko (2008, pp. 426–427) cite instances in which attacks from a group's enemies (as in Al Qaeda's September 11 attacks) can increase support for extreme responses against those enemies.

In his nomination acceptance speech, Trump (2016) explained the economic decline of American workers as due to politicians abandoning them for financial gain provided by corporate lobbyists. This fit with beliefs of most Americans, 65% of whom agreed (Pew Research Center, 2015) that "the economic system in this country unfairly favors powerful interests" (only 31% agreed that it "is generally fair to most Americans"). The proof of his ability to "make our country rich again" was the claim that "I have made billions of dollars in business making deals" (Trump, 2016, p. 20), and Trump's alleged business success was cited repeatedly as a rationale by some who voted for him (Perry, 2017).

3.2   Dramatic Structure of the Narrative

According to our theory, the five belief components do not exist in isolation from each other, but are typically woven together into a dramatic story that tells of diverging paths toward very bad vs. very good outcomes (Roseman, 1994). The story tends to have a predictable structure. It says that truly terrible things have happened, or could happen unless we act; but if we take the proper actions, then the terrible outcomes will be reversed or averted, and the enormously better outcomes will result. Political versions of this dramatic story tend to emphasize *group* identities, conflicts, and outcomes: Individuals and groups who are opposed to us (because of their bad motives or inferior abilities) are taking unjust actions that will lead to ruinous outcomes for our group; but if we do what we should, we can defeat them and survive and prosper.

According to Schmid (2013), in Al Qaeda's narrative the basic grievance is that the Zionist-Christian alliance is mistreating Muslims. There is a vision of the good society, the Caliphate, where Sharia law would rule. The path from the grievance to realization of the vision is jihad conducted by a heroic vanguard.

In one version of Trump's 2016 Republican convention narrative, as shown in Fig. 1, politicians, for their own benefit, were keeping in place a rigged system that sent factories overseas, while allowing illegal aliens to take jobs that rightfully belonged to Americans and to murder innocent citizens. Voting for Trump—the successful plain-speaking businessman who is the voice of the abandoned and forgotten people—would allow him to restrict illegal immigration, crack down on crime, and negotiate great trade deals, which would make America safe, rich, and great again.

3.3   Emotions in the Narrative

Grounded in the Emotion System theory (Roseman, 2011, 2013), and related empirical research (e.g., Fischer & Roseman, 2007; Goodvin, 2019; Roseman, Antoniou, & Jose, 1996; Steele, 2020), this model was elaborated by Roseman, Steele, and Goodvin (2019b) to encompass the influence of emotions. As in other types of stories, including narrative fiction (Oatley, 2002), autobiographical narratives (Habermas, 2019), historical narratives (e.g., Kane, 2001), and narratives constructed in the course of psychotherapy (e.g., Angus & Greenberg, 2011), emotions are generated toward the agents and recipients of action in ideological narratives, as well as in response to the specified actual, anticipated, and hypothetical situations, events, and actions, and appraisals of their moral aspects.

For example: insofar as outcomes are presented as unwanted, possible, and imminent, fear can be created; desired potential outcomes can generate hope; unfair actions may elicit anger; beneficial outcomes attributed to leaders may produce affection; and successful outcomes seen as caused by oneself or members of one's group can engender pride. As shown in Fig. 1, the emotions accompanying, supporting, and amplifying portions of Trump's narrative include fear (e.g., of crime and terrorism), anger (at immigrants taking Americans' jobs), contempt (for crooked Hillary), hope (e.g., of jobs brought back), affection (for Trump, whose "pledge reads: 'I'M WITH YOU – THE AMERICAN PEOPLE … I will fight for you, and I will win for you'"; Trump, 2016, p. 27; Reicher & Haslam, 2017), and pride (about being great again).

Another emotion, which is likely to be particularly important for extremism, is hatred. Indeed the way that Trump depicts many individuals and groups as malevolent enemies makes him a purveyor of hate (Roseman, Steele, & Goodvin, 2019b). According to appraisal theories (Ellsworth & Scherer, 2003; Roseman & Smith, 2001; Scherer & Moors, 2019), emotions are typically elicited by evaluations of the relevance of events for a person's motives (goals and preferences), with different patterns of appraisal eliciting distinct emotions (along with the phenomenology, physiology, expressive displays, action tendencies, and goals that tend to be characteristic of each emotion; Roseman, 2011). For example, research indicates that

- interpersonal dislike is characterized by appraisals that other persons are causing undesirable but not blameworthy events that must be accepted (Roseman, Steele, & Goodvin, 2019a);
- anger is elicited by unwanted events (e.g., Roseman et al., 1996) such as goal blockages (e.g., Ceulemans, Kuppens, & Van Mechelen, 2012), especially if perceived as caused by other persons (e.g., Frijda, Kuipers, & ter Schure, 1989) and unjust (e.g., Averill, 1982), and it seems that one should be able to do something about them (Kuppens, Van Mechelen, Smits, & De Boeck, 2003);
- contempt is characterized by perceptions of people as having undesirable qualities (Roseman, Steele, & Goodvin, 2019a), such as being immoral (Pilecki, 2015) or stupid or incompetent (Hutcherson & Gross, 2011);
- hatred is characterized by thoughts that an individual or group is evil and cannot be changed (Steele, 2020), and may be elicited by such perceptions (Fischer, Halperin, Canetti, & Jasini, 2018).

Thus attributions of unchangeable malevolence distinguish the phenomenology of hatred from that of interpersonal dislike, anger, and contempt. Labelling people as terrorists (Trump, 2016), rapists (see Washington Post, 2015), or thugs (see Chavez & Sanchez, 2020) characterizes them as inherently evil, bent on harm. In the same vein, Trump has repeatedly described Muslims as having "hatred of us" (Johnson & Hauslohner, 2017). Unchangeably malevolent people are likely to hurt us in the future if allowed to do so. Unlike in anger, where criticism and confrontation could change the target's behavior (Fischer & Roseman, 2007), or in contempt, where shaming or shunning could prompt the target to inhibit or reform an undesirable quality (Roseman, 2018), in hatred the only way to prevent future harm is to incapacitate such enemies, either by destroying them (Fischer et al., 2018) or otherwise getting them out of one's life forever (Steele, 2020), e.g., by segregating or deporting them. When feeling hatred, people are more likely than when feeling other negative emotions to fantasize about bad things happening to the object of their emotion, look for an opportunity to take action against them, attack them verbally or physically, encourage others to attack them, and want to get back at them, hurt them, have them suffer, and get rid of them (Steele, 2020). Experiencing hatred, people feel justified in attacking those who are seen as evil (Steele, 2020). For example, if immigrants from Mexico are criminals and rapists, one might ask for cost estimates to build an electrified border fence, topped with spikes that could pierce a person's flesh, and surrounded by a moat filled with alligators or snakes, as Trump is reported to have done (Shear & Davis, 2019). If protesters at Trump rallies are "thugs," "lowlifes," and "very bad people…doing bad things," then they might not be treated so well (Chavez & Sanchez, 2020). Such extreme behaviors can also be instrumental responses to the appraisals of unchangeable malevolence, even in the absence of hatred, or if hatred had once accompanied or generated the appraisals but is no longer actively present (e.g., Fischer et al., 2018).

Particular emotions also have differing implications for belief (e.g., Brader & Marcus, 2013) and action (e.g., Fontaine & Scherer, 2013; Frijda et al., 1989; Roseman, Wiest, & Swartz, 1994). Fear tends to increase seeking information about threats (e.g., Valentino, Hutchings, Banks, & Davis, 2008), and can thus decrease reliance on existing beliefs (MacKuen, Marcus, Neuman, & Keele, 2007) and increase openness to persuasion (Nai, Schemeil, & Marie, 2017)—although this may depend on the intensity of the fear and whether the new information or the existing information seems more relevant to the threat (e.g., Albertson & Gadarian, 2015; Easterbrook, 1959). In contrast, anger tends to boost confidence and certainty about one's existing beliefs (Lerner & Tiedens, 2006), and resistance to discrepant information (Suhay & Erisen, 2018). Thus fear could increase support for extremist narratives and candidates (Karwowski et al., 2020), particularly if they appear to provide relief from uncertainty (Thórisdóttir & Jost, 2011). But anger can have similar or greater downstream effects (Vasilopoulos et al., 2019). If individuals already have or are leaning toward extremist views, anger can increase confidence in them and decrease openness to opposing arguments or considerations, thus promoting belief rigidity.

With regard to the impact of specific emotions on behavior, Fischer and Roseman (2007) found that experiences of anger were characterized by short-term verbal attacks to try to force change in a target's behavior or get revenge, whereas experiences of contempt were associated more with relationship termination. Tausch et al. (2011) found that feeling anger was associated with self-reported likelihood of participating in normative protest activities such as demonstrations, and moderate nonnormative but nonviolent actions such as blocking highways. In contrast, contempt was associated with support for nonnormative violent actions such as setting fire to buildings and violence against military and civilian targets. However, in a study by Cheung-Blunden and Blunden (2008), rated anger (after seeing photographs of the September 11 attacks) fully mediated the effects of anti-terrorism attitudes on support for the wars in Afghanistan and Iraq, and for killing terrorists, government officials, soldiers, and civilians in those countries. Participants induced to feel anger toward an outgroup in an experiment by Mackie, Devos, and Smith (2000) reported greater motivation to confront, oppose, or argue with them, whereas those induced to feel contempt reported wanting to have nothing to do with them, avoid them, or keep them at a distance. Studies of autobiographical experiences of four interpersonal negative emotions indicate that interpersonal dislike is most characterized by avoidance (of the disliked person); contempt by ridicule and looking down on the person; anger by yelling at the person; and hatred by fantasizing about bad things happening to the person, seeking vengeance, and encouraging attacks against the person (Goodvin, 2019; Roseman, Steele, & Goodvin, 2019a; Steele, 2020). Hatred was also the emotion most associated with wanting to get the target person out of one's life forever (Steele, 2020) and to suffer (Goodvin, 2019).

The combined influence of multiple emotions was suggested in a study by Pilecki (2015). He measured (1) the extent to which online participants perceived particular groups (e.g., immigrants) as violating moral principles; (2) the "other-condemning" emotions of contempt, anger, and disgust (Haidt, 2003); and (3) participants' support for policies varying in extremity, e.g., from allowing organizations to exclude those engaging in homosexual behavior (low extremity) to having homosexual behavior punishable by the death penalty (high extremity). He found that combined ratings of the other-condemning emotions mediated the relationship between the rated immorality of a group and the extremity of policies against them that participants supported. Matsumoto, Hwang, and Frank (2014) found that increased anger, contempt, and disgust in leaders' speeches in several countries preceded acts of aggression (e.g., revolution, invasion, or war) rather than nonviolent protest.

Felt emotions also produce tendencies to perceive situations and events in ways consistent with the appraisals that elicit those emotions (Han, Lerner, & Keltner, 2007). Thus, emotions can lead to extreme belief and behavior both directly (via the action tendencies characteristic of particular emotions) and indirectly (by priming emotion-related appraisals). For example, the perceived danger of terrorism is heightened by fear (e.g., Lerner, Gonzalez, Small, & Fischhoff, 2003); opposition to citizenship for undocumented immigrants is amplified by anger (Banks, 2016); the prospect of prosperity is enhanced by hope (Reicher & Haslam, 2017); and the appeal of regaining lost status is magnified by envisioned pride (Hochschild, 2016). Abandoning beliefs that elicit emotions, or that are anchored by motives, may then be much more difficult insofar as this entails loss of the relevant feeling (e.g., of hope or pride) or associated goal (e.g., of prosperity or significance), or creates alternative unwanted affective states (e.g., hopelessness or depression; cf. Corner & Gill, 2019).

In presenting a story of vastly differing outcomes that are imminent and contingent on the actions of the audience (here, their votes; in narratives of radicalization, their joining a militant group, taking to the streets, or taking up arms), the dramatic structure of such narratives can engender passion—strong emotion created by the prospect of transformative events (Roseman, 2017). Movement between an intensely negative outcome (such as "death, destruction, terrorism and weakness;" Trump, 2016) and deliverance (Jamieson & Taussig, 2017) is proposed to produce greater passion, and thereby greater ability to produce extreme belief and behavior: (1) the greater the relevance of the outcomes for an individual's goals, (2) the greater the importance of those goals for the individual, (3) the greater the difference in desirability between the outcomes, and (4) the more imminent the outcomes appear to be (Roseman, 2011).

4   Applying the Narrative Theory to Help Explain Extreme Beliefs and Behavior of Trump and His Supporters

Taken together these five belief components and related emotions form a powerfully appealing narrative that may help explain the intense and enduring devotion of Trump's loyal supporters (Hibbing, 2020) despite his many norm-shattering behaviors (e.g., proposing a ban on travel to the U.S. based on people's religion, Rucker, DelReal, & Stanley-Becker, 2020; refusing to release his tax returns, Harwell, 2016) and scandals that would seemingly derail a presidential candidate (e.g., being accused of multiple sexual assaults, supported by being caught on tape talking of grabbing women by their genitals; agreeing to a $25 million settlement of lawsuits over claims that Trump University was a scam; see Graham, 2017). Indeed at a 2016 Iowa campaign rally Trump famously boasted that his supporters were so loyal that he could stand in the middle of Fifth Avenue and shoot someone and not lose any voters.[1] Such steadfast loyalty continued after his inauguration among 35% to 49% of U.S. adults,[2] despite a continuing stream of serious norm-violating actions, such as refusal to put his assets into a blind trust (Harwell, 2017); saying he believed Russian president Putin's denial of election interference over the consensus assessments of American intelligence agencies (Elving, 2020); and mocking the emoluments clause of the Constitution as "phony" (Collins, Jackson, & Subramanian, 2019).

Even before the 2020 election a number of Trump's behaviors resembled prototypes of political extremism. For example, on multiple occasions he encouraged, advocated, or directed violence and other punitive actions against political opponents. These include

- suggesting that his 2016 Democratic opponent should be imprisoned (Krieg, 2016), and, at his rallies, encouraging supporters to call for this (Washington Post, 2016);
- suggesting that she might be killed by "Second Amendment people" if she were elected and then appointed judges who curtailed gun rights (Corasaniti & Haberman, 2016);
- advocating and condoning physical attacks against protesters at rallies in Iowa ("Knock the crap out of him, will you"), Alabama ("Maybe he should have been roughed up"), and Nevada ("You know what they used to do to guys like that… they'd be carried out on a stretcher"), and promising to defend and pay legal fees for the attackers (Tiefenthaler, 2016);
- implying that those who provided information to the Ukraine scandal whistleblower should be executed (Levin, 2019).
- sending armed Federal agents into Portland to confront demonstrators despite opposition from the local governor and mayor (Bernton, 2020).

---

[1] https://www.youtube.com/watch?v=iTACH1eVIaA

[2] https://www.statista.com/statistics/666113/approval-rate-of-donald-trump-for-the-presidential-job/

In other instances, Trump acted or raised the prospect of acting in defiance of the Constitution, laws, or norms in order to gain or maintain power. For example:

- unlawfully soliciting the assistance of foreign governments in his election and reelection efforts (Rampton & Zengerie, 2019; Wertheimer & Eisen, 2019), which led to his impeachment.
- repeatedly talking about the possibility of remaining in office beyond the constitutionally set limit of two terms (e.g., Sonmez, 2019).
- during the third 2016 presidential debate and again on Election Day, Trump refused to say that he would accept the results of the 2016 election, if he lost (Kaczynski & McDermott, 2016),
- engaging in a sustained, multipronged effort to overturn his loss in the 2020 election. It included pressuring the Georgia Secretary of State to "find" enough votes to overturn his loss there, and warning that Raffensperger might be criminally prosecuted if he didn't report the ballot counting as corrupt (Gardner & Firozi, 2021); pressuring state legislators and governors to ignore the popular vote and instead appoint a pro-Trump slate to the Electoral College (Fearnow, 2020); pressuring members of Congress to challenge electors from states he lost (Bade et al., 2020); and calling on Vice President Pence to reject Electoral College votes from states that Biden won (Schmidt, 2021). When these efforts and court challenges failed, on the day that Congress would meet to count the Electoral College votes and declare Biden the winner, Trump (who'd urged people to come to Washington for a "big" and "wild" protest; Berry & Frenkel, 2021) repeated to a large crowd the false claim that an election he'd won "by a landslide" had been "stolen from you, from me and from the country." In his speech (Associated Press, 2021) Trump said that "We will not let them silence your voices. We're not going to let it happen." Challenging the certification of the election results was "a matter of national security," necessary to "save our democracy." He told them that "We must stop the steal" and made it seem feasible: "All Vice President Pence has to do is send it back to the states to recertify and we become president and you are the happiest people." Though he had said that people would march "to the Capitol building to peacefully and patriotically make your voices heard," toward the end of his remarks he told the crowd that "We fight like hell. And if you don't fight like hell, you're not going to have a country anymore...So...we're going to the Capitol, and we're going to try...and give our Republicans, the weak ones...the kind of pride and boldness that they need to take back our country." At the Capitol, where Congress was meeting, people had begun to clash with police and break through barricades before Trump's speech ended, and when more from the rally arrived, agitation increased, and eventually the crowd stormed the building (New York Times, 2021). Watching the events on TV at the White House, Trump failed to deploy the National Guard to protect legislators or the Capitol (Giella, 2021) and initially resisted appeals from former and current aides and advisers to condemn the insurrection or demand that it end (Haberman, 2021). It wasn't until 20 minutes after rioters broke into the building that Trump tweeted that people should support the police and "stay peaceful." Then it wasn't until

shortly after President-elect Biden appeared on national TV and called on Trump to demand an end to the siege that Trump released a video on Twitter (Ortutay, 2021), repeating the false claim that the election was stolen, but telling his supporters "We have to have peace. We have to have law and order... So go home. We love you. You're very special." Finally, it was only after he was impeached by the House of Representatives a week later that Trump released a video condemning the violence (Haberman & Schmidt, 2021). Whether or not Trump's actions (and inaction once the riot had begun) qualify as involvement in an attempted *coup d'etat* (Snyder, 2020), they clearly violated constitutional norms and laws, were consistent with his earlier receptivity to the use of violence for political ends, and by the definition articulated above, confirmed him as an extremist.

At least some Trump supporters endorsed or acted in accordance with his extreme words and deeds. Recordings of Trump rallies show cheers and applause in response to his comments about remaining in office beyond his legal term, and condoning violence against protesters (Sonmez, 2019; Tiefenthäler, 2016). According to ABC News (Levine, 2020), as of May 30, 2020 there had been at least 54 incidents in which individuals or groups invoked Trump in connection with documented or alleged threats of violence, or actual attacks. Following Trump's refusal to recognize the results of the 2020 election in November, there were death threats against election officials in states that failed to vote for Trump, protests by armed Trump supporters outside the homes of state and local officials, and attacks on black churches by Trump-supporting members of the Proud Boys, a right-wing organization that has been classified as a hate group (Southern Poverty Law Center, n.d.), which Trump refused to condemn in the presidential debate on September 29 (Derysh, 2020).

Thousands of people heeded Trump's call to come to Washington on January 6: police estimated that between 25,000 and 35,000 heard his speech at the Ellipse (Knowles et al., 2021). Online, a number of participants had offered to help people bring guns and other weapons to Washington, and some protesters thought their efforts would make it possible for Trump to remain in power (Barry et al., 2021). When Trump told the crowd "We will not let them silence your voices" the audience chanted "Fight for Trump" (Associated Press, 2021). At the conclusion of Trump's speech, hundreds online called for the storming of the Capitol (Frenkel, 2021). Many at the Capitol wore Trump regalia or carried Trump flags, and a large Trump 2020 banner was draped on the balcony. Some rioters explicitly invoked Trump's call, like the man who said "I believed I was following the instructions of former President Trump (Rubin et al., 2021). Men in the crowd were seen carrying plastic zip ties used as handcuffs by police, perhaps suggesting they intended to take hostages (Barrett et al., 2021). A gallows had been erected near the Capitol Reflecting Pool, and a noose hung from it; inside, some searched for legislators, and one said later "We were looking for Nancy to shoot her in the friggin' brain" (Papenfuss, 2021). During the insurrection, Trump tweeted that Pence "didn't have the courage to do what should have been done to protect our Country and our Constitution," and about ten minutes later some in the crowd chanted "Hang Mike Pence" (Evon,

2021). Police officers defending the Capitol were dragged and beaten by the mob, and one died after being attacked (Hill et al., 2021). After the insurrection, the Department of Homeland Security warned of a heightened threat environment posed by "ideologically motivated violent extremists" with grievances "fueled by false narratives"–an apparent reference to Trump's claim that the 2020 election had been stolen (Kanno-Youngs & Sanger, 2021).

Our analysis suggests that Trump's extremist behavior, as well as that of his most loyal supporters, may be initiated and maintained by the five specified belief components and supporting emotions, organized into or consistent with dramatic narratives, as discussed above. We use the plural "narratives" because the communications presented by extremist political figures and groups are multifaceted, potentially comprising an infinite number of combinations which may constitute equipotent variations that appeal to different audiences. For example, considering just the evaluative component, as shown in Fig. 1, for some Trump supporters attaining prosperity or wealth (as opposed to lost jobs or lowered wages; Blendon, Casey, & Benson, 2017) may be most important, while for others regaining status and respect (Lamont, 2018) may be paramount. Regarding the identificational component, adherents may be drawn into the narrative through a variety of social identities: political party (Jacobson, 2017), Christian religion (Martí, 2019), racial identification with whites (Tesler & Sides, 2016) or against blacks (e.g., Schaffner et al., 2018) or immigrants (Sides, Tesler, & Vavreck, 2017). Regarding what we have termed the explanatory component, some may have been convinced or reassured that Trump's narrative was true because they believed his claims of great business success (Perry, 2017), while others trusted supportive coverage from Fox News or its commentators (Mitchell, Gottfried, & Barthel, 2017). In terms of emotions, some adherents may have resonated with Trump's anger (at illegal immigrants portrayed as taking Americans' jobs; Smith & Hanley, 2018), or contempt (at Trump's allegedly corrupt, incompetent opponent), or, for those afraid of terrorists or criminals, felt hope (Roseman, Abelson, & Ewing, 1986; cf. Reicher & Haslam, 2017) that Trump's restricting immigration or cracking down on crime would make them safe. The variations would seem to converge on the behavior of voting for Trump, though support may also have been increased or diminished based on agreement with or opposition to the particular actions Trump promised to carry out. For example, those high in authoritarianism might be especially attracted to his promise to enforce the country's laws (there were 21 mentions of law, laws, lawful, or lawlessness in his nomination acceptance speech), while those low in agreeableness might find appealing his refusal to be "politically correct" (Trump, 2016).

In contrast to the varied motives, identifications, explanations, and emotions that may distinguish subgroups of his supporters, Trump's personal narrative may be considerably simpler. Its evaluative component may center around self-glorification (McAdams, 2020) or feeling special (Malkin, 2019) rather than hated (Madhani, 2020). Observers see an extreme need for self-aggrandizement and superiority (Zimbardo & Sword, 2019) manifest, for example, in claiming that he is a "genius" (Diaz, 2018), that he was successful at everything he ever did (Wall Street Journal, 2018) and that even his questionable actions are "perfect" (Kiely, Robertson, &

Gore, 2019). He seems to need praise constantly (Schwartz, 2019) and to find criticism intolerable (Ayer et al., 2016). He angrily and contemptuously belittles detractors (Zimbardo & Sword, 2019), rivals (Malkin, 2019), and any who dare to raise doubts about even his demonstrably erroneous pronouncements (Law & Martinez, 2019). Central to his identity is being a "winner" rather than a "loser" (Jamieson & Taussig, 2017).

Personally powerful emotions seem to include: shame, as Trump frequently speaks of humiliation and other countries "laughing at us" (Chokshi, 2016); contempt (e.g., for rivals, seen as "failed" or "weak" losers, and for critics, characterized as "fake" or "dishonest"; Bump, 2019); and pride (about what he regards as his towering achievements, which he often represents as the greatest or biggest "in history"; e.g., Woodward & Yen, 2020). Behaviors Trump tends to rely on as instrumental to his goals involve verbal denigration (Jamieson & Taussig, 2017; Lee & Quealy, 2019), which can be an action tendency of contempt (Fischer & Roseman, 2007) or of anger (Averill, 1982); and sometimes encouraging or authorizing physical aggression, as reviewed above, which can also be an action tendency of anger (Berkowitz, 2012). Within the explanatory component, evidence for the validity of Trump's narrative include (1) a zero-sum conception of international and social relations (e.g., Stiglitz, 2018), in which one party's win requires another's loss; and (2) Trump's successes, such as winning the approval and affection of his supporters and becoming President (McAdams, 2020, p. 149; Russell, 2017; Wall Street Journal, 2018).

5 Testing the Narrative Theory in Predicting Support and Voting for Trump

Roseman, Mattes, and Redlawsk (2019) tested the narrative theory using a module that they created for the 2016 Cooperative Congressional Election Study (CCES; Ansolabehere & Schaffner, 2017). The CCES provided a probability sample of 1000 voting-age American adults. Although its "common content" portion was not designed to measure specific variables in the narrative theory, it contained items that could be used to assess those belief components not covered in the module.

To measure the identificational component, Roseman, Mattes, and Redlawsk (2019) averaged the strength of participants' Republican partisanship; the extent to which their self-reported position on the continuum from extremely liberal to extremely conservative matched the position they assigned to Donald Trump; and how well they thought "cares about people like you" described Trump (Cronbach's alpha for this 3-item index was 0.78). They also assessed identification *against* Blacks (with 7 items assessing anti-black racism and racial resentment, $\alpha = 0.81$) and against immigrants (2 items, $\alpha = 0.60$). The behavioral component was assessed via endorsement of three actions Trump said that he would take as President: deporting illegal immigrants, repealing the Affordable Care Act, and opposing EPA regu-

Table 1 OLS regression weights predicting Trump thermometer ratings from Trump belief system components and relevant emotions, including identification against Blacks

Model component	Unstandardized coefficients		Standardized coefficients		
	B	Std. error	Beta	t	Sig.
(Constant)	9.103	1.119		8.132	0.000
Identification with Trump[a]	23.717	2.668	0.275	8.889	0.000
Identification against Blacks[b]	4.640	2.619	0.039	1.772	0.077
Evaluative[c]	6.985	1.941	0.084	3.599	0.000
Behavioral[d]	13.155	1.825	0.177	7.210	0.000
Normative[e]	4.059	1.513	0.055	2.683	0.007
Explanatory[f]	21.663	2.798	0.232	7.743	0.000
Hope re Trump	10.428	3.262	0.106	3.197	0.001
Enthusiasm re Trump	8.477	3.678	0.082	2.304	0.021
Pride re Trump	−6.579	3.705	−0.059	−1.776	0.076
Fear re Clinton	4.355	2.706	0.049	1.610	0.108
Anger re Clinton	4.941	2.772	0.060	1.783	0.075
Contempt re Clinton	5.484	2.611	0.061	2.100	0.036

[a]Republican partisanship, perceived liberal-conservative fit with Trump, and perception that Trump cares about people like you. [b]Racial resentment and racism index. [c]Abortion and gay rights restricted; gun rights strengthened; economy not deteriorating. [d]Deporting illegal immigrants, repealing Obamacare, opposing EPA regulation. [e]Authoritarianism. [f]Perceiving Trump qualified to be President.
Adjusted $R^2 = 0.70$

lation of carbon emissions ($\alpha = 0.63$). The evaluative component was assessed by endorsement of three outcomes that Trump said would contrast with those that he attributed to Hillary Clinton (involving support for gun rights, and opposition to abortion and gay marriage) as well as the belief that the economy had gotten worse during the previous year (which Trump promised to reverse; alpha for this 4-item index was 0.63). The normative component was assessed using the 4-item American National Election Studies (ANES) authoritarianism scale (MacWilliams, 2016), which measures the relative importance of respect for elders, obedience, good manners, and being well-behaved (as opposed to independence, self-reliance, curiosity, and being considerate; $\alpha = 0.64$). The explanatory component was measured by participants' rating of the extent to which Trump was "qualified to be President" (to reflect acceptance of the idea that his experience and talent as a businessman meant that he would be able to run the country). Participants also rated how often they felt three positive emotions (hope, enthusiasm, pride) and three negative emotions (fear, anger, contempt) when thinking of Trump and when thinking of Clinton, using questions in the format of the affect battery from the 2012 ANES.

These variables were then used to predict feeling thermometer evaluations of Trump (Tables 1 and 2), and voting for Trump as opposed to Clinton (Table 3). As shown in Table 1, measures of each of the five belief components, as well as hope

Table 2 OLS regression weights predicting Trump thermometer ratings from Trump belief system components and relevant emotions, including identification-against-immigrants

Model component	Unstandardized coefficients		Standardized coefficients		
	B	Std. error	Beta	t	Sig.
(Constant)	8.502	1.140		7.459	0.000
Identification with Trump[a]	23.582	2.662	0.273	8.858	0.000
Identification against immigrants[b]	4.643	1.759	0.061	2.640	0.008
Evaluative[c]	6.979	1.926	0.084	3.623	0.000
Behavioral[d]	12.033	1.889	0.162	6.370	0.000
Normative[e]	3.882	1.511	0.052	2.569	0.010
Explanatory[f]	21.495	2.791	0.230	7.700	0.000
Hope re Trump	10.617	3.255	0.108	3.262	0.001
Enthusiasm re Trump	8.781	3.662	0.085	2.398	0.017
Pride re Trump	−6.622	3.696	−0.060	−1.792	0.074
Fear re Clinton	4.881	2.708	0.055	1.802	0.072
Anger re Clinton	4.584	2.770	0.056	1.655	0.098
Contempt re Clinton	5.180	2.609	0.058	1.986	0.047

[a]Republican partisanship, perceived liberal-conservative fit with Trump, and perception that Trump cares about people like you. [b]No legal status to illegal immigrant dreamers or nonfelons. [c]Abortion and gay rights restricted; gun rights strengthened; economy not deteriorating. [d]Deporting illegal immigrants, repealing Obamacare, opposing EPA regulation. [e]Authoritarianism. [f]Perceiving Trump qualified to be President.
Adjusted $R^2 = 0.70$

and enthusiasm when thinking about Trump, significantly predicted more positive evaluations of Trump. Identification against Blacks was a marginally significant predictor.

As shown in Table 2, measuring identification against immigrants instead of identification against blacks produced a very similar pattern, though with identification against the outgroup and contempt when thinking about Clinton becoming significant (rather than marginal) predictors.

Table 3 shows results when predicting the Trump vs. Clinton vote (rather than Trump evaluations) and therefore including emotions favoring Clinton (as well as those favoring Trump). As shown in Table 3, the identificational, evaluative, behavioral, and explanatory components were significant predictors of voting for Trump, as was contempt for Clinton. Fear when thinking about Trump predicted voting for Clinton.[3]

---

[3] In this analysis, enthusiasm when thinking about Trump predicted voting for Clinton. That could have occurred because the ANES question asks about enthusiasm when thinking about Trump, but does not specify about what or toward whom the enthusiasm is felt. Thus enthusiasm occasioned by thinking about Trump (and the kind of person he is) could actually be enthusiasm about voting for Clinton, in light of her opponent's character or actions.

Table 3 Logistic regression predicting voting for Trump (rather than Clinton) from Trump belief system components and all emotions (re Trump and Clinton)

Model component	B	S.E.	df	Sig.	Exp(B)	95% CI for Exp(B)	
						Lower	Upper
Identification with Trump[a]	2.811	1.080	1	0.009	16.622	2.003	137.927
Identification against blacks[b]	0.622	0.851	1	0.464	1.863	0.352	9.871
Evaluative[c]	1.197	0.521	1	0.022	3.309	1.192	9.185
Behavioral[d]	2.211	0.429	1	0.000	9.123	3.938	21.138
Normative[e]	0.347	0.422	1	0.412	1.415	0.618	3.237
Explanatory[f]	3.891	1.274	1	0.002	48.944	4.033	593.948
Hope re Trump	3.213	2.180	1	0.141	24.841	0.346	1781.810
Enthusiasm re Trump	−4.499	1.770	1	0.011	0.011	0.000	0.357
Pride re Trump	1.530	1.578	1	0.332	4.616	0.209	101.796
Fear re Clinton	2.230	1.729	1	0.197	9.296	0.314	275.478
Anger re Clinton	1.306	0.936	1	0.163	3.691	0.589	23.115
Contempt re Clinton	1.897	0.910	1	0.037	6.665	1.119	39.698
Hope re Clinton	−1.351	0.995	1	0.175	0.259	0.037	1.822
Enthusiasm re Clinton	−0.391	1.115	1	0.726	0.676	0.076	6.015
Pride re Clinton	−2.154	1.479	1	0.145	0.116	0.006	2.104
Fear re Trump	−2.930	1.115	1	0.009	0.053	0.006	0.475
Anger re Trump	−0.864	0.591	1	0.143	0.421	0.132	1.341
Contempt re Trump	−1.097	0.785	1	0.163	0.334	0.072	1.556
Constant	−1.481	0.313	1	0.000	0.227		

[a]Republican partisanship, perceived liberal-conservative fit with Trump, and perception that Trump cares about people like you. [b]Racial resentment and racism index. [c]Abortion and gay rights restricted; gun rights strengthened; economy not deteriorating. [d]Deporting illegal immigrants, repealing Obamacare, opposing EPA regulation. [e]Authoritarianism. [f]Perceiving Trump qualified to be President.
Nagelkerke $R^2 = 0.88$

In sum, this study found a significant amount of evidence for the narrative theory in predicting support for and voting for Trump. All belief components predicted Trump support, and all but the normative component predicted vote choice. Predictions about the co-occurrence of components were not supported, as no significant interactions were observed--perhaps because many different combinations of components could result in support for Trump. Interestingly, the most consistent emotion predictor across our dependent variables was contempt when thinking about Clinton. This echoes recent results showing felt contempt to be the most important negative emotion predicting voting against three out of four candidates in two U.S. Senate races in 2014 (Roseman, Mattes, Redlawsk, & Katz, 2020), as well as a significant predictor of voting in the 2016 Iowa GOP caucuses (Redlawsk, Roseman, Mattes, & Katz, 2018).

It is important to note that while we have presented evidence that Trump has made statements and taken actions that meet the criteria for extremism, this does *not* mean that all or even most of his supporters are perceiving him or his words and deeds as extremist. As shown in Fig. 1, there are many different versions of the Trump narrative. Many who voted for him in 2016 may not have approved of the extremist aspects of his rhetoric and behavior—instead casting their ballots primarily against his Democratic opponent, Hillary Clinton (e.g., Margolis, 2020; Saad, 2016), or for Trump primarily because he was their party's candidate (Jacobson, 2017) or because they thought that he'd bring back jobs and prosperity (Perry, 2017) or appoint anti-abortion judges to the Supreme Court (Edgar, 2020). Voters, and especially partisans, are notoriously selective in the information to which they attend, and how they interpret it and weigh its importance (e.g., Barnidge et al., 2020; Iyengar & Hahn, 2009; Redlawsk, 2006). A limitation of this study in shedding light on the focal questions of this chapter is that support and voting for Trump are not necessarily linked to his extreme words and actions, however salient these may be to his detractors.

On the other hand, the number and prominence of news reports about Trump's controversial words and deeds suggest that many people simply looked past them to vote for him; and a significant proportion of his strong supporters seem to approve of his extremist rhetoric, judging by audience responses at pro-Trump rallies (see, e.g., Tiefenthäler, 2016). Despite his extreme statements and actions once in office, more than 74 million Americans voted for him in the 2020 election (46.8% of the votes that were cast).

Another obvious limitation is that the survey by Roseman, Mattes, and Redlawsk (2019) gathered correlational, not causal, data. Future research assessing the narrative theory's variables as prospective predictors and determinants of specifically extreme beliefs and behaviors is clearly needed.

6   Using the Theory to Counteract Extremist Narratives

Our theory suggests at least three general ways to counteract extremist narratives, each of which has many variations.

6.1   Challenging Extremist Narratives

Insofar as extreme beliefs and actions are produced or maintained by narratives of the sort that we have discussed, it would seem they could be tempered or altered by modifying narrative components. Effective counter-narratives might alter any of the key belief components or emotions. For example, a counter-narrative to the one shown in Fig. 1 might target the identificational component, e.g., with evidence that Donald Trump really does *not* care about "people like you." One might highlight the fact that Trump knowingly downplayed the severity of the coronavirus and discouraged wearing masks, endangering the lives of many Americans (Gangel, Herb, & Stuart, 2020); held rallies that endangered the health of his supporters (Carlisle, 2020); and tried to pressure schools to reopen even as cases of COVID-19 were at unprecedented levels and increasing (Sullivan & Green, 2020). Instances like these suggest that Trump puts his own political interests above the health of both the general public and his supporters.

The evaluative component of Trump's narrative might be challenged with facts about outcomes of concern to potential adherents (e.g., that, while violent crime in the U.S. had indeed increased in 2015, it was down sharply since Obama became President, part of a decades-long trend; Berman, 2016). The behavioral component might be challenged with information that illegal immigrants commit *fewer* crimes than native-born citizens (Ingraham, 2018). The normative component might be addressed by documented accounts of Trump's illegal actions, discussed above. The explanatory component might be disputed by factual information about Trump's business successes and failures (e.g., Buettner & Craig, 2019).

Of course, it can be difficult to alter strong beliefs with facts. Facts may be in dispute, and the importance of a given set of facts can be hard to determine. Thus people with opposing views often talk past each other (Goertzel, 1992). Interventions employing the cognitive route must contend with selective exposure (Smith, Fabrigar, & Norris, 2008), selective recall (Kahan, Jenkins-Smith, & Braman, 2011), and motivated reasoning (Kunda, 1990) operating through defensive processes such as viewing belief-consistent evidence as high in quality, and inconsistent evidence as deficient (Visser, Krosnick, & Norris, 2016). However, even if strong partisans may be resistant to persuasion, it seems that continued accretion of incongruent information over time can alter people's views (Redlawsk, Civettini, & Emmerson, 2010).

6.2   Inducing Belief-Altering Emotions

Insofar as emotions are producing or strengthening extremist narratives, efforts could be made to reduce, alter, or redirect them; or create emotions that would be incompatible with them or that support competing narratives.

Studies examining why some individuals leave extremist groups have found that one common reason is anger at the group or group leaders, e.g., for failing to deal with infighting (Simi, Windisch, Harris, & Ligon, 2019), or for actions that have led to many deaths (Jacobson, 2010). Thus, anger might also be directed at Trump for his divisiveness, or for delaying the government response to the coronavirus pandemic, which is estimated to have cost thousands of lives (Glantz & Robertson, 2020). Research has also found that disillusionment (Simi et al., 2019) or lack of respect for leaders (Jacobson, 2010) is sometimes cited by former members as a reason for disengaging from a terrorist group, and a number of authors suggest using satire (Task Force on Confronting the Ideology of Radical Extremism, 2009), ridicule (Kessels, 2010), or negative portrayals of extremist leaders (e.g., as common criminals; Jacobson, 2010) as one part of efforts aimed at "rewriting the narrative" (Task Force on Confronting the Ideology of Radical Extremism, 2009) promulgated by extremist groups. This suggests employing the emotion of contempt, which is associated with perceiving others as having bad qualities and therefore rejecting them (Roseman, 2018). Contempt might be focused on Trump's ignorance (e.g., in suggesting unsound, unsafe coronavirus treatments; Dale, McDermott, Cohen, Vazquez, Steck, & Fossum, 2020); or incompetence (in mismanagement of the coronavirus crisis; cf. Hutcherson & Gross, 2011); or for his violation of moral standards (Bell, 2013) in lying continually (Kessler, Rizzo, & Kelly, 2020), or in hiding evidence (e.g., financial records, tax returns, subpoenaed documents in his impeachment trial), which resembles the behavior of ordinary criminals concealing their misdeeds (PBS Newshour, 2020). Counter-narratives might also attempt to elicit guilt (e.g., about ignoring Trump's association with white supremacists)—another emotion suggested as an antecedent of disengagement from terrorism (as when feeling "sinful" about causing harm; Jacobson, 2010).

Insofar as effective counter-narratives must also provide a pathway to a preferred outcome, including the emotion of hope is also likely to be important (Just, Crigler, & Belt, 2007). Indeed, Schmid's (2013) review concludes that using positive inducements rather than negative ones is the approach to deradicalization that has gotten the strongest empirical support. For example, the fear of crime might be assuaged by displays of hope, e.g., for unity, racial justice, and peace. Anger at undocumented immigrants might be countered by depictions of gratitude to immigrants for their contributions (e.g., as technological innovators, doctors and nurses, caregivers for the elderly, etc.), or empathic portrayals showing personal stories (cf. Task Force on Confronting the Ideology of Radical Extremism, 2009) of immigrants dealing with the same problems (e.g., economic struggles, illnesses) as other Americans, and, like others, working hard to achieve their dreams. A counter-narrative might also encompass affection for an empathic, genuinely caring leader (Roseman, Steele, & Goodvin, 2019b).

6.3   Constructing Counter-Narratives

One interesting question is whether it may sometimes or even typically be more effective to construct a competing narrative (e.g., Dahlstrom, 2014; Gaard, 2014) rather than to challenge (in whole or in part) an existing one. For example, in court cases, the prosecution and defense offer different theories of the case, which are typically competing stories (Pennington & Hastie, 1992), each one specifying eliciting events, actors, motives, actions, and outcomes. Competing narratives are also offered by political campaigns (e.g., in presidential elections; Neville-Shepard, 2017; Smith, 1989), and in attempts at deradicalization (Da Silva, Fernández-Navarro, Gonçalves, Rosa, & Silva, 2020).

Our theory suggests that the most successful counter-narrative should contain all of the components of a coherent narrative, structured as a dramatic story. That is, it should specify alternative outcomes differing in desirability; actions that can be taken which affect those outcomes; groups and individuals with whom the audience can identify, who take the actions and are affected by the outcomes; moral grounds on which the actions are justified and the outcomes are deserved; reasons to believe the narrative is true; and emotions which support the narrative. Due to their dramatic structure, cohesiveness, motive-relevance, and emotional impact, competing counter-narratives may be considerably more effective in reaching and persuading audiences than attempting to correct particular factual inaccuracies or challenging only one or two components of extremist ideologies.

For example, a counter-narrative to the one that Trump used to justify extreme behaviors might contrast the outcomes of unity and peace with those of division and conflict-related injury and death; actions of cooperation and compromise, rather than competition and attacks; superordinate inclusive group identities (e.g., as Americans) rather than partisan ones; the morality of reciprocity (fairness) and care as more important than authority, loyalty and purity (or cast authority and loyalty as pertaining to an overarching group identity, and purity in terms of standards of god-like love or kindness); and culturally accepted explanatory truths, principles, or historical examples of how cooperation resolves social dilemmas or other conflicts, and results in preferable outcomes for all in the long run. For example, one such narrative might say that Donald Trump, to further his personal political ambitions, has attacked minorities, immigrants, and political opponents (setting Americans against their fellow citizens) and violated the Constitution and the law to gain power and try to remain in power. His unlawful actions and their negative effects on people make us angry (and we have contempt for the selfishness that they demonstrate). But if people come together and support a leader who will pursue policies aimed at improving the welfare of *all* Americans, then all will benefit. We know that divided we fall, and we can hope that united we will stand. If we love our neighbors and support each other, as we did when facing the Depression and powerful foes in World War II, we can overcome the problems that we face, restoring peace and prosperity.

Note that the preceding paragraph provides merely an illustration of how a counter-narrative might be constructed from belief components and emotions. We are not claiming it is the best narrative, or even a superior one. We would predict that the more that a narrative can address the most important current concerns of its target audience, connect with their salient identities, offer justifiable actions that will attain their goals (according to the ways that they believe the world works), and resonate with their emotions, the more likely it will attract their strong belief. The specific contents of effective narratives will vary over time, as situations, concerns, and beliefs change.

6.4   Addressing Grievances and Aspirations

At the heart of strongly held systems of belief are the motivations of believers (Roseman, 1994), such as desires for safety, prosperity, and respect (e.g., see Trump, 2016). In addition, the ground that underlies, rationalizes, or allows many cases of seeking, accepting, or acting on political extremist ideology is perceived injustice (Dalgaard-Nielsen, 2010; Moghaddam, 2005), seeing desired outcomes as wrongfully denied or unfairly distributed.

To be more than empty rhetoric, efforts to counter extremism must go beyond constructing stories about desirable and just outcomes. They must create those outcomes in reality. According to the report of the Presidential Task Force on Confronting the Ideology of Radical Extremism (2009), "political and economic reform" is "the best strategic response" for "reducing the pool of recruits to radical extremism" (p. 9). "If grievances can be expressed peacefully and mediated through democratic institutions, citizens are less apt to turn to more extreme options… Prosperous democratic societies that respect the rights of their citizens are more resilient and less susceptible to political instability and radicalization" (p. 13).

When such recommendations are implemented, there is evidence that they work. In a careful analysis of the history of popular response to the Euskadi Ta Askatasuna (ETA) terrorist group in Spain, Alonso (2010) found that political reforms preceded dramatic declines in ETA's support. Public views of ETA were changed by democratization that involved granting significant political autonomy to the Basque region, including the creation of regional legislative, judicial, and executive institutions, along with recognition of the Basque language. Whereas in 1978 almost half of Basque adults viewed ETA members as patriots or idealists, by 1989 less than a quarter viewed them favorably (Alonso, 2010, pp. 24–25).

7 Looking Back and Looking Ahead

7.1 What Have We Learned?

This chapter offered a conceptualization of extremism as significantly norm-violating beliefs and behaviors, with a focus on prototypical political extremism that involves acceptance of violence and illegal means to achieve political ends. We discussed cognitive, motivational, behavioral and emotional pathways to extremism, and integrated these influences within a narrative theory with identificational, behavioral, evaluative, normative, and explanatory components structured into a dramatic story of justified action taken to overcome an imminent threat (supported and amplified by particular negative and positive emotions). We described survey research that tested the ability of variables from the theory to predict Americans' support and voting for Donald Trump, which found some empirical evidence for each of the five hypothesized belief components and the emotions of enthusiasm, hope, fear, and contempt. We also discussed how our theory might be used to challenge extremist narratives and construct effective counter-narratives.

7.2 Future Research Needed

Going forward, this narrative theory requires replication and extension. Can it help explain additional diverse examples, such as extremism in different societies and cultures (Gelfand, LaFree, Fahey, & Feinberg, 2013); religious fundamentalism as well as terrorism (Pratt, 2010); left-wing as well as right-wing populism (Mudde & Rovira Kaltwasser, 2012)? Attempted replications might test:

1. whether all five belief components are *necessary* for persuasive narratives. Roseman, Mattes, and Redlawsk (2019) found they each predicted thermometer evaluations of Trump, but the normative component did not independently predict vote choice;
2. whether some components are more important than others. Roseman, Mattes, and Redlawsk (2019) found that the identificational and explanatory components accounted for the largest share of variance, but this could have reflected the particular measures used—research with alternative measures is needed;
3. whether some emotions are more potent amplifiers of the narrative than others. For example, Schmid's (2013) review concluded that positive inducements for disengagement from terrorism were generally more effective than negative ones. Do findings about motivational influences (rewards vs. punishments) extend to positive vs. negative emotions? Are hope and anger, whose associated appraisals involve potential positive outcomes, and the power or ability to attain them (Lerner & Tiedens, 2006; Roseman & Evdokas, 2004) particularly potent emotions (Roseman et al., 2012)?
4. whether the various belief components and emotions have *interactive* effects. If narratives tell coherent stories (e.g. Pennington & Hastie, 1992; Roseman, 1994) then combinations of multiple components should have synergistic effects on the strength of belief and on behavior. In contrast, Roseman, Mattes, and Redlawsk (2019) found only main effects of the belief components and emotions.

7.3 Applications Needed

This chapter has suggested how our theory could be used to counteract extremist narratives, applying it to the example of Donald Trump's rhetoric. Would this actually affect people's beliefs and behaviors? Would such interventions succeed in preventing people from adopting extreme populist beliefs or joining extremist groups in other countries, or help in convincing them to disengage from such beliefs and organizations?

One interesting question is whether aiming to change behavior is generally more likely to succeed than attempting to change attitudes. Research from a dissonance theory perspective finds that when beliefs and behavior are in conflict, people tend to alter their beliefs (e.g., Fotuhi et al., 2013). Based on interviews with former members, Horgan (2008) concludes that leaving a terrorist group rarely results from, and is rarely accompanied by, abandonment of radical beliefs. More often, the departure may be occasioned by competing role demands such as becoming a parent (Jacobson, 2010) or getting a job (Bjørgo, 2009). Over time, depending on the extent to which alternative behaviors, coping responses, engagement, and supports are established, extremist narratives may be gradually abandoned or replaced (Barrelle, 2015).

Another question is the extent to which one should focus on social processes when attempting to counter extremist narratives. Extremist behavior is almost always a group or relational phenomenon (Schuurman et al., 2019). Entry into such groups is typically through familial and other social networks (Sageman, 2004) or outreach from group members (Hafez & Mullins, 2015); group processes (e.g., social learning, conformity) are often involved in the acquisition and maintenance of extremist beliefs (e.g., Goodwin & Darley, 2012); whether friends and associates leave or remain in extremist groups affects the related decisions of individuals (Simi et al., 2019); relationships with family and friends are often cited as reasons for leaving extremist groups (Simi et al., 2019); and the formation of supportive social contacts and relationships is important to successful reintegration of former extremist group members (Sulkowski & Picciolini, 2018). The operation of social processes is not inconsistent with the narrative model we have outlined. Rather, acknowledgement of their influence reminds us that social motives may be prominent in the evaluative component; the behavioral component often consists largely of collective actions; the identificational component typically involves social identity (Seyle & Besaw, 2021); norms are socially defined; and explanations are socially constructed and validated (Berger & Luckmann, 1966). Applying our model to understanding or altering extremist narratives must take into account, and often work through, social and group mechanisms.

Our approach implies that applications of the theory must proceed from particular conditions in each instance, such as the specific grievances and aspirations of potential adherents (e.g., correcting racial inequities; attaining political autonomy; providing economic betterment). Best might be a multifaceted approach, like that exemplified by the Presidential Task Force report (Task Force on Confronting the Ideology of Radical Extremism, 2009), which offered numerous theoretically and empirically grounded specific recommendations. It would also be useful to identify which among them has greatest support from extant research (as per Schmid's, 2013 review) or are likely to have greatest impact according to new theorical formulations.

In applying the theory, it is important to recognize that different interventions are likely to work best for different audiences and under differing conditions (Kessels, 2010). Even within a given extremist group, different members may join through different processes (McCauley & Moskalenko, 2008) and disengage for different reasons (Windisch, Simi, Ligon, & McNeel, 2016). In addition to the different motives of different individuals and groups in the evaluative component, different worldviews will make different arguments, historical examples, and metaphors relevant and convincing in the explanatory component.

Finally, we would be remiss if we failed to acknowledge that extremism might be necessary or beneficial in some instances (see, e.g., Rovira Kaltwasser's 2012 discussion of populism functioning as both a threat and a corrective for democracy). As citizens of a country born of violent revolution against an exploitative colonial power, Americans remain aware that sometimes prevailing norms, laws, and political institutions are unjust and oppressive, and need to be reformed or even overthrown. Similarly, many would maintain that some wars, which employ violence for political and other ends, need to be fought (e.g., to prevent fascist conquest, or end slavery). The difficulty, of course, is knowing when resorting to unlawful means or violence are truly necessary. While extremist narratives often contend that they are the only ways to attain vital and legitimate goals (Berger, 2018), the enormous costs of uprisings, revolutions, and wars (e.g., Hacker & McPherson, 2011), and the history of would-be tyrants, groups, and nations misrepresenting their private aims as beneficial and necessary for the general welfare (e.g., Crossman, 1950) argues that the bar for accepting such assertions should be very, very high.

References

Abelson, R. P. (1995). Attitude extremity. In R. E. Petty & J. A. Krosnick (Eds.), *Attitude strength: Antecedents and consequences* (pp. 25–41). Mahwah, NJ: Erlbaum.

Ahmed, Z. S., & Bashirov, G. (2020). Religious fundamentalism and violent extremism. In F. R. Aravena (Ed.), *The difficult task of peace: Crisis, fragility and conflict in an uncertain world* (pp. 245–260). Cham: Palgrave Macmillan.

Albertson, B., & Gadarian, S. K. (2015). *Anxious politics: Democratic citizenship in a threatening world*. New York: Cambridge University Press.

Alonso, R. (2010). Counter-narratives against ETA's terrorism in Spain. In E. J. A. M. Kessels (Ed.), *Countering violent extremist narratives* (pp. 26–35). The Hague: National Coordinator for Counter-Terrorism.

Altemeyer, B. (1981). *Right-wing authoritarianism*. Winnipeg: University of Manitoba Press.

American Heritage Dictionary. (n.d.-a). *Extreme*. Retrieved July 23, 2020, from https://ahdictionary.com/word/search.html?q=extreme

American Heritage Dictionary. (n.d.-b). *Extremist*. Retrieved July 23, 2020, from https://ahdictionary.com/word/search.html?q=extremist

American Immigration Council. (n.d.). *Government documents on family separation*. Retrieved from https://www.americanimmigrationcouncil.org/FOIA/government-documents-family-separation-tracking-policys-evolution-implementation-and-harm

Angus, L. E., & Greenberg, L. S. (2011). *Working with narrative in emotion-focused therapy: Changing stories, healing lives*. Washington, DC: American Psychological Association.

Ansolabehere, S., & Schaffner, B. F. (2017). *CCES Common Content, 2016*. Cambridge, MA: Harvard University [producer].

Associated Press (2021, January 13). Transcript of Trump's speech at rally before US Capitol riot. *US News & World Report*. Retrieved from https://www.usnews.com/news/politics/articles/2021-01-13/transcript-of-trumps-speech-at-rally-before-us-capitol-riot.

Aumer, K., & Erickson, M. A. (2021). Shared hatred: Bringing people together and creating bonds. In K. Aumer (Ed.), *The psychology of extremism*. Cham: Springer.

Averill, J. R. (1982). *Anger and aggression: An essay on emotion*. New York: Springer-Verlag.

Ayer, D. B. et al. (2016). *Statement by former national security officials.* Retrieved from https://apps.washingtonpost.com/g/documents/national/read-the-letter-by-former-gop-national-security-officials-opposing-trump/2116/

Backes, U. (2010). *Political extremes: A conceptual history from antiquity to the present.* London: Routledge.

Bade, R., Dawsey, J., & Hamburger, T. (2020, December 10). Trump pressures congressional Republicans to help in his fight to overturn the election. *The Washington Post.* https://www.washingtonpost.com/politics/trump-republicans-biden-election/2020/12/09/abd596ea-3a4e-11eb-9276-ae0ca72729be_story.html

Bakker, E. (2006). *Jihadi terrorists in Europe.* The Hague: Cliengendael.

Bandura, A. (1990). Mechanisms of moral disengagement in terrorism. In W. Reich (Ed.), *Origins of terrorism: Psychologies, ideologies, states of mind* (pp. 161–191). New York: Cambridge University Press.

Bandura, A. (1997). *Self-efficacy: The exercise of control.* New York: Freeman.

Banks, A. J. (2016). Are group cues necessary? How anger makes ethnocentrism among whites a stronger predictor of racial and immigration policy opinions. *Political Behavior, 38*(3), 635–657.

Barnidge, M., Gunther, A. C., Kim, J., Hong, Y., Perryman, M., Tay, S. K., & Knisely, S. (2020). Politically motivated selective exposure and perceived media bias. *Communication Research, 47*(1), 82–103.

Barrelle, K. (2015). Pro-integration: Disengagement from and life after extremism. *Behavioral Sciences of Terrorism and Political Aggression, 7*(2), 129–142.

Barrett, D., Hsu, S. S., & Zapotsky, M. (2021, January 8). FBI focuses on whether some Capitol rioters intended to harm lawmakers or take hostages. *The Washington Post.* Retrieved from https://www.washingtonpost.com/national-security/capitol-riot-fbi-hostages/2021/01/08/df99ae5a-5202-11eb-83e3-322644d82356_story.html.

Barry, D., McIntire, M., & Rosenberg, M. (2021, January 9). 'Our President wants us here': The mob that stormed the Capitol. *The New York Times.* Retrieved from https://www.nytimes.com/2021/01/09/us/capitol-rioters.html.

Baumeister, R. F. (1991). *Meanings of life.* New York: Guilford.

Bélanger, J. J., Caouette, J., Sharvit, K., & Dugas, M. (2014). The psychology of martyrdom: Making the ultimate sacrifice in the name of a cause. *Journal of Personality and Social Psychology, 107*(3), 494–515.

Bell, M. (2013). *Hard feelings: The moral psychology of contempt.* New York: Oxford University Press.

Berger, A. L. (2018). Religious fundamentalism and political extremism. *Journal of Ecumenical Studies, 53*(4), 608–615.

Berger, J. M. (2019). *Researching violent extremism: The state of play.* Washington, DC: Resolve Network.

Berger, P. L., & Luckmann, T. (1966). *The social construction of reality: A treatise in the sociology of knowledge.* New York: Penguin.

Berkowitz, L. (2012). A different view of anger: The cognitive-neoassociation conception of the relation of anger to aggression. *Aggressive Behavior, 38*(4), 322–333.

Berman, M. (2016, July 21). What Trump says about crime in America and what is really going on. *The Washington Post.* Retrieved from https://www.washingtonpost.com/news/post-nation/wp/2016/07/21/what-trump-says-about-crime-in-america-and-what-is-really-going-on/

Bernton, H. (2020, July 20). Dynamic of Portland protests shifts as Trump administration ratchets up federal pressure on cities. *The Seattle Times.* Retrieved from https://www.seattletimes.com/seattle-news/dynamic-of-portland-protests-shifts-as-trump-administration-ratchets-up-federal-pressure-on-cities/

Berry, D., & Frenkel, S. (2021, January 6). 'Be there. Will be wild!': Trump all but circled the date. *The New York Times.* Retrieved from https://www.nytimes.com/2021/01/06/us/politics/capitol-mob-trump-supporters.html.

Bertrand, N., & Samuelsohn, D. (2019, June 21). What if Trump won't accept 2020 defeat? *Politico.* Retrieved from https://www.politico.com/story/2019/06/21/trump-election-2020-1374589

Bettencourt, B. A., Talley, A., Benjamin, A. J., & Valentine, J. (2006). Personality and aggressive behavior under provoking and neutral conditions: A meta-analytic review. *Psychological Bulletin, 132*(5), 751–777.

Betz, H. G. (1994). *Radical right-wing populism in Western Europe.* London: Macmillan.

Bjørgo, T. (2009). Processes of disengagement from violent groups of the extreme right. In T. Bjørgo & J. G. Horgan (Eds.), *Leaving terrorism behind: Individual and collective disengagement* (pp. 30–48). New York: Routledge.

Bjørgo, T. (2011). Dreams and disillusionment: Engagement in and disengagement from militant extremist groups. *Crime, Law and Social Change, 55*(4), 277–285.

Blendon, R. J., Casey, L. S., & Benson, J. M. (2017). Public opinion and Trump's jobs and trade policies. *Challenge, 60*(3), 228–244.

Bobo, L. D. (2017). Racism in Trump's America: Reflections on culture, sociology, and the 2016 US presidential election. *The British Journal of Sociology, 68*, S85–S104.

Borum, R. (2011). Radicalization into violent extremism I: A review of social science theories. *Journal of Strategic Security, 4*(4), 7–36.

Borum, R. (2014). Psychological vulnerabilities and propensities for involvement in violent extremism. *Behavioral Sciences & the Law, 32*(3), 286–305.

Brader, T., & Marcus, G. E. (2013). Emotion and political psychology. In L. Huddy, D. O. Sears, & J. S. Levy (Eds.). *The Oxford handbook of political psychology* (pp. 165–204). New York: Oxford University Press.

Brandstätter, H., & Opp, K. D. (2014). Personality traits ("Big Five") and the propensity to political protest: Alternative models. *Political Psychology, 35*(4), 515–537.

Buettner, R., & Craig, S. (2019, May 8). Decade in the red: Trump tax figures show over $1 billion in business losses. *The New York Times.* Retrieved from https://www.nytimes.com/interactive/2019/05/07/us/politics/donald-trump-taxes.html

Bump, P. (2019, August 20). The expansive, repetitive universe of Trump's Twitter insults. *The Washington Post.* Retrieved from https://www.washingtonpost.com/politics/2019/08/20/expansive-repetitive-universe-trumps-twitter-insults/

Bump, P. (2020, May 6). A review of Trump's many unsubstantiated allegations of voter fraud. Retrieved from https://www.washingtonpost.com/politics/2020/05/26/review-trumps-many-unsubstantiated-allegations-voter-fraud/

Burnstein, E., & Vinokur, A. (1977). Persuasive argumentation and social comparison as determinants of attitude polarization. *Journal of Experimental Social Psychology, 13*(4), 315–332.

Cannon, W. B. (1932). *The wisdom of the body.* New York: Norton.

Carlisle, M. (2020, July 11). Three weeks after Trump's Tulsa rally, Oklahoma reports record high COVID-19 numbers. *Time.* https://time.com/5865890/oklahoma-covid-19-trump-tulsa-rally/

Ceulemans, E., Kuppens, P., & Van Mechelen, I. (2012). Capturing the structure of distinct types of individual differences in the situation-specific experience of emotions: The case of anger. *European Journal of Personality, 26*(5), 484–495.

Chavez, N., & Sanchez, R. (2020, June 20). Trump calls protesters 'thugs' despite peaceful demonstrations in Tulsa and much of the US. *CNN.* Retrieved from https://www.cnn.com/2020/06/20/us/nationwide-protests-saturday/index.html

Cheung-Blunden, V., & Blunden, B. (2008). The emotional construal of war: Anger, fear, and other negative emotions. *Peace and Conflict, 14*(2), 123–150.

Chokshi, N. (2016, January 27). The 100-plus times Donald Trump assured us that America is a laughingstock. *The Washington Post.* Retrieved from https://www.washingtonpost.com/news/the-fix/wp/2016/01/27/the-100-plus-times-donald-trump-has-assured-us-the-united-states-is-a-laughingstock/

Cofer, C. N., & Appley, M. H. (1964). *Motivation: Theory and research.* New York: Wiley.

Collins, M., Jackson, D., & Subramanian, C. (2019, October 21). 'Phony.' Donald Trump mocks 'emoluments' clause of U.S. constitution that bans foreign gifts. *USA Today.* Retrieved from https://www.usatoday.com/story/news/politics/2019/10/21/donald-trump-mocks-constitution-emoluments-clause-phony/4055162002/

Corasaniti, N., & Haberman, M. (2016, August 9). Donald Trump suggests 'Second Amendment People' could act against Hillary Clinton. *The New York Times*. Retrieved from https://www.nytimes.com/2016/08/10/us/politics/donald-trump-hillary-clinton.html

Corner, E., & Gill, P. (2019). Psychological distress, terrorist involvement and disengagement from terrorism: A sequence analysis approach. *Journal of Quantitative Criminology*, 1–28.

Crossman, R. H. S. (Ed.). (1950). *The God that failed: Six studies in Communism*. London: Hamilton.

Dale, D., McDermott, N., Cohen, M., Vazquez, M., Steck, E., & Fossum, S. (2020, April 24). Fact check: Trump dangerously suggests sunlight and ingesting disinfectants could help cure coronavirus. *CNN*. https://www.cnn.com/2020/04/23/politics/fact-check-coronavirus-briefing-april-23/index.html

Da Silva, R., Fernández-Navarro, P., Gonçalves, M. M., Rosa, C., & Silva, J. (2020). Disengagement from political violence and deradicalization: A narrative-dialogical perspective. *Studies in Conflict & Terrorism, 43*(6), 444–467.

Dahlstrom, M. F. (2014). Using narratives and storytelling to communicate science with non-expert audiences. *Proceedings of the National Academy of Sciences, 111*(Supplement 4), 13614–13620.

Dalgaard-Nielsen, A. (2010). Violent radicalization in Europe: What we know and what we do not know. *Studies in Conflict & Terrorism, 33*(9), 797–814.

Daniels, B. C. (1993). Sober mirth and pleasant poisons: Puritan ambivalence toward leisure and recreation in colonial New England. *American Studies, 34*(1), 121–137.

della Porta, D. (2018). Radicalization: A relational perspective. *Annual Review of Political Science, 21*, 461–474.

Derysh, I. (2020, December 14). Hate crime probe launched in wake of violent pro-Trump rally: Vandals attack historic Black churches. *Salon*. https://www.salon.com/2020/12/14/hate-crime-probe-launched-in-wake-of-violent-pro-trump-rally-vandals-attack-historic-black-churches/

Deutsch, M., & Gerard, H. B. (1955). A study of normative and informational social influences upon individual judgment. *The Journal of Abnormal and Social Psychology, 51*(3), 629–636.

Diaz, D. (2018, January 6). Trump: I'm a 'very stable genius'. Retrieved from https://www.cnn.com/2018/01/06/politics/donald-trump-white-house-fitness-very-stable-genius/index.html

Easterbrook, J. A. (1959). The effect of emotion on cue utilization and the organization of behavior. *Psychological Review, 66*(3), 183–201.

Edgar, E. A. (2020). A rational continuum: Legal and cultural abortion narratives in Trump's America. *European Journal of American Studies, 15*(15–2).

Ellsworth, P. C., & Scherer, K. R. (2003). Appraisal processes in emotion. In R. J. Davidson, K. R. Scherer, & H. H. Goldsmith (Eds.), *Handbook of affective sciences* (pp. 572–595). Oxford: Oxford University Press.

Elving, R. (2020, July 17). Trump's Helsinki bow To Putin leaves world wondering: Why? *NPR*. https://www.npr.org/2018/07/17/629601233/trumps-helsinki-bow-to-putin-leaves-world-wondering-whats-up

Evon, D. (2021). *Was 'Hang Mike Pence' chanted at Capitol riot?* Retrieved from https://www.snopes.com/fact-check/hang-mike-pence-chant-capitol-riot/

Fearnow, B. (2020, December 12). Trump urges base in Georgia, Arizona to oust governors who 'allowed' election to be 'stolen.' *Newsweek*. Retrieved from https://www.newsweek.com/trump-urges-base-georgia-arizona-oust-governors-who-allowed-election-stolen-1554330.

Federal Bureau of Investigation Counterterrorism Division. (2006). *The radicalization process: From conversion to Jihad*. Retrieved from https://the-eye.eu/public/Books/campdivision.com/Sensitive/Leaked%20Docs/fbi-jihad.pdf

Festinger, L. (1957). *A theory of cognitive dissonance*. Palo Alto, CA: Stanford University Press.

Fischer, A., Halperin, E., Canetti, D., & Jasini, A. (2018). Why we hate. *Emotion Review, 10*(4), 309–320.

Fischer, A. H., & Roseman, I. J. (2007). Beat them or ban them: The characteristics and social functions of anger and contempt. *Journal of Personality and Social Psychology, 93*, 103–115.

Fiske, S. T. (2010). *Social beings: Core motives in social psychology* (2nd ed.). New York: Wiley.

FiveThirtyEight. (2020). *How popular is Donald Trump?* Retrieved on December 16, 2020 from https://projects.fivethirtyeight.com/trump-approval-ratings/

Fontaine, J. J. R., & Scherer, K. R. (2013). Emotion is for doing: The action tendency component. In J. J. R. Fontaine, K. R. Scherer, & C. Soriano (Eds.), *Components of emotional meaning: A sourcebook* (pp. 170–185). Oxford: Oxford University Press.

Fotuhi, O., Fong, G. T., Zanna, M. P., Borland, R., Yong, H. H., & Cummings, K. M. (2013). Patterns of cognitive dissonance-reducing beliefs among smokers: A longitudinal analysis from the International Tobacco Control (ITC) Four Country Survey. *Tobacco Control, 22*(1), 52–58.

Frankl, V. (2000). *Man's ultimate search for meaning.* Cambridge, MA: Perseus.

Frenkel, S. (2021, January 6). The storming of Capitol Hill was organized on social media. *The New York Times.* Retrieved from https://www.nytimes.com/2021/01/06/us/politics/protesters-storm-capitol-hill-building.html.

Frijda, N. H. (1986). *The emotions.* New York: Cambridge University Press.

Frijda, N. H., Kuipers, P., & ter Schure, E. (1989). Relations among emotion, appraisal, and emotional action readiness. *Journal of Personality and Social Psychology, 57*, 212–228.

Gaard, G. (2014). What's the story? Competing narratives of climate change and climate justice. *Forum for World Literature Studies, 6*(2), 272–291.

Gangel, J., Herb, J., & Stuart, E. (2020, September 9). 'Play it down': Trump admits to concealing the true threat of coronavirus in new Woodward book. *CNN.* https://www.cnn.com/2020/09/09/politics/bob-woodward-rage-book-trump-coronavirus/index.html

Gardner, A., & Firozi, P. (2021, , January 5). Here's the full transcript and audio of the call between Trump and Raffensperger. *The Washington Post.* Retrieved from https://www.washington-post.com/politics/trump-raffensperger-call-transcript-georgia-vote/2021/01/03/2768e0cc-4ddd-11eb-83e3-322644d82356_story.html

Garrett, K. N., & Bankert, A. (2018). The moral roots of partisan division: How moral conviction heightens affective polarization. *British Journal of Political Science*, 1–20.

Gelfand, M. J., LaFree, G., Fahey, S., & Feinberg, E. (2013). Culture and extremism. *Journal of Social Issues, 69*(3), 495–517.

Giella, L. (2021, January 8). Fact check: Did Trump call in the National Guard after rioters stormed the Capitol? *Newsweek.* Retrieved from https://www.newsweek.com/fact-check-did-trump-call-national-guard-after-rioters-stormed-capitol-1560186.

Glantz, J., & Robertson, C. (2020, May 20). Lockdown delays cost at least 36,000 lives, data show. *The New York Times.* Retrieved from https://www.nytimes.com/2020/05/20/us/coronavirus-distancing-deaths.html

Goertzel, T. G. (1992). *Turncoats & true believers: The dynamics of political belief and disillusionment.* Buffalo, NY: Prometheus Books.

Goodvin, A. (2019). *Is hate a distinct emotion?* Unpublished Master's thesis. Camden, NJ: Rutgers University.

Goodwin, G. P., & Darley, J. M. (2012). Why are some moral beliefs perceived to be more objective than others? *Journal of Experimental Social Psychology, 48*(1), 250–256.

Graham, D. A. (2017). The many scandals of Donald Trump: A cheat sheet. *The Atlantic.* Retrieved from https://www.theatlantic.com/politics/archive/2017/01/donald-trump-scandals/474726/

Haberman, M. (2021, January 6). Trump told crowd 'You will never take back our country with weakness.' *The New York Times.* Retrieved from https://www.nytimes.com/2021/01/06/us/politics/trump-speech-capitol.html

Haberman, M., & Schmidt, M. S. (2021, January 13). Under heavy pressure, Trump releases video condemning Capitol siege. *The New York Times.* Retrieved from https://www.nytimes.com/2021/01/13/us/politics/trump-video-capitol-riot.html.

Habermas, T. (2019). *Emotion and narrative: Perspectives in autobiographical storytelling.* New York: Cambridge University Press.

Hacker, J. D., & McPherson, J. M. (2011). A census-based count of the civil war dead: With introductory remarks by James M. McPherson. *Civil War History, 57*(4), 307–348.

Hafez, M., & Mullins, C. (2015). The radicalization puzzle: A theoretical synthesis of empirical approaches to homegrown extremism. *Studies in Conflict & Terrorism, 38*(11), 958–975.

Haidt, J. (2003). The moral emotions. In R. J. Davidson, K. R. Scherer, & H. H. Goldsmith (Eds.) *Handbook of affective sciences* (pp. 852–870). Oxford, UK: Oxford University Press

Han, S., Lerner, J. S., & Keltner, D. (2007). Feelings and consumer decision making: The appraisal-tendency framework. *Journal of Consumer Psychology, 17*(3), 158–168.

Harwell, D. (2016, September 15). All the excuses Trump has given for why he won't release his tax returns. *The Washington Post.* https://www.washingtonpost.com/news/business/wp/2016/09/15/a-running-tally-of-trumps-many-excuses-for-why-he-wont-release-his-tax-returns/

Harwell, D. (2017, April 3). Trump can quietly draw money from trust whenever he wants, new documents show. *The Washington Post.* Retrieved from https://www.washingtonpost.com/politics/trump-can-quietly-draw-money-from-trust-whenever-he-wants-new-documents-show/2017/04/03/7f4c0002-187c-11e7-9887-1a5314b56a08_story.html

Hassan, G., Brouillette-Alarie, S., Alava, S., Frau-Meigs, D., Lavoie, L., Fetiu, A., Varela, W., Borokhovski, E., Venkatesh, V., Rousseau, C., & Sieckelinck, S. (2018). Exposure to extremist online content could lead to violent radicalization: A systematic review of empirical evidence. *International Journal of Developmental Science, 12*(1–2), 71–88.

Hatemi, P. K., & McDermott, R. (2012). A neurobiological approach to foreign policy analysis: Identifying individual differences in political violence. *Foreign Policy Analysis, 8*(2), 111–129.

Hibbing, J. R. (2020). *The securitarian personality: What really motivates Trump's base and why it matters for the post-Trump era.* New York: Oxford University Press.

Hill, E., Botti, D., Khavin, D., Jordan, D., & Browne, M. (2021, March 24). Officer Brian Sicknick died after the Capitol riot. New videos show how he was attacked. *The New York Times.* Retrieved from https://www.nytimes.com/interactive/2021/03/24/us/officer-sicknick-capitol-riot.html

Hirschberger, G., Ein-Dor, T., Leidner, B., & Saguy, T. (2016). How is existential threat related to intergroup conflict? Introducing the multidimensional existential threat (MET) model. *Frontiers in Psychology, 7*, 1877.

Hirschberger, G., Pyszczynski, T., & Ein-Dor, T. (2009). Vulnerability and vigilance: Threat awareness and perceived adversary intent moderate the impact of mortality salience on intergroup violence. *Personality and Social Psychology Bulletin, 35*(5), 597–607.

Hochschild, A. R. (2016). *Strangers in their own land: Anger and mourning on the American right.* New York: The New Press.

Hogg, M. A. (2014). From uncertainty to extremism: Social categorization and identity processes. *Current Directions in Psychological Science, 23*(5), 338–342.

Horgan, J. (2003). The search for the terrorist personality. In A. Silke (Ed.), *Terrorists, victims and society* (pp. 3–27). Hoboken, NJ: Wiley.

Horgan, J. (2008). Deradicalization or disengagement? A process in need of clarity and a counter-terrorism initiative in need of evaluation. *Perspectives on Terrorism, 2*(4), 3–8.

Howe, L. C., & Krosnick, J. A. (2017). Attitude strength. *Annual Review of Psychology, 68*(1), 327–351.

Hull, C. L. (1943). *Principles of behavior.* New York: Appleton-Century-Crofts.

Hutcherson, C. A., & Gross, J. J. (2011). The moral emotions: A social–functionalist account of anger, disgust, and contempt. *Journal of Personality and Social Psychology, 100*(4), 719–737.

Ingraham, C. (2018, June 19). Two charts demolish the notion that immigrants here illegally commit more crime. *The Washington Post.* Retrieved from https://www.washingtonpost.com/news/wonk/wp/2018/06/19/two-charts-demolish-the-notion-that-immigrants-here-illegally-commit-more-crime/

Iyengar, S., & Hahn, K. S. (2009). Red media, blue media: Evidence of ideological selectivity in media use. *Journal of Communication, 59*(1), 19–39.

Izard, C. E. (1991). *The psychology of emotions.* New York: Plenum Press.

Jacobson, G. C. (2017). The triumph of polarized partisanship in 2016: Donald Trump's improbable victory. *Political Science Quarterly, 132*(1), 9–42.

Jacobson, M. (2010). Learning counter-narrative lessons from cases of terrorist dropouts. In E. J. A. M. Kessels (Ed.), *Countering violent extremist narratives* (pp. 72–83). The Hague: National Coordinator for Counter-Terrorism.

Jamieson, K. H., & Taussig, D. (2017). Disruption, demonization, deliverance, and norm destruction: The rhetorical signature of Donald J. Trump. *Political Science Quarterly, 132*(4), 619–651.

Johnson, J., & Hauslohner, A. (2017, May 20). 'I think Islam hates us': A timeline of Trump's comments about Islam and Muslims. *The Washington Post*. Retrieved from https://www.washingtonpost.com/news/post-politics/wp/2017/05/20/i-think-islam-hates-us-a-timeline-of-trumps-comments-about-islam-and-muslims/

Just, M. R., Crigler, A. N., & Belt, T. L. (2007). Don't give up hope: Emotions, candidate appraisals, and votes. In W. R. Neuman, G. E. Marcus, A. N. Crigler, & M. MacKuen (Eds.), *The affect effect: Dynamics of emotion in political thinking and behavior* (pp. 231–259). Chicago: The University of Chicago Press.

Kaczynski, A., & McDermott, N. (2016, November 8). On election day, Trump still signaling he may not accept results. *CNN*. Retrieved from https://www.cnn.com/2016/11/08/politics/trump-election-day-accepting-results/index.html

Kahan, D. M., Jenkins-Smith, H., & Braman, D. (2011). Cultural cognition of scientific consensus. *Journal of Risk Research, 14*(2), 147–174.

Kane, A. (2001). Finding emotion in social movement processes: Irish land movement metaphors and narratives. In J. Goodwin, J. M. Jasper, & F. Polletta (Eds.), *Passionate politics: Emotions and social movements* (pp. 251–266). Chicago: University of Chicago Press.

Kanno-Youngs, Z., & Sanger, D. (2021, January 27). Extremists emboldened by Capitol attack pose rising threat, Homeland Security says. *The New York Times*. Retrieved from https://www.nytimes.com/2021/01/27/us/politics/homeland-security-threat.html.

Karwowski, M., Kowal, M., Groyecka, A., Białek, M., Lebuda, I., Sorokowska, A., & Sorokowski, P. (2020). When in danger, turn right: Does Covid-19 threat promote social conservatism and right-wing presidential candidates? *Human Ethology, 35,* 37–48.

Katz, D. (1960). The functional approach to the study of attitudes. *Public Opinion Quarterly, 24*(2), 163–204.

Keniston, K. (1968). *Young radicals: Notes on committed youth*. New York: Harcourt, Brace & World.

Kessels, E. J. A. M. (Ed.). (2010). *Countering violent extremist narratives*. The Hague: National Coordinator for Counter-Terrorism.

Kessler, G., Rizzo, S., & Kelly, M. (2020, June 1). President Trump made 19,127 false or misleading claims in 1,226 days. *The Washington Post*. Retrieved from https://www.washingtonpost.com/politics/2020/06/01/president-trump-made-19127-false-or-misleading-claims-1226-days/

Kiely, E., Robertson, L., & Gore, D. (2019). Trump's inaccurate claims about his 'perfect' call. *FactCheck.org*. Retrieved from https://www.factcheck.org/2019/10/trumps-inaccurate-claims-about-his-perfect-call/

Knowles, D., Walker, H., & Winter, J. (2021, January 6). Trump supporters storm Congress, halting electoral vote certification debate. *Yahoo!News*. Retrieved from https://www.yahoo.com/news/trump-supporters-storm-congress-halting-electoral-vote-certification-debate-200312508.html

Krieg, G. (2016, October 10). Trump threatens to jail Clinton if he wins election. *CNN*. Retrieved from https://www.cnn.com/2016/10/09/politics/eric-holder-nixon-trump-presidential-debate/index.html

Kruglanski, A. W., Gelfand, M. J., Bélanger, J. J., Sheveland, A., Hetiarachchi, M., & Gunaratna, R. (2014). The psychology of radicalization and deradicalization: How significance quest impacts violent extremism. *Political Psychology, 35,* 69–93.

Kunda, Z. (1990). The case for motivated reasoning. *Psychological Bulletin, 108*(3), 480–498.

Kuppens, P., Van Mechelen, I., Smits, D. J. M., & De Boeck, P. (2003). The appraisal basis of anger: Specificity, necessity, and sufficiency of components. *Emotion, 3*(3), 254–269.

Lamont, M. (2018). Addressing recognition gaps: Destigmatization and the reduction of inequality. *American Sociological Review, 83*(3), 419–444.

Lamont, M., Park, B. Y., & Ayala-Hurtado, E. (2017). Trump's electoral speeches and his appeal to the American white working class. *The British Journal of Sociology, 68,* S153–S180.

Law, T., & Martinez, G. (2019). NOAA disputes its own experts, siding with president Trump over hurricane Dorian and Alabama. Here's a full timeline of the controversy. *Time*. Retrieved from https://time.com/5671606/trump-hurricane-dorian-alabama/

Lee, J. C., & Quealy, K. (2019, May 24). The 598 people, places and things Donald Trump has insulted on Twitter: A complete list. *The New York Times*. Retrieved from https://www.nytimes.com/interactive/2016/01/28/upshot/donald-trump-twitter-insults.html

Lerner, J. S., Gonzalez, R. M., Small, D. A., & Fischhoff, B. (2003). Effects of fear and anger on perceived risks of terrorism: A national field experiment. *Psychological Science, 14*(2), 144–150.

Lerner, J. S., & Tiedens, L. Z. (2006). Portrait of the angry decision maker: How appraisal tendencies shape anger's influence on cognition. *Journal of Behavioral Decision Making, 19*(2), 115–137.

Levin, B. (2019, September 26). Trump suggests executing the whistle-blower's sources like "in the old days." *Vanity Fair*. https://www.vanityfair.com/news/2019/09/trump-whistleblower-spies-treason

Levine, M. (2020, May 30). 'No blame?' ABC news finds 54 cases invoking 'Trump' in connection with violence, threats, alleged assaults. *ABC News* https://abcnews.go.com/Politics/blame-abc-news-finds-17-cases-invoking-trump/story?id=58912889.

Mackie, D. M., Devos, T., & Smith, E. R. (2000). Intergroup emotions: Explaining offensive action tendencies in an intergroup context. *Journal of Personality and Social Psychology, 79*(4), 602–616.

MacKuen, M., Marcus, G. E., Neuman, W. R., & Keele, L. (2007). The third way: The theory of affective intelligence and American democracy. In G. E. Marcus, W. R. Neuman, M. MacKuen, & A. N. Crigler (Eds.), *The affect effect: Dynamics of emotion in political thinking and behavior.* (pp. 124–151). University of Chicago Press.

MacWilliams, M. C. (2016). Who decides when the party doesn't? Authoritarian voters and the rise of Donald Trump. *PS: Political Science & Politics, 49*(4), 716–721.

Madhani, A. (2020, June 19). Trump turns virus conversation into 'US vs. THEM' debate. *The Associated Press*. Retrieved from https://apnews.com/fe8d83b196f703520495ab7a92ba4dcc

Malkin, C. (2019). Pathological narcissism and politics: A lethal mix. In B. X. Lee (Ed.), *The dangerous case of Donald Trump: 37 psychiatrists and mental health experts assess a president* (2nd ed., pp. 46–63). New York: St. Martin's.

Manchia, M., Booij, L., Pinna, F., Wong, J., Zepf, F., & Comai, S. (2020). Neurobiology of violence. In B. Carpiniello, A. Vita, & C. Mencacci (Eds.), *Violence and mental disorders* (pp. 25–47). Cham: Springer.

Margolis, M. F. (2020). Who wants to make America great again? Understanding evangelical support for Donald Trump. *Politics and Religion, 13*(1), 89–118.

Martí, G. (2019). The unexpected orthodoxy of Donald J. Trump: White evangelical support for the 45th President of the United States. *Sociology of Religion, 80*, 1–8.

Matsumoto, D., Hwang, H. C., & Frank, M. G. (2014). Emotions expressed in speeches by leaders of ideologically motivated groups predict aggression. *Behavioral Sciences of Terrorism and Political Aggression, 6*(1), 1–18.

McAdams, D. P. (2020). *The strange case of Donald J. Trump: A psychological reckoning.* New York: Oxford University Press.

McCauley, C., & Moskalenko, S. (2008). Mechanisms of political radicalization: Pathways toward terrorism. *Terrorism and Political Violence, 20*(3), 415–433.

McDermott, R., & Hatemi, P. K. (2017). The relationship between physical aggression, foreign policy and moral choices: Phenotypic and genetic findings. *Aggressive Behavior, 43*(1), 37–46.

McDermott, R., Tingley, D., Cowden, J., Frazzetto, G., & Johnson, D. D. P. (2009). Monoamine oxidase A gene (MAOA) predicts behavioral aggression following provocation. *Proceedings of the National Academy of Sciences, 106*(7), 2118–2123.

Midlarsky, M. I. (2011). *Origins of political extremism: Mass violence in the twentieth century and beyond.* New York: Cambridge University Press.

Miklikowska, M. (2017). Development of anti-immigrant attitudes in adolescence: The role of parents, peers, intergroup friendships, and empathy. *British Journal of Psychology, 108*(3), 626–648.

Mitchell, A., Gottfried, J., & Barthel, M. (2017). Trump, Clinton voters divided in their main source for election news. *Pew Research.* Retrieved from https://www.journalism.org/2017/01/18/trump-clinton-voters-divided-in-their-main-source-for-election-news/

Mitchell, L. (2020, June 23). What if Trump rejects the election result? *CNN.* Retrieved from https://www.cnn.com/2020/06/23/opinions/what-if-trump-rejects-election-result-mitchell/index.html

Moghaddam, F. M. (2005). The staircase to terrorism: A psychological exploration. *American Psychologist, 60*(2), 161–169.

Mudde, C., & Rovira Kaltwasser, C. (2012). Populism and (liberal) democracy: A framework for analysis. In *Populism in Europe and the Americas: Threat or corrective for democracy* (pp. 1–26). New York: Cambridge University Press.

Murray, H. A. (1938). *Explorations in personality: A clinical and experimental study of fifty men of college age.* New York: Oxford University Press.

Nai, A., Schemeil, Y., & Marie, J-L. (2017). Anxiety, sophistication, and resistance to persuasion: Evidence from a quasi-experimental survey on global climate change. *Political Psychology, 38*(1), 137–156.

Neumann, P. R., & Rogers, B. (2007). *Recruitment and mobilisation for the Islamist militant movement in Europe.* London: International Centre for the Study of Radicalisation and Political Violence.

Neville-Shepard, R. (2017). Constrained by duality: Third-party master narratives in the 2016 presidential election. *American Behavioral Scientist, 61*(4), 414–427.

New York Times (2021, January 12). How a Presidential rally turned into a Capitol rampage. *The New York Times.* Retrieved from https://www.nytimes.com/interactive/2021/01/12/us/capitol-mob-timeline.html.

Nicholas, P. (2020, June 16). Trump could still break democracy's biggest norm. *The Atlantic.* Retrieved from https://www.theatlantic.com/politics/archive/2020/06/when-does-trump-leave-white-house/613060/

Nickerson, R. S. (1998). Confirmation bias: A ubiquitous phenomenon in many guises. *Review of General Psychology, 2*(2), 175–220.

Nisbett, R. E., & Cohen, D. (1996). *Culture of honor: The psychology of violence in the South.* Boulder, CO: Westview Press.

Oatley, K. (2002). Emotions and the story worlds of fiction. In M. C. Green, J. J. Strange, & T. C. Brock (Eds.), *Narrative impact: Social and cognitive foundations* (pp. 39–69). Mahwah, NJ: Erlbaum.

Ortutay, B. (2021, January 6). Twitter, Facebook remove Trump video amid Capitol violence *Fox 13.* Retrieved from https://www.fox13now.com/news/national-news/twitter-facebook-remove-trump-video-amid-capitol-violence

Papenfuss, M. (2021, January 31). FBI: Capitol rioter arrested after she boasted on video she wanted to shoot Nancy Pelosi. *Huffington Post.* Retrieved from https://www.huffpost.com/entry/dawn-bancroft-diana-santos-smith-shooting-pelosi-capitol-selfie_n_60150b9ac5b6bde2f5bf9fbd.

Pauwels, L., & Schils, N. (2016). Differential online exposure to extremist content and political violence: Testing the relative strength of social learning and competing perspectives. *Terrorism and Political Violence, 28*(1), 1–29.

PBS Newshour. (2020, January 21). 'Only guilty people try to hide the evidence,' Rep. Nadler says. *PBS Newshour.* Retrieved from https://www.youtube.com/watch?v=AE0Vqi4qNkA

Pelinka, A. (2013). Right-wing populism: Concept and typology. In R. Wodak, M. Khosravinik, & B. Mral (Eds.), *Right-wing populism in Europe: Politics and discourse* (pp. 3–22). New York: Bloomsbury.

Pennington, N., & Hastie, R. (1992). Explaining the evidence: Tests of the story model for juror decision making. *Journal of Personality and Social Psychology, 62*(2), 189–206.

Perry, C. (2017). *In America: Tales from Trump country*. Dublin: Gill & Macmillan.

Pew Research Center (2015). *Beyond distrust: How Americans view their government*. Retrieved from https://www.pewresearch.org/politics/wp-content/uploads/sites/4/2015/11/11-23-2015-Governance-release.pdf

Piazza, J. A. (2017). The determinants of domestic right-wing terrorism in the USA: Economic grievance, societal change and political resentment. *Conflict Management and Peace Science, 34*(1), 52–80.

Pilecki, A. (2015). *Doing unjust things in a 'just' society: The moral justification of structural violence* (Publication No. 3730002) [Doctoral dissertation, UC Santa Cruz]. ProQuest Dissertations and Theses Global.

Plutchik, R. (1980). A general psychoevolutionary theory of emotion. In R. Plutchik & H. Kellerman (Eds.), *Emotion: Theory, research, and experience: Vol. 1. Theories of emotion* (pp. 3–33). New York: Academic Press.

Pratt, D. (2010). Religion and terrorism: Christian fundamentalism and extremism. *Terrorism and Political Violence, 22*(3), 438–456.

Pyszczynski, T., Abdollahi, A., Solomon, S., Greenberg, J., Cohen, F., & Weise, D. (2006). Mortality salience, martyrdom, and military might: The great Satan versus the axis of evil. *Personality and Social Psychology Bulletin, 32*(4), 525–537.

Rampton, R., & Zengerle, P. (2019, October 3). Trump publicly asks China to probe Biden, even amid impeachment inquiry. *Reuters*. Retrieved from https://www.reuters.com/article/us-usa-trump-whistleblower/trump-publicly-asks-china-to-probe-biden-even-amid-impeachment-inquiry-idUSKBN1WI0BC

Redlawsk, D. P. (2006). Motivated reasoning, affect, and the role of memory in voter decision making. In *Feeling politics: Emotion in political information processing* (pp. 87–107). New York: Palgrave Macmillan.

Redlawsk, D. P., Civettini, A. J. W., & Emmerson, K. M. (2010). The affective tipping point: Do motivated reasoners ever "get it"? *Political Psychology, 31*(4), 563–593.

Redlawsk, D. P., Roseman, I. J., Mattes, K., & Katz, S. (2018). Donald Trump, contempt, and the 2016 GOP Iowa caucuses. *Journal of Elections, Public Opinion and Parties, 28*(2), 173–189.

Reeve, J. (2018). *Understanding motivation and emotion* (7th ed.). Hoboken, NJ: Wiley.

Reicher, S., & Haslam, S. A. (2017). The politics of hope: Donald Trump as an entrepreneur of identity. In M. Fitzduff (Ed.), *Why irrational politics appeals: Understanding the allure of Trump* (pp. 25–40). Santa Barbara, CA: Praeger.

Reicher, S., Haslam, S. A., & Rath, R. (2008). Making a virtue of evil: A five-step social identity model of the development of collective hate. *Social and Personality Psychology Compass, 2*(3), 1313–1344.

Reicher, S., Haslam, S. A., & Rath, R. (2019, July). On the virtues of hate: The mobilisation discourse of Donald Trump and ISIS. In I. Roseman & A. Fischer (Chairs), *Creating hate, eliminating hate: Some timely insights*. [Symposium]. International Society for Research on Emotions 23rd Conference, Amsterdam.

Reif, A., Rösler, M., Freitag, C. M., Schneider, M., Eujen, A., Kissling, C., Wenzler, D., Jacob, C. P., Retz-Junginger, P., Thome, J., Lesch, K.-P., & Retz, W. (2007). Nature and nurture predispose to violent behavior: Serotonergic genes and adverse childhood environment. *Neuropsychopharmacology, 32*(11), 2375–2383.

Rip, B., Vallerand, R. J., & Lafrenière, M. A. K. (2012). Passion for a cause, passion for a creed: On ideological passion, identity threat, and extremism. *Journal of Personality, 80*(3), 573–602.

Roseman, I. J. (1994). The psychology of strongly-held beliefs: Theories of ideological structure and individual attachment. In R. C. Schank & E. Langer (Eds.), *Beliefs, reasoning, and decision making: Psycho-logic in honor of Bob Abelson* (pp. 175–208). Hillsdale, NJ: Erlbaum.

Roseman, I. J. (2011). Emotional behaviors, emotivational goals, emotion strategies: Multiple levels of organization integrate variable and consistent responses. *Emotion Review, 3*(4), 434–443.

Roseman, I. J. (2013). Appraisal in the emotion system: Coherence in strategies for coping. *Emotion Review, 5*(2), 141–149.

Roseman, I. J. (2017). Transformative events: Appraisal bases of passion and mixed emotions. *Emotion Review, 9*(2), 133–139.

Roseman, I. J. (2018). Rejecting the unworthy: The causes, components, and consequences of contempt. In M. Mason (Ed.), *The moral psychology of contempt* (pp. 107–130). London: Rowman & Littlefield.

Roseman, I. J., Abelson, R. P., & Ewing, M. F. (1986). Emotion and political cognition: Emotional appeals in political communication. In R. R. Lau & D. O. Sears (Eds.), *Political cognition: The 19th annual Carnegie symposium on cognition* (pp. 279–294). Hillsdale, NJ: Erlbaum.

Roseman, I. J., Antoniou, A. A., & Jose, P. E. (1996). Appraisal determinants of emotions: Constructing a more accurate and comprehensive theory. *Cognition and Emotion, 10,*(3) 241–277.

Roseman, I. J., & Evdokas, A. (2004). Appraisals cause experienced emotions: Experimental evidence. *Cognition and Emotion, 18*(1), 1–28.

Roseman, I. J., Johnston, B. M., Garguilo, S., Floman, J. L., Bryant, A. D., Frazier, I. R., & Nugent, M. K. (2012, May). *Are some emotions more politically potent than others?* [Poster presentation]. Association for Psychological Science 24th Annual Convention, Chicago, IL.

Roseman, I. J., Mattes, K., & Redlawsk, D. P. (2019, August). Testing an integrative theory of beliefs and emotions predicting Trump support. In A. Podob (Chair), *The causes and consequences of the rise of populist sentiments.* [Symposium]. American Political Science Association Annual Meeting, Washington, DC.

Roseman, I. J., Mattes, K., Redlawsk, D. P., & Katz, S. (2020). Reprehensible, laughable: The role of contempt in negative campaigning. *American Politics Research, 48*(1), 44–77.

Roseman, I. J., & Smith, C. A. (2001). Appraisal theory: Overview, assumptions, varieties, controversies. In K. R. Scherer, A. Schorr, & T. Johnstone (Eds.), *Appraisal processes in emotion: Theory, methods, research* (pp. 3–19). New York: Oxford University Press.

Roseman, I. J., Steele, A. K., & Goodvin, A. (2019a, May). Interpersonal dislike, contempt, anger, and hate: Distinct emotions? In K. Aumer (Chair), *What is hate? Evaluating the conceptualization, categorization, and function of our hate.* [Symposium]. Association for Psychological Science 31st Annual Convention, Washington, DC.

Roseman, I. J., Steele, A. K., & Goodvin, A. (2019b, July). Out of the darkness: Appraisals, responses, and narratives of hatred and related emotions. In I. Roseman & A. Fischer (Chairs), *Creating hate, eliminating hate: Some timely insights.* [Symposium]. International Society for Research on Emotions 23rd Conference, Amsterdam.

Roseman, I. J., Wiest, C., & Swartz, T. S. (1994). Phenomenology, behaviors, and goals differentiate discrete emotions. *Journal of Personality and Social Psychology, 67,* 206–221.

Rovira Kaltwasser, C. (2012). The ambivalence of populism: Threat and corrective for democracy. *Democratization, 19*(2), 184–208.

Rubin, O., Mallin, A., & Hosenball, A. (2021, February 9). 'Because President Trump said to': Over a dozen Capitol rioters say they were following Trump's guidance. *ABC News.* Retrieved from https://abcnews.go.com/US/president-trump-dozen-capitol-rioters-trumps-guidance/story?id=75757601

Rucker, P., DelReal, J. A., Stanley-Becker, I. (2020, June 13). Trump pushes expanded ban on Muslims entering the U.S. *The Washington Post.* https://www.washingtonpost.com/politics/trump-pushes-expanded-ban-on-muslims-and-other-foreigners/2016/06/13/c9988e96-317d-11e6-8ff7-7b6c1998b7a0_story.html

Ruiter, R. A. C., Kessels, L. T. E., Peters, G-J. Y., & Kok, G. (2014). Sixty years of fear appeal research: Current state of the evidence. *International Journal of Psychology, 49*(2), 63–70.

Russell, G. J. (2017, July 2). 'I'm president, they're not': Donald Trump savages media at veterans rally. *The Guardian.* Retrieved from https://www.theguardian.com/us-news/2017/jul/02/im-president-theyre-not-donald-trump-savages-media-at-veterans-rally

Saad, L. (2016). Aversion to other candidate key factor in 2016 vote choice. *Galllup*. Retrieved from https://news.gallup.com/poll/196172/aversion-candidate-key-factor-2016-vote-choice.aspx

Sageman, M. (2004). *Understanding terror networks*. Philadelphia: University of Pennsylvania Press.

Schachter, S. (1951). Deviation, rejection, and communication. *The Journal of Abnormal and Social Psychology, 46*(2), 190–207.

Schaffner, B. F., MacWilliams, M., & Nteta, T. (2018). Understanding white polarization in the 2016 vote for president: The sobering role of racism and sexism. *Political Science Quarterly, 133*(1), 9–34.

Scherer, K. R., & Moors, A. (2019). The emotion process: Event appraisal and component differentiation. *Annual Review of Psychology, 70*, 719–745.

Schmid, A. P. (2013). Radicalisation, de-radicalisation, counter-radicalisation: A conceptual discussion and literature review. *ICCT Research Paper, 97*(1), 22.

Schmid, A. P. (2014). *Violent and non-violent extremism: Two sides of the same coin?* The Hague: International Centre For Counter-Terrorism. Retrieved on December 16, 2020 from https://wb-iisg.com/wp-content/uploads/bp-attachments/4803/ICCT-Schmid-Violent-Non-Violent-Extremism-May-2014.pdf

Schmidt, M. S. (2021, January 5). Trump says Pence can overturn his loss in congress. That's not how it works. *The New York Times*. Retrieved from https://www.nytimes.com/2021/01/05/us/politics/pence-trump-election.html

Schuurman, B., Lindekilde, L., Malthaner, S., O'Connor, F., Gill, P., & Bouhana, N. (2019). End of the lone wolf: The typology that should not have been. *Studies in Conflict & Terrorism, 42*(8), 771–778.

Schwartz, T. (2019). I wrote the art of the deal with Donald Trump. In B. X. Lee (Ed.), *The dangerous case of Donald Trump: 37 psychiatrists and mental health experts assess a president* (2nd ed., pp. 64–69). New York: St. Martin's.

Sedgwick, M. (2007). Inspiration and the origins of global waves of terrorism. *Studies in Conflict & Terrorism, 30*(2), 97–112.

Seyle, C., & Besaw, C. (2021). Identity, extremism, and (de) radicalization. In K. Aumer (Ed.), *The psychology of extremism*. Cham: Springer.

Shear, M. D., & Davis, J. H. (2019, October 2). Shoot migrants' legs, build alligator moat: Behind Trump's ideas for border. *The New York Times*. Retrieved from https://www.nytimes.com/2019/10/01/us/politics/trump-border-wars.html

Siddique, Q. (2009). *Weapons of mass instruction? A preliminary exploration of the link between madrassas in Pakistan and militancy*. Oslo: Norwegian Defense Research Establishment.

Sides, J., Tesler, M., & Vavreck, L. (2017). The 2016 US election: How Trump lost and won. *Journal of Democracy, 28*(2), 34–44.

Simi, P., Windisch, S. Harris, D., & Ligon, G. (2019). Anger from within: The role of emotions in disengagement from violent extremism. *Journal of Qualitative Criminal Justice & Criminology, 7*(2), 3–28. Retrieved on December 16, 2020 from https://epps.utdallas.edu/jqcjc/documents/v7i2.pdf

Smith, D. N., & Hanley, E. (2018). The anger games: Who voted for Donald Trump in the 2016 election, and why? *Critical Sociology, 44*(2), 195–212.

Smith, L. D. (1989). A narrative analysis of the party platforms: The Democrats and Republicans of 1984. *Communication Quarterly, 37*(2), 91–99.

Smith, S. M., Fabrigar, L. R., & Norris, M. E. (2008). Reflecting on six decades of selective exposure research: Progress, challenges, and opportunities. *Social and Personality Psychology Compass, 2*(1), 464–493.

Snyder, T. (2020, January 9). The American abyss. *The New York Times*. Retrieved from https://www.nytimes.com/2021/01/09/magazine/trump-coup.html

Sonmez, F. (2019). Trump says supporters might 'demand' that he serve more than two terms as president. *The Washington Post*. Retrieved from https://www.washingtonpost.com/politics/trump-says-supporters-might-demand-that-he-serve-more-than-two-terms-as-president/2019/06/16/4b6b9ae2-9041-11e9-b570-6416efdc0803_story.html

Southern Poverty Law Center (n.d.). *Proud boys*. Retrieved on December 17, 2020 from https://www.splcenter.org/fighting-hate/extremist-files/group/proud-boys

Spencer, H., & Stolberg, S. G. (2017, August 11). White nationalists march on University of Virginia. *The New York Times*. Retrieved from https://www.nytimes.com/2017/08/11/us/white-nationalists-rally-charlottesville-virginia.html

Staub, E. (1989). *The roots of evil: The origins of genocide and other group violence*. New York: Cambridge University Press.

Steele, A. K. (2020). *Are interpersonal dislike and hatred discrete emotions?* (Publication No. 28262389) [Master's thesis, Rutgers University]. ProQuest Dissertations and Theses Global.

Stern, J. (2003). *Terror in the name of God: Why religious militants kill*. New York: Harper Collins.

Stiglitz, J. E. (2018). Trump and globalization. *Journal of Policy Modeling, 40*, 515–528.

Suhay, E., & Erisen, C. (2018). The role of anger in the biased assimilation of political information. *Political Psychology, 39*(4), 793–810.

Sulkowski, M. L., & Picciolini, C. (2018). The path into and out of violent extremism—part 2: Deradicalizing and leaving violent extremism. *Communiqué, 47*(2), 1–18.

Sullivan, E., & Green, E. L. (2020, July 10). As Trump demanded schools reopen, his experts warned of 'highest risk.' *The New York Times*. Retrieved from https://www.nytimes.com/2020/07/10/us/politics/trump-schools-reopening.html

Task Force on Confronting the Ideology of Radical Extremism. (2009). *Rewriting the narrative—An integrated strategy for counter radicalization*. Washington, DC: The Washington Institute.

Tausch, N., Becker, J. C., Spears, R., Christ, O., Saab, R., Singh, P., & Siddiqui, R. N. (2011). Explaining radical group behavior: Developing emotion and efficacy routes to normative and nonnormative collective action. *Journal of Personality and Social Psychology, 101*(1), 129–148.

Tesler, M., & Sides, J. (2016, March 3). How political science helps explain the rise of Trump: The role of white identity and grievances. *The Washington Post*. Retrieved from https://www.washingtonpost.com/news/monkey-cage/wp/2016/03/03/how-political-science-helps-explain-the-rise-of-trump-the-role-of-white-identity-and-grievances/

Tesser, A., Martin, L., & Mendolia, M. (1995). The impact of thought on attitude extremity and attitude-behavior consistency. In R. E. Petty & J. A. Krosnick (Eds.), *Attitude strength: Antecedents and consequences* (pp. 73–92). Mahwah, NJ: Erlbaum.

Thórisdóttir, H., & Jost, J. T. (2011). Motivated closed-mindedness mediates the effect of threat on political conservatism. *Political Psychology, 32*(5), 785–811.

Tiefenthäler, A. (2016, March 14). Trump's history of encouraging violence. *The New York Times*. Retrieved from https://www.nytimes.com/video/us/100000004269364/trump-and-violence.html

Tomkins, S. S. (1970). Affect as the primary motivational system. In M. B. Arnold (Ed.), *Feelings and emotions: The Loyola symposium* (pp. 101–110). New York: Academic Press.

Trump, D. J. (2016). *Donald J. Trump Republican nomination acceptance speech*. Retrieved from http://assets.donaldjtrump.com/DJT_Acceptance_Speech.pdf

Valentino, N. A., Hutchings, V. L., Banks, A. J., & Davis, A. K. (2008). Is a worried citizen a good citizen? Emotions, political information seeking, and learning via the internet. *Political Psychology, 29*(2), 247–273.

van den Bos, K. (2020). Unfairness and radicalization. *Annual Review of Psychology, 71*, 563–588.

Van Hiel, A., & Mervielde, I. (2003). The measurement of cognitive complexity and its relationship with political extremism. *Political Psychology, 24*(4), 781–801.

van Zalk, M. H. W., Kerr, M., van Zalk, N., & Stattin, H. (2013). Xenophobia and tolerance toward immigrants in adolescence: Cross-influence processes within friendships. *Journal of Abnormal Child Psychology, 41*(4), 627–639.

van Zomeren, M., Spears, R., Fischer, A. H., & Leach, C. W. (2004). Put your money where your mouth is! Explaining collective action tendencies through group-based anger and group efficacy. *Journal of Personality and Social Psychology, 87*(5), 649–664.

Vasilopoulos, P., Marcus, G. E., Valentino, N. A., & Foucault, M. (2019). Fear, anger, and voting for the far right: Evidence from the November 13, 2015 Paris terror attacks. *Political Psychology, 40*(4), 679–704.

Venhaus, J. M. (2010). *Why youth join al-Qaeda*. Washington, DC: United States Institute for Peace.

Visser, P. S., Krosnick, J. A., & Norris, C. J. (2016). Attitude importance and attitude-relevant knowledge. In J. A. Krosnick, I-C. A. Chiang, & T. H. Stark (Eds.), *Political psychology: New explorations* (pp. 203–245). New York: Routledge.

Wall Street Journal. (2018, January 14) *Transcript of Donald Trump interview with the Wall Street Journal*. Retrieved from https://www.wsj.com/articles/transcript-of-donald-trump-interview-with-the-wall-street-journal-1515715481

Washington Post. (2015, June 16). *Full text: Donald Trump announces a Presidential bid*. Retrieved from https://www.washingtonpost.com/news/post-politics/wp/2015/06/16/full-text-donald-trump-announces-a-presidential-bid/?arc404=true

Washington Post. (2016, October, 10). *Trump on Clinton: 'Lock her up is right.'* Retrieved from https://www.washingtonpost.com/video/politics/trump-on-clinton-lock-her-up-is-right/2016/10/10/fd56d59e-8f51-11e6-bc00-1a9756d4111b_video.html

Weaver, M., & Ackerman, S. (2017, January 26). Trump claims torture works but experts warn of its 'potentially existential' costs. *The Guardian*. Retrieved from https://www.theguardian.com/us-news/2017/jan/26/donald-trump-torture-absolutely-works-says-us-president-in-first-television-interview

Wertheimer, F., & Eisen, N. (2019, January 2). Trump illegally asked Russia to help him win in 2016. He shouldn't get away with it. *USA Today*. Retrieved from https://www.usatoday.com/story/opinion/2019/01/02/trump-broke-law-russia-clinton-emails-hold-him-accountable-column/2449564002/

Wiktorowicz, Q. (2005). *Radical Islam rising: Muslim extremism in the west*. Lanham, MD: Rowman & Littlefield.

Williams, A. (2020, June 17). Attendees of President Trump's Tulsa rally must agree to a coronavirus liability waiver. *Fox 10 Phoenix*. Retrieved from https://www.fox10phoenix.com/news/attendees-of-president-trumps-tulsa-rally-must-agree-to-a-coronavirus-liability-waiver

Williams, J. A. (2007). *Turning to nature in Germany: Hiking, nudism, and conservation, 1900–1940*. Palo Alto, CA: Stanford University Press.

Windisch, S., Simi, P., Ligon, G. S., & McNeel, H. (2016). Disengagement from ideologically-based and violent organizations: A systematic review of the literature. *Journal for Deradicalization, 9*, 1–38.

Woodward, C. & Yen, H. (2020, January 18). AP FACT CHECK: Trump's compulsive claims of 'biggest' ever. *Associated Press*. Retrieved from https://apnews.com/d5f3863f3924033f71afdc0abcdcaa80

Zimbardo, P., & Sword, R. (2019). Unbridled and extreme present hedonism: How the leader of the free world has proven time and again he is unfit for duty. In B. X. Lee (Ed.), *The dangerous case of Donald Trump: 37 psychiatrists and mental health experts assess a* president (2nd ed., pp. 25–50). New York: St. Martin's.

Identity, Extremism, and (De) Radicalization

Conor Seyle and Clayton Besaw

To paraphrase an old saying, every generation thinks they invented terrorism: there is a tendency to look at modern terrorist violence as something particularly unique to either the geopolitics of the twenty-first century or due to a fundamental incompatibility between perpetrators of terrorism and the cultural expectations of the developed world (Neumayer & Plümper, 2009). In part this reflects a bafflement with the decision process that leads supporters of different political perspectives to commit incredibly destructive acts at high cost to themselves. It is easy to dismiss perpetrators of terrorist violence as irrational or to focus on the specifics of their claims and their situation to understand them. However, terrorist attacks, including violently self-destructive attacks, have taken place since at least the nineteenth century and have been associated with a wide variety of ideologies from anarchism to leftist to religious movements (Rapoport, 2004). What is consistent across these different movements, across time and geography, is a willingness to exert incredible effort and run high risk of harm to the self in support of a political movement. The behavior of a suicide terrorist, or even someone who chooses to leave a relatively comfortable life for the rigors of life in an armed insurgency (Henck, 2007), challenges the traditional psychological understanding of motivations. At the level of conscious thought, if not necessarily at the level of evolved predispositions (Henrich et al., 2006), a standard tenant in psychology is that core social motives tend to revolve around the enhancement and continuation of the self (Fiske, 2009). Therefore, it is clear that these groups must provide a powerful draw to their participants to offset the existing pressures to maintain the self.

While there are multiple arguments currently developing that explore why and how someone may choose to engage in extreme behavior, in this chapter we argue that the prevailing data show that identity-related issues are central to the attraction of extremist groups, and that joining extremist groups is an attempt to respond to

C. Seyle (✉) · C. Besaw
OEF Research, One Earth Future Foundation, Broomfield, CO, USA
e-mail: dcseyle@oneearthfuture.org

© Springer Nature Switzerland AG 2020
K. V. Aumer (ed.), *The Psychology of Extremism*,
https://doi.org/10.1007/978-3-030-59698-9_3

identity-related uncertainty. Extremist groups allow people to solicit strongly confirmatory information about uncertain aspects of their identity. At the same time, the ideology of the groups that they align with can condition what the identity means to the group member, and tip their behavior towards violence or more positive political behavior. This chapter engages with the current research on what that psychological draw might be, and how violent groups create and support a psychological state that encourages recruitment and continued participation. We review and define extremism as a construct, review the literature on the identity-related pathways to extremism and radicalization and the existing research on what works in deradicalization, and develop some suggested implications for programming focusing on preventing/combating violent extremism.

1 Defining Extremism

Violent extremism in current political discourse is a slippery concept and one that verges on tautological. Similar to the definition given in the introduction, a Federal Bureau Investigation (FBI) website aimed at countering violent extremism defines it as "encouraging, condoning, justifying, or supporting the commission of a violent act to achieve political, ideological, religious, social, or economic goals" (Federal Bureau of Investigations, n.d.-a). In other words, violent extremism is defined by the FBI as the decision to use violence to achieve ideological goals. The risk with this definition is that by focusing on the decision to use violence, it may conflate strategic calculations made at the level of the group with individual psychological characteristics that endorse the use of violence. There is no evidence, as described above, that violent extremists are inherently more violent or more likely to use violence across all contexts. At the same time, there is evidence that shows that the decision to use violence and what types of violence to use is a conscious and strategic decision in the service of many groups' political goals (McCartan, Masselli, Rey, & Rusnak, 2008; Santifort, Sandler, & Brandt, 2013). The result is that a definition focusing specifically on the willingness to use violence captures something about the strategic context in which a specific group operates, rather than something about why recruits are attracted to these extremist groups. For example, the FBI currently still lists the Colombian leftist group the Revolutionary Armed Forces of Columbia (FARC) as an international violent extremist group (FBI, n.d.-b). However, the FARC has formally signed a peace agreement with the Colombian government that includes the renunciation of violence as a strategy without necessarily changing core beliefs about the ideology or desires of the group itself. As the demobilization and reintegration process in Colombia develops, the likelihood that the FARC chooses to use violence declines due to the changes in strategic context. The ideology and the strategic goals that underpinned the FARC will certainly change as it integrates into Colombian society—but there remains a substantial correspondence between the political and social goals of the FARC as an armed group and as a political segment of Colombian society. This suggests that a definition that defines violent extremism solely in terms of the strategic choice of a group is unsatisfying in explaining radicalization, as it says more about the strategic context of a group than the underlying psychology that supports the use of violence.

Extant literature on the psychology of extremism has suggested that there are elements of alignment with a group or ideology that can be identified as characterizing extremism separate from the decision of that group to engage in violence or not. For the purpose of this chapter, we define extremism as *a psychological state of alignment with a group such that the aligned person sees belonging to the group as carrying moral weight and that belonging to the group is a moral imperative, sees the group as being absolutely correct in its teachings such that it is difficult to legitimately challenge or change the group's beliefs, and sees the group as actively under threat* (Seyle, 2007). In this definition, we draw from research on the psychology of members of radical or extremist groups. When radicalism or extremism is defined in terms of groups that are either far outside of mainstream perspectives or are more likely to use violence in the service of their groups, studies of members of these groups can provide important insight into the domain-independent psychology of extremism, if such a phenomenon exists. Research has tended to support the idea that there are some similarities in the psychology of members of these groups, independent of ideology. Specifically, absolutism and group-based moral authority are frequently identified as key elements which characterize the members of radical or extremist groups (Atran, 2003; Crenshaw, 2000; McCormick, 2003; Smith, 2004).

It is important to note that nothing in this definition is inherently tied to the choice to use violence, avoiding the tautological definition. However, extremism according to our definition does make it significantly easier to support violence, and it is useful to specify the mechanisms through which extremists justify or endorse violent behavior against out-group members. We argue that there is a two-stage process through which extremism may result in violence.

1. *Strategic reification* of out-group members as *enemies* or *targets*.
2. Using *norms, anger, and punishment* defined by the extremist movement to catalyze negative emotions like anger tied to perceived and actual norm violations by out-group targets.

Finally, we discuss how extremist movement outcomes regarding violence may have a degree of equifinality. Namely that extremism alone does not always result in violence and may depend on the social construction of identity among individuals belonging to an extremist movement or holding extremist ideologies.

1.1   Stage 1: The Strategic Reification of the Enemy

The first step towards violence for extremist movements entails some degree of so-called target setting. Oftentimes this manifests as what can be called a reification of the enemy. Individuals belonging to an extremist movement are primed for this target setting through the adoption of an extremist psychological state. These individuals already hold some degree of belief in the primacy of their in-group and the threat that out-group members may pose to their beliefs regarding in-group cohesion, process, and success. Because of this extremist state of mind, it is important to recognize the salience of extremist beliefs at the individual level regarding out-group behavior in this strategic target setting. The strategic use of violence by any extremist movement implicitly, or even explicitly, leverages this psychological state accordingly. The combination of dehumanization of out-group members and the reification of the threat they pose is key to target setting.

Reification of the enemy occurs when the abstract threats (i.e. they, them, the man, shadowy forces, deep state, etc.) to an extremist movement are given explicit inter-subjective substance (i.e. Jews, Muslims, Freemasons, Catholics, Leftists, Fascists, etc.). The substance of the threat refers to the ability for extremist movements to directly connect the abstract threats that bind their individual members around a specific and culturally shared target. Hatred of an abstract and ambiguous force that besieges an extremist movement is unlikely to galvanize support for violence due to the inability to concretely specify the source of the extremist's fear and anguish regarding the integrity of their respective in-group. It may make extremists angry that their in-group suffers economic or political deprivation, but total ambiguity regarding the source of the extremists' grievances provides no signal regarding the perpetrator or the specific normative catalysts that the perpetrator has violated. By making real the actual or perceived source of these threats, extremist movements can begin to more concretely catalyze violent behavior through the use of norm violations and calls for punishment. See Fig. 1 for examples from two modern extremist movements.

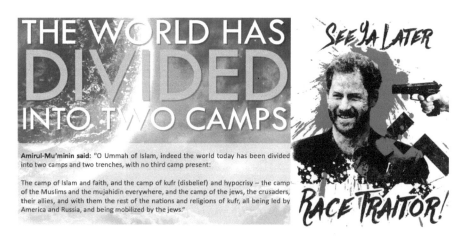

Fig. 1 Extremist propaganda showing the use of reification to strategically set targets for in-group members. Left image shows Islamic State propaganda from their English language publication *Dabiq*. Right image shows propaganda from the transnational neo-nazi group Atomaffen

1.2   Stage 2: Norms, Anger, and Punishment

Once strategic target setting has occurred, extremist movements can then attempt to galvanize members to participate in extremist violence against perceived and real out-group threats. Parochial altruistic punishment theory, or the theory of biased strong reciprocity, may provide clues into how extremist individuals decide to condone or directly engage in political violence (Besaw, 2018; Choi & Bowles, 2007; Tezcür & Besaw, 2020). From an evolutionary perspective, humans acquired behaviors intended to promote cooperation and survivability in harsh environments. Selfish behavior may endanger the social grouping, and costly punishment behaviors are thought to have been key to understanding when shared norms regarding cooperative behavior were punished (Fehr & Gaechter, 2002). Punishers usually take a cost to themselves (calories, injury, etc.) to punish in-group members who violate shared norms but provide greater fitness to the social whole as a result. Altruistic costly punishment serves as a strong signal of deterrence against free-riding and defection regarding shared cooperative norms (Fehr & Gaechter, 2002; Fiske & Rai, 2014).

The main mechanism of costly punishment behavior in this setting is somewhat contested, but extant scholarship argues that anger tied to norm violations is the proximate catalyst for engagement in costly punishment (Fehr & Gaechter, 2002). The role of emotion, specifically anger, is key here. Altruistic punishment behavior occurs even in nonrepeated interactions in which shared understanding and reputation are minimal. Cooperative norms are thus powerful drivers of behavior, and anger tied to their violation can cause seemingly irrational costly punishment in one-off cooperation games. Generalizing to extremist movements that induce regular interpersonal interaction, the emotional reaction to inter-subjectively held norms is likely to be far stronger than what is observed in an abstract laboratory setting.

From a neurological perspective, there has been strong evidence for this anger–punishment pathway. Directly priming for anger increases altruistic punishment in third-party sanction games (Nelissen & Zeelenberg, 2009) and can regulate the level of cooperation found within inter-group settings (Burton-Chellew, Ross-Gillespie, & West, 2010). Examining fMRI data concerning the activation of neural "anger" centers have been linked to perceptions of unfair behavior (Sanfey, Aronson, Nystrom, & Cohen, 2003). More specifically looking at instances of norm violation, anger has been found to be a salient regulator of decision making and risk assessment following violation simulation (Montague & Lohrenz, 2007; Singer, Critchley, & Preuschoff, 2009). De Quervain, Fischbacher, Treyer, & Schellhammer (2004) found that anger tied to norm violation was linked to anticipated satisfaction resulting from punishment. Further research has suggested that dopamine production in the brain is suggested to be such a driver in engaging in altruistic punishment, having an almost drug-like effect regarding behavior on the punisher (Strobel et al., 2011). Finally, these neurological mechanisms connecting anger tied to norm violation tied to altruistic punishment behavior is conditioned on identity. Baumgartner, Goette, Guegler, & Fehr (2012) found that punishment induced by anger tied to violations by out-group members were significantly greater than those tied to in-group members. This suggests that the psychological urge to engage in costly punishment is stronger against out-group norm violators than in-group ones.

Whether it is realized or not, leaders of extremist movements are potentially tapping into a powerful evolutionary mechanism to drive human violence. Identity-based parochial altruistic punishment is argued to be a significant driver of human inter-group violence ranging from small-group resource competition to inter-state war (Bernhard, Fehr, & Fischbacher, 2006; Bowles, 2006; Choi & Bowles, 2007; Rusch, 2014). Members of an in-group are thought to see out-group norm violators are inherently degrading the integrity of one's in-group identity and the inter-subjectively held norms that constitute it (Rusch, 2014). Thus, actual or perceived out-group norm violations are argued to be an evolutionary adaptation used for eliciting potentially powerful emotional responses, including ones that result in "corrective" violence against the perpetrators. To the parochial altruistic punisher, acts of violent punishment against out-group violators are justified as a means for defending in-group integrity and cooperation.

Connecting anger-driven parochial altruistic punishment to the strategic reification of an out-group enemy within extremist movement discourse produces a clear pathway to potential extremist violence adoption. For example, a radicalization pipeline for members of the modern White Nationalist Atomwaffen group whose propaganda was presented above may follow a process where existing grievances stoked by propaganda and pointed at out-group members in ways that lead the extremist to believe that he can fight for the group through taking violent action. Given time and exposure, members of extremist movements can move from nascent supporters to users of kinetic violence. Strategic enemy targeting is likely to elicit greater amounts of anger over time as the extremist movement members are continuously bombarded with a greater quantity of norm violation examples and greater emotional buy-in as they become more familiar with the beliefs and norms that constitute the social identity of an extremist movement. If self-association is a prerequisite for prejudice, then the identity-laden reification of the out-group norm violator is likely a prerequisite for extremist violence.

2 Violent Extremism Types and Trends

Existing research on motivated self-sacrifice in the service of groups has tended to refer to the phenomenon of non-state violence as extremist violence, a term that has become a fixture of the modern conflict landscape. For the purpose of this chapter, by extremist violence we mean *the use of kinetic action to kill, harm, or threaten another in pursuit of ideological goals.* Harm, in this definition, can encompass the destruction of nonhuman life or property in an effort to damage a target indirectly as well. This definition is useful because it focuses on the source of the behavior and does not unduly restrict the instrumental manifestation of violence. As such, it can include a number of violent actions including but not limited to:

1. Terrorism, or the use and threatened use of violence to intimidate targets beyond the victim(s).
2. Guerilla warfare, or the use of indirect or surprising violent actions to inflict damage against a more powerful adversary when power asymmetries exist.
3. Conventional warfare, or the use of direct violence and maneuvers to degrade the fighting ability of an adversary.
4. Genocide, or the intentional destruction of a group of people based on their identified characteristics.

Note that this list includes some elements popularly associated with extremist violence, such as terrorism or genocide, but it also includes some elements that are not, such as conventional warfare. This is partly because the choice of strategies by a group appears to be a reflection more of its specific capacities and abilities than an inherent desire to use some form of violence (Freedman, 2007; Merari, 1993). Additionally, we seek to develop a domain-neutral approach to understanding the psychology of actors motivated to engage in extreme acts in the service of a group. Such a definition must necessarily include the more prosocial or socially acceptable forms of extreme actions such as radical self-sacrifice in the service of patriotism or other positive goals.

In the current landscape of violent extremism, three broad categories can be seen as capturing the current state of violent extremism. These are (1) non-state-organized actors, (2) individual "lone-wolf" actors, and (3) state institutions. For the remainder of this chapter the focus will remain on 1 and 2, but it is acknowledged that the state can play a powerful role in shaping and directing extremist violence.

2.1   Organized Non-state Extremism vs. State Extremism

The study of political violence has traditionally centered topics related to war, revolution and rebellion (Valentino, 2014). Historical and scientific analyses alike have often focused on the development of general theories regarding the role of political elites and state infrastructure in galvanizing and enabling forms of extremist violence such as genocide, ethnic cleansing and political terrorism.

It stands that state actors have influenced and will continue to influence outcomes concerning mass political violence and extremism for the foreseeable future; however we believe that there is good reason to both delineate between state and non-state extremism and to focus the bulk of our attention here to the latter.

First, general theories of extremist violence that focus on the comorbidity of armed conflict and political violence patterns are inherently problematic from an ecological perspective. Extremist violence exists regardless of state behavior and purely state-based theories fail to adequately address the deeply personal mechanisms that drive individuals towards kinetic violence against another human for ideological reasons whether it be for a state or non-state actor respectively (Besaw, 2018; Kalyvas, 2006; Valentino, 2014). Given this observation, focusing on individual-level theories of extremist violence for those belonging to non-state actors can provide insight into both phenomena from a theoretical stance.

Second, modern data collection efforts have strengthened a growing consensus that while armed interstate conflict has steadily declined over time the manifestation of non-state political violence has continued to grow (Pettersson & Eck, 2018; Valentino, 2014). The most damaging applications of violent non-state extremism as manifest in terrorism, rebellion, and genocide are highly organized and social phenomena. Recent estimates find that while internationalized intrastate conflict deaths have steadily declined in the previous 5 years, deaths involving the actions of non-state extremist actors have continued to increase (Pettersson & Eck, 2018) (Fig. 2).

Organized violent non-state actors are groups that utilize extremist violence and who are wholly or partially independent from the state (Hofmann & Schneckener, 2011). The distinction between non-state-organized extremism and state-organized extremism is an important one to address for two reasons. First, states have coercive capabilities that often exceed non-state groups and organizations. Access to resources and personnel to carry out potentially extremist policy objectives is assumed to be easier and more far-reaching. Second, states are often at the forefront of norm development and enforcement within any society. Extremist ideas may be more easily propagated by state entities using mass media or may come from broadly held societal norms regarding the role of "other" and nurtured accordingly by the state. Non-state extremist movements on the other hand often find themselves at odds with the state or even broader societal norms. These movements lack readily accessible and effective coercive capacity beyond their membership or immediate

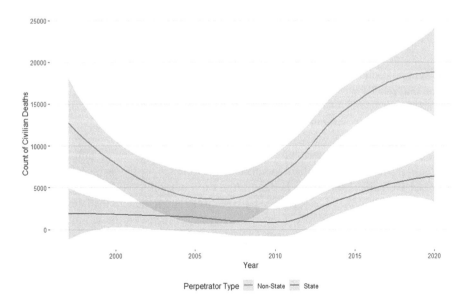

Fig. 2 Civilian victimization by state and non-state armed actors from January 1997 to June 2020. (Source: Armed Conflict Location & Event Data Project (ACLED); https://www.acleddata.com)

surroundings. Their beliefs can often be met with severe hostility by society at large and must invest in maintenance regarding membership and ideological cohesion.

It is possible that states can sanction organized non-state extremist movements as well, but it is unlikely that such sanctioning will mitigate the relative disadvantages that non-state movements face without full cooptation or participation. Regardless, there are salient asymmetries in the type of outcomes experienced between state and non-state-organized extremist movements.

State-organized extremism will continue to play a powerful role in violence for the foreseeable future, but our focus privileges non-state extremism for two reasons. First, increasing economic and social globalization has given rise to increasingly complex networks of non-state extremist actors and pools of recruitment. Second, modern political violence has taken an increasingly sharp turn away from interstate war and towards low-intensity intrastate armed conflict often involving multiple non-state and state actors (citation here). Because of these trends, we believe that non-state extremist movements will continue to play an increasingly important role in the patterns of political change and violence going forward.

2.2   Lone Wolf Extremism

Lone Wolf extremism is a difficult concept to deal with but has become increasingly more common over the past 30 years (Spaaij, 2010). Lone wolf violence is characterized by individuals planning and/or executing attacks in support of a political group or ideology without strategy and extensive direction from the group's leadership. While lone wolf political violence has been documented throughout much of recorded human history (Kaplan, Lööw, & Malkki, 2014), the proliferation of communications technologies and the increasing lethality of modern weaponry has increased the lone wolf's ability to communicate with people who share his (or her, but mostly his as stated in Lafree, Jensen, James, & Safer-Lichtenstein, 2018) perspectives and engage in increasingly high thresholds of violence. The difficulty underlying the study of lone wolf extremism is that it can be difficult, if not impossible, to understand completely the motivations and triggers of resulting violence. From a counter-extremism perspective, it may also be nearly impossible to discover ways in which to forecast and mitigate the manifestation of lone wolf violence in the same way that many counterterrorism and counterinsurgency doctrines can with organized extremist violence across the globe.

In general, lone wolf extremism is thought to have the following characteristics. First, lone wolf extremist violence is considered to be a type of "black swan" event (Bakker & de Graaf, 2011). The reason for this unpredictability is that lone wolf extremists are often highly idiosyncratic in their genesis towards violent extremism and highly varied in their methodology of violence. Second, lone wolf extremists also tend to be less lethal than their organized counterparts (Spaaij, 2010). Third, the rates of psychological health issues and social personality disorder tend to manifest more commonly in lone wolf extremists than those that belong to organized movements (Spaaij, 2010).

The presence of potential pathological triggers of lone wolf violence is what makes these actors highly unusual when compared to those individuals that are found in non-state-organized extremism. We argue that the psychological underpinnings of organized extremist violence are fundamentally "normal" in the context of social behavior. More work needs to be done on the potential pathological genesis of these lone wolf actors before the pathology argument can be made with more certainty, but contemporary evidence suggests that organized extremists are unlikely to be driven by pathological factors in the same way that lone wolf actors might be (Rash, 1979; Victoroff, 2005). Because of the highly idiosyncratic, and potentially pathological, motivations behind lone wolf extremist violence, we make the choice to exclude it from our broader analysis. Like state-organized violence, lone wolf violence requires a separate dedication to understanding the drivers of behavior.

2.3   The Normalcy Underpinning Organized Violent Extremism

Considering the sometimes-brutal and senseless acts of killing, it can be tempting to cast all violent extremists as irrational or otherwise driven to violence. The decision of a suicide bomber to sacrifice his life to kill civilians appears to be a fundamentally irrational, if not insane, decision. Despite this, there's been significant and consistent research showing that members of violent extremist groups are not typically people with psychological disorders or significant mental health issues (Crenshaw, 2000; Rash, 1979; Victoroff, 2005). We discuss later in this chapter the psychological elements that may predict support for extremist groups or the development of extremist views; however, it's not the case that all extremists are suffering from mental health issues. Research shows that at the level of the organization as a whole the decision to use violence (up to and including suicide terror) is almost always a conscious and strategic decision (Pape, 2006). Additionally, the selection of targets and strategies consistently shows violent groups to be thoughtful and selective in their decision about whether to use violence and which targets to focus on (Carter, 2016; Polo & Gleditsch, 2016).

Given that it would be an error to believe that all extremists are psychologically ill, it would also be an error to dismiss psychological issues as completely irrelevant for understanding extremism and extremist violence. Although the use of violence may be strategic it's also the case that the willingness to use violence for political ends is closely related to issues of individual psychology. There is some evidence that support for political violence is related to exposure to previous political violence (Hayes & McAllister, 2001), personality variables associated with interpersonal aggression (Kalmoe, 2014), and political or religious ideology that wouldn't necessarily be considered extremist (Zaidise, Canetti-Nisim, & Pedahzur, 2007).

In the case of extremist violence, whether associated with a group or an individual act, a developing body of research has explored the pathway to radicalization, and the deepening development of the extremist mindset that moves a potential extremist from a neutral state into an attitude that endorses and supports the use of violence (Kruglanski, Jasko, Chernikova, Dugas, & Webber, 2017; Post, 2007). However, this radicalization process only takes place in the case of some listeners—not everyone who is exposed to the same messaging or information will go on to develop extremist attitudes. This suggests that a deeper understanding of the psychology of extremism can help develop better approaches to preventing radicalization and supporting the deradicalization and reintegration of former members of extremist groups.

Current research on the psychology of extremism includes several perspectives on what may lead people to be susceptible to radicalization. A debate is ongoing about the relative influence of ideology, personality, norms, and other elements. Human behavior is almost always multicausal—there are few phenomena that can easily be traced to a single source, whether personal or situational (Swann & Seyle, 2005). Hence, in the case of extremism it's likely that any given example of radicalization or extremist violence is the result of multiple different pressures. Despite that, there is strong and consistent research that one core element of extremism, both in questions of what predisposes people to joining extremist groups and also in the question of what psychological state underlies an extremist point of view, is the element of identity. Specifically, there is strong evidence that people are most at risk for joining extremist groups when they face uncertainty about core aspects of their identity (Hogg, 2014). In addition, there is evidence that extremists are characterized in part by an extreme commitment to a specific group identity (Swann, Gómez, Seyle, Francisco, & Huici, 2009). This work allows for a framing for understanding some pressures that support radicalization and extremist violence, and based on that it can perhaps give insights into how to structure prevention and deradicalization programs that ensure participants will meet their psychological needs.

The remainder of this chapter defines extremism while reviewing the existing research on violent extremism, with a focus on what this implies for why and how people may be attracted to extremist ideologies. It will also review the current research on preventing or combating violent extremism (P/CVE) and suggest what alternate approaches to P/CVE models may be on the basis of the review of psychological literature.

3   Theories of Extremism

A key question is why some people develop extremist orientations to specific groups while others do not. Considering organized violence taken in support of specific political groups or ideologies, it's almost always the case that the supporters or perpetrators of organized violence represent a subset of the larger identity or political ideology. Not everyone exposed to extremist groups finds themselves drawn to the group as a whole, if that is true, then why are some people attracted to an extremist orientation to the group? While it is true that research has tended to conclude that there is no one answer to this question—in general, people are drawn to extremist orientations through several different pathways—there have been several overall answers proposed including ideology, rational choice theory, individual pathology, and identity-related drivers. The remainder of this section briefly reviews these approaches.

3.1 Ideology and Extremist Violence

A prominent approach to understanding extremism comes from both popular discussion and some security analysts, which emphasizes the idea that extremism is an element of specific ideologies. From this perspective, individual psychological characteristics are secondary to a process of learning about and aligning with a formal ideology which presents arguments for the use of violence. One clean example of this approach comes from a report developed by the Intelligence Division of the New York City Police Department in 2007. This report was a review of radicalization and selection into terrorist groups, but specifically defined radicalization in terms of alignment with "Jihadi-Salafi Ideology." In the words of the authors, the answer to the question of why people may choose to support terrorist groups or engage in extremist violence was "ideology." Ideology is the bedrock and catalyst for radicalization. Ideology is defined as "the conflict, guides movements, identifies the issues, drives recruitment, and is the basis for action" (Silber, Bhatt & Analysts, 2007, p. 16). Although current research on ideology and violence has tended to focus primarily on Islamist ideologies as a driver of conflict, violence as a tool for political ends has a long history. Even focusing specifically on terrorism, or the use of violence against civilians, over time this has been a favored strategy of groups from almost every part of the political spectrum from ethno-nationalists to anarchists, anticolonial and left-wing groups (Rapoport, 2004).

In the scholarly analysis of violent extremism, ideology has become a predominant lens in which variation in violent extremist group behavior has been filtered. Bruce Hoffman (1998) postulated early on that ideological typologies can explain considerable variation in the degree to which violent political organizations engage in violence. Religiously motivated movements were argued to engage in the most widespread and destructive violence, only followed by ethno-nationalist movements. In contrast, leftist movements in an effort to gain the support of a wider constituency were seen to be more moderate in their choice to engage in violence against outsiders (Laqueur, 2000). The logic here is that religious and ethno-nationalist movements center more strongly around easily defined in-group and out-group markers. Individuals either meet the membership criteria or they don't, and Hoffman (1998) placed special emphasis on the role that religion had on the ability for individuals to justify increasingly violent behavior against nonmembers. More recently Hoffmann (2019) has reiterated the centrality of ideology in shaping violence with a specific focus on jihadist ideology in particular, arguing that ideology can only be fought by stronger counter-ideologies and less reliance on kinetic counterterrorism.

Regardless of what role ideology may play, a focus on ideology alone is incomplete for understanding the mechanisms through which extremist violence is adopted. A broad focus on ideology can't fully explain variation in the adoption of violence between co-ideologues and struggles to account for ethno-nationalist and religious movements that fail to adopt extremism, violence, or both. It is possible that an exclusive focus on ideology is analogous to mistaking the symptoms of a disease for the cause. There is no doubt that ideology matters. Ideology organizes individuals around a world view, can promote cohesion, and delineate friend from foe. As implicated above, ideology can be highly strategic. However, why do some extremist ideologies adopt violence when others don't?

3.2   Rational Choice and Extremist Violence

Another prominent theoretical approach in the study of violent extremism posits that the choice to adopt violence is tied to preferences and the conditions that enable the strategic achievement of preferences. The rational actor model (Allison, 1969; Von Neumann & Morgenstern, 1944) argues that individuals can define known preferences and rank them accordingly. Rationality occurs in that an actor is assumed to not knowingly choose a "lower" ranked preference over a higher ranked one given a permissive choice environment. However, an actor's environment may contain constraints regarding information asymmetries and rival actors that result in the need to choose a lower preference option when higher ranked preferences are unobtainable (Gintis, 2014).

An application of this rational actor model has been a dominant paradigm for studying the choice to adopt extremist violence and variation in violent extremist behavior for the past two decades. Early approaches focused on a bargaining theory model of extremism (Sandler, Tschirhart, & Cauley, 1983) in which violent extremist behavior is characterized as a type of negotiation behavior meant to influence an out-group opponent such as a government. The rational actor model has been used to explain a diverse set of violent extremist behavior including the escalation and severity of extremist violence (Bloom, 2004; Conrad & Greene, 2015; Kydd & Walter, 2006; Nemeth, 2014), recruitment patterns (Weinstein, 2006), and the choice to target noncombatants (Kalyvas, 2006; Wood, 2015). The rational choice model has even argued that increasingly extremist ideology has an advantage in civil conflict (Walter, 2017). The main conclusion from the above research is that seemingly irrational extremist behavior can have strategic considerations behind them. Highly visible and brutal violence combined with increasingly dogmatic extremism can serve as a tool for successfully competing against a range of rival extremist organizations and for signaling ideological resolve and capability. As Walter (2017) states argues, extremist leaders may not necessarily believe fully in the ideological tenets of a violent extremist movement but may promote them for strategic purposes.

The rational actor paradigm is helpful in that it provides a clear theoretical link between incentives, environment, and extremist behavior while also correctly dismissing the argument that extremist violence is driven by some degree of irrational pathology. However, it suffers from a number of shortcomings that make it difficult to use as a singular approach to understanding extremist radicalization and the adoption of violence.

First, incentive-driven models of participation in violent extremist movements fails to account for variation in participation. This is highlighted by the fact that participation is generally a rare event and that the proportion of participants is considerably small when compared to a larger constituent in-group (Victoroff, 2005). A strand of rational choice theories surrounding participation in violent extremist movements argues that incentives and selfish motivations regarding social achievement, material gain, and individual safety are necessary to explain participation in extremist movements (Lee, 2011; Tullock, 1971). The problem with the incentive/selfish motivation argument is that it often fails to explain why individuals with objectively favorable socioeconomic achievements choose to leave their conditions for more dangerous ones (i.e. western foreign fighters). The second problem with rational actor models concerns the "black box" nature of the incentive-driven extremist. If incentive structures fail to adequately model participation variation broadly, then it is clear that any rationalist approach is potentially under specifying individual-level models of extremist radicalization and violence adoption (List & Spiekermann, 2013; Victoroff, 2005).

As a result of these problems, the rational actor model relies too heavily on reified assumptions regarding the primacy of the incentive structure. It also too often dismisses variation in extremist radicalization in favor of focusing on symptoms of extremism (i.e., violent behavior). Thus, missing the point of why actors are using extremist violence to begin with. While the rationalist paradigm has played an important role in the scientific understanding of extremist violence, we turn to psychological theories of violent extremism to fill the conceptual gaps left by both the rationalist and ideology approaches outlined above.

3.3   Psychology and Violent Extremism

The psychological approach to extremism, while having a rich history in the psychology and psychiatric traditions, has been more nascent in traditional security related fields with a focus on violent extremism. The psychology approach can be distilled into two sets of extant work. The pathology approach and the psychological approach.

The application of pathological psychology to violent extremism is simultaneously popular among nonscholars and deeply controversial within academia. The primary argument made by this approach is that individuals who participate in violent extremism do so as a result of identifiable clinical disorders that cause them to deviate from the psychological "norm" (Hacker & Hacker, 1976; Victoroff, 2005). Pathological mechanisms can manifest as either Axis I disorders (mental illness, psychosis) or Axis II disorders (personality disorders). In terms of empirical evidence, there is currently nothing that can support a strong linkage between Axis I disorders and broad participation in violent extremist movements (Victoroff, 2005), which is not surprising as Axis I disorders often result in serious distortion of reality that would make participation in any social movement challenging.

Due to the dearth of evidence regarding the Axis I disorder pathway, pathology arguments have predominantly focused on personality disorders as a potential mechanism for participation. Anti-social personality disorder (APD) has been a widely held candidate for the connection between pathology and extremist violence. APD often entails a high disregard for the "other" and produces a broad dehumanization for those that are not belonging to the self. Like Axis I disorders though, extant studies have found little to no evidence regarding APD or Axis II disorders among the majority of violent extremists (Crenshaw, 1981; Post, Sprinzak, & Denny, 2003; Rasch, 1979). It is entirely possible that Axis II disorders manifest in some subset of violent extremist movements, but the prevailing evidence suggests that this is not broadly the case. An extremist movement with only individuals that fit an APD diagnosis would likely suffer from a lack of social and ideological cohesion or serious internal violence and infighting.

If clinical psychological disorders fail as a candidate for explaining participation in violent extremist movements, then what aspects of psychology are useful? Scholarship regarding personality, cognitive traits, and identity formation may be prime candidates for a more efficacious approach to the psychology of participation in violent extremism.

Personality approaches to participation in violent extremism tends to focus predominantly on the role of narcissism or narcissistic wounds in early personality formation. Narcissism may play a role in magnifying actual and perceived humiliation against one's self and group and make an individual more susceptible to extremist radicalization (Akhtar, 1999; Cohen, Johansson, Kaati, &Mork, 2014; Feddes, Mann, & Doosje, 2015). The predisposition towards narcissism could be the result of early family fragmentation, trauma, or the combination of these events (Post, 1990). The problem with a focus on narcissistic personality is that much of the research has focused on a psychoanalytic process tracing of known extremist actors. It is unclear if the narcissism of the violent extremist is distinguishable from the narcissism of the everyday selfish acquaintance or office rival. Additionally, there is the problem of variation. Almost everyone can name a potential narcissist in their recent past, but almost no one can name a violent extremist that they knew personally. Narcissism may play a role in the genesis of many violent extremists, but it doesn't appear to be the definitive factor.

Another psychological strand of research focuses on cognitive traits. Cognitive traits entail the ways in which we process information regarding the environment around ourselves. In particular, variations concerning cognitive capacity and style are suggested to have strong linkages to the decision to endorse and participate in extremist political views and movements (Victoroff, 2005). Cognitive capacity refers to ability regarding information processing and decision making. Actions such as memory formation, concentration, language development, learning, and judgment on novel information are all influenced by our ability to process a certain degree of data and to synthesize it accordingly with past information (Victoroff, 2005). Cognitive style is related to ways of thinking. This includes things like biases, heuristics, stereotyping, and tendencies (Victoroff, 2005). Regarding cognitive traits, style has seen the most focus. Conceptual complexity seems to be strongly linked to at least the endorsement of extremist and exclusionary attitudes. Low conceptual complexity individuals are typically more inflexible and uncomfortable by judgments that contain uncertainty or *shades of gray*. Black and white thinking has been empirically connected to the endorsement of extremism, ethnocentrism, and racism within the laboratory (Canetti & Pedahzur, 2002; Sidanius, 1985).

While there is indirect evidence regarding conceptual complexity and the endorsement of extremist attitudes, it is unclear whether this is enough to create a direct linkage between such cognitive variation and participation in violent extremism. Many individuals know someone who may be inflexible or slow to embrace uncertainty regarding complex ideas or ambiguous concepts, but is it enough to jump to violent extremism? Probably not. Moreover, personality variables are by definition traits, while extremism as we describe it is more accurately considered a state. That is, while the developing research on personality does suggest that some people are more likely to develop extremist orientation towards groups, nobody is born an extremist. Any understanding of the development of extremism must necessarily be able to explain both variation in extremism among similarly predisposed people as well as describe the process by which people become more aligned. An approach focused purely on individual differences fails to meet this standard.

The remainder of this chapter focuses on the fourth approach proposed in the psychological research: the idea that extremism is rooted in identity-related concerns. From our perspective, while there is evidence that ideology, rational choice, and individual differences all come into play and parallel evidence that no one theory is universally centered across all cases of extremism, it is the research on identity which best captures the majority of variation in radicalization.

4   Violent Extremism and Identity

The term "identity" is used by a variety of disciplines and in a variety of ways, and is closely related to the idea of the "self." One framing of the literature around this concept identified ten separate aspects of the self or identity, ranging from the base fact of awareness through more complex sets of beliefs about how people understand their own characteristics and their relationship with the wider world (Decety & Sommerville, 2003). For the purpose of this chapter, we are most focused on identity as captured in the discussion around "self-concept," or the set of beliefs that people carry about who they are (Baumeister, 1999). The self-concept is one example of a schema, a generalized set of beliefs that allow us to establish a basic understanding of how objects or situations can be expected to operate. Humans use schema, broadly, to organize our world and reduce the cognitive load associated with making decisions on a day-to-day basis (Fiske & Taylor, 1991). This is certainly true for the self-concept, where research has suggested that the self-concept affects behavior through a variety of different ways. Broadly, humans have several "core social motives" that describe what we seek from different social interactions (Fiske, 2007, 2009). While the details of these motives are still in debate, one framing identifies them as belonging or affiliation with groups, understanding the world, having control over the environment, feeling positive about the self (self-enhancement), and viewing the world as benevolent and other people as trustworthy (Fiske, 2009). Collectively, these core social motives allow the human cognitive system to maintain stable beliefs about the world that minimize cognitive load and support positive and evolutionarily rewarded behavior.

As with the self or identity more broadly, the self-concept has been conceptualized as a multifaceted construct with many different layers or elements. Of particular importance to the question of extremism is a distinction that has been drawn between the personal and social selves (Brewer, 1991; Postmes, Baray, Haslam, Morton, & Swaab, 2006; Seyle & Swann, 2007). The individual self includes elements of the self-concept which describe people as individuals—traits such as "tall," "nice," or "athletic"—while the social self includes elements which connect the self to larger social groups or relations. The social self may include beliefs about a person as a sister or brother, an American, or other groups. While the conceptual distinction between the personal and social self goes back to William James in the late nineteenth century (James, 1890), research in social cognition has confirmed that this is more than a theoretical distinction. Priming studies show that the personal and social self appear to be stored as distinct and non-overlapping schema in the brain, and can be primed separately (Trafimow, Triandis, & Goto, 1991). Social neuroscience research has extended this, with FMRI research suggesting that while there are distinct patterns of neural activation associated with different aspects of the self, it's also the case that these patterns are not wholly distinct and that the association between self and others can be blurred particularly in cases where the participants were asked to think about other people very closely associated with themselves (Decety & Sommerville, 2003; Vanderwal, Hunyadi, Grupe, Connors, & Schultz, 2008). Conceptually, this is reasonable, as the different levels of the self-concept directly relate to each other. Social groups carry information about what they expect from their members, or stereotypes in the broader population about what characteristics their members have. Some identity theorists have described this as the "group prototype"—the model for what characteristics and attributes are expected from group members and in particular those characteristics which describe members of the group as distinct from other people or other groups (Hogg & Terry, 2000). This means that membership in groups carries information about the personal characteristics that may be expected from group memberships, and provides a pathway for the two elements of the self to interact.

The self-concept is complex (Linville, 1985, 1987) and can be somewhat self-contradictory. It's not at all unusual for people to contain beliefs about the self which are incongruous with each other. This is because not all aspects of the self-concept are active at the same time (Markus & Wurf, 1987). As with any complex cognitive schema, a distinction can be drawn between the elements of the self-concept as a whole and the elements which are active at any given point. Some aspects of the self-concept are going to be relevant in different situations, and hence more likely to be active (McConnell, 2011). For example, a study of racial and gender identity showed that White American students did not see their racial identity as particularly salient or active in most situations, but this changed if they were in the racial minority in a specific context (Aries et al., 1998). Markus and Kunda (1986) proposed that the aspects of the self which were active in any given moment could be termed the "working self-concept." Because not every aspect of the self is active simultaneously, it's possible for people to hold self-contradictory self-concepts so long as the contradictory aspects are not associated with aspects of the self-concept likely to be activated simultaneously.

Consistent with this, the dominant understanding of the relationship between the personal and social selves has assumed that they are primarily in contrast with each other, with activation of one separate from activation of the other. Broadly, research has tended to assume that to the extent that the social self is activated, the personal self is not and vice-versa. Under this basic assumption, several broad theories about how the personal and social selves interact have developed. Optimal Distinctiveness Theory (Brewer, 1991, 2011) argues that in the service of core social motives including self-enhancement and self-certainty, people are motivated to affiliate with social groups and accordingly adopt social prototypes. However, at the same time people are motivated to see themselves as distinct from the group and a valued individual. The tension between these two drives leads people to seek a relationship with groups of "optimal distinctiveness" in which they are associated closely enough with a group to feel accepted and included in that group, but separate enough to be seen as a distinct individual. These two different needs are essentially diametrically in opposition to each other, with affiliation coming at the expense of differentiation and vice-versa. Laboratory research has supported the idea that the needs for affiliation and differentiation can be triggered separately and lead to increased alignment with groups or distancing from them (Leonardelli, Pickett, & Brewer, 2010). Similarly, Self-Categorization Theory (SCT) (Turner, 1985) sees the relationship between the personal and social self as somewhat in tension. Specifically, SCT proposes that groups value those people who are closest to the group prototype, and those who either naturally or through activation of selected parts of the personal self show greater alignment with the group prototype are more valued by the group as a whole (Hogg & Terry, 2000; Turner & Reynolds, 2011). Further, SCT theorists would argue that the activation of a group identity by contextual salience in turn triggers the activation of those elements of the self-concept associated with the group prototype, emphasizing the similarity of the individual to the group (Hogg & Turner, 1987).

An alternate approach posits that to the extent that personal self-views are strongly in alignment with the expectations of social groups, there may not be a tension. In general, people are strongly motivated to seek out information or feedback which confirms existing beliefs they have about themselves (Swann, 1984). Given a choice of contexts in which to interact, people will actively seek out settings and contexts which reinforce existing beliefs about the self, even when those beliefs are negative (Swann, Rentfrow, & Guinn, 2003). Specifically because the group prototype contains information about what characteristics are expected of the group member, this means that group membership can be a powerful tool for eliciting confirmatory feedback (Swann et al., 2009). Research on "identity fusion" has suggested that when group prototypes include characteristics that members either see as central and important to their personal identity or are otherwise very close to their existing self-views, activation of the collective identity would in parallel activate the personal identity. Research from self-verification would suggest that in this case, group membership would be strongly valued and indeed research in identity fusion has suggested that people with high degrees of overlap between the group and their self-concept are much more likely to endorse costly behavior in support of the group (Swann, Gómez, Dovidio, Hart, & Jetten, 2010; Swann, Gómez, Huici, Morales, & Hixon, 2010; Whitehouse, 2018).

In considering the identity-based links of extremism, this body of work collectively invokes a few predictions. Social identity theorists have proposed two primary motivations for strong identification with groups. Consistent with broad social motives relating to identity, they have proposed that identification with the group (and with the group social prototype) is a result of human motivations either for self-enhancement or self-certainty (Hogg & Terry, 2000). Recent work in political extremism has focused on uncertainty avoidance specifically as more important than self-enhancement for extremism (Hogg, 2014; Seyle, 2007; Swann et al., 2009). People often identify with low-status groups (Turner, Hogg, Turner, & Smith, 1984), and there is no strong evidence that enhancement motivations underlie outgroup derogation and the kind of group-based privileging that defines extremism (Rubin & Hewstone, 1998). As discussed above, certainty about the self is a core social motive—something that humans hold as a core expectation from the social environments in which they operate.

One significant debate in the psychological literature is over the mechanism by which these certainty concerns affect behavior, harkening back to the differing models for how the personal and social selves interact. One community, affiliated primarily with the self-categorization model for this interaction, sees these two differing aspects of the self as essentially hydraulic, with identification with the social group coming at the expense of activation and focus on the personal self (Turner & Reynolds, 2011). From this perspective, the dominant tool for group-related uncertainty reduction is a group which is very clearly and tightly defined, with a strong and explicit social identity and very clear and rigid rules about belonging (Hogg, 2014). In this understanding of the uncertainty-extremism link, uncertainty reduction can be achieved either by affiliating with groups with strong social prototypes and clear expectations for group members or alternately by increasing the clarity and distinctiveness of the identity associated with an existing group. This model emphasizes group members' perspective about the group as a whole, and argues for a psychology of extremism which emphasizes very clear expectations about group members, very strong boundaries between in-group and out-group, and some elements of strong positive associations with the group as a whole. It makes less predictions about whether the content of the individual group identities matters—in principle, any group of any type which is able to meet the goals of strong social prototypes and clear in- and out-groups would meet their needs.

For those researchers focused on a more holistic relationship between the personal and social selves, this approach is unsatisfying because to the extent that alignment with the social prototype requires people to challenge or change their personal self-views, such alignment will increase rather than decrease uncertainty. An alternate theory, based in the research on self-verification, suggests that uncertainty reduction is achieved by identifying groups where the social prototype emphasizes elements of the personal self which are closely held or important (Swann et al., 2009). From this perspective, groups provide reassuring feedback to people who feel uncertain by emphasizing key elements that they see in themselves. Recruitment campaigns for many legitimate organizations often play into this, emphasizing the perceived characteristics of group members in ways that appeal to people who want to see those characteristics in themselves but may doubt that they exist. Consider advertising campaigns designed to promote enlistment in the armed forces: many of them explicitly emphasize the idea that joining the military is a way of supporting and demonstrating a specific idealized self-image. For example, in 2019 the US Army launched a recruitment campaign titled "What's your warrior" that was explicitly intended to communicate the idea that "through Army service, Soldiers can both contribute to something greater than themselves while improving who they will become" (Army Enterprise Marketing, 2019). This model emphasizes the role that group membership plays in allowing people to demonstrate their commitment to specific identities, whether personal or social, and predicts that group membership is attractive to the extent that the group membership reinforces existing or desired personal or social self-view. This orientation is associated with the "Identity Fusion" theory of extremism, because it would predict that extremely strong or extremist alignment with groups would only be possible to the extent that soliciting confirmatory feedback about a social identity did not in turn challenge personal self-views.

As of this writing, there is an ongoing debate between proponents of these two theories and developing research in both camps. In considering the practical implications of this for work in CVE, however, the specific predictions of both approaches overlap in significant ways. They both argue that people are most susceptible to recruitment into extremist groups when their identities are undermined or challenged. Both would suggest that such a challenge could be to either personal or social self-views. The primary distinction would be a prediction about which group might be most attractive to the potential recruit. Uncertainty reduction based on self-categorization theory would argue that the characteristics of the group itself is more important, with groups that have clearer and more distinct social prototypes being more attractive to potential recruits than groups with less clear prototypes (Hogg, 2014). The content of the group's social prototype is less important than its clarity, while in contrast, theories of uncertainty reduction based in self-verification would suggest that the content of the group's social prototype is the most important element determining whether or not someone was at risk of a strong identification with the group that might contribute to extremism. Regardless of how the debate settles, the unified prediction of both approaches is that people are susceptible to recruitment into extremist groups when their self-concept is uncertain or challenged. To the extent that identity-related issues are truly involved in the attraction or commitment to radical groups, the psychological research would suggest that uncertain or challenged identity elements should be a predictor. The research on radicalization suggests that this prediction is borne out, as the next section will discuss.

5   Identity, Radicalization and Deradicalization

In existing research and policy discussion, the term "radicalization" is used to refer to the process of aligning with a violent group or moving along a spectrum from identification to action. Although, importantly, there is much more conceptual confusion around specifically how radicalization should be defined than the typical discourse acknowledges (Sedgwick, 2010), in general radicalization in the context of violent extremism can be thought of as the process of growing psychological and ideological commitment to a group which promotes violence. Specifically, if extremism is defined as the psychological relationship to a specific group or identity as described above, radicalization can be thought of as the dual process of (1) developing the psychological state of extremism and (2) accepting the ideology of a specific group which encourages or promotes this psychological state. This means that mechanisms for preventing radicalization or encouraging deradicalization should operate on one or both of these pathways.

To the extent that identity-related motivations are present in extremism, radicalization processes are the point at which they should become most obvious. Although the details of radicalization remain contested and there are few universally established evidence-based approaches to understanding radicalization, there has been sufficient research to determine that "that no single pathway or explanatory theory exists that would apply to all types of groups or to all individuals." (Borum, 2011, p. 15). Instead, there are a number of different pressures or elements which vary in importance from one case to another, and understanding the radicalization pathway should involve understanding a framework of pressures that can include individual readiness to affiliate with groups, individual perceptions about the value and status of violent groups or perpetrators of violence, the presence of specific groups and ideologies, and other contextual variables (Horgan, 2008). One model for capturing this diversity, developed by psychologists, posits that radicalization is a process that proceeds along a pathway from sensitivity to group alignment and finally action, driven by an interaction of individual-level sensitivity ("micro" level pressures), connections to specific groups or group ideologies (the "meso" level pressures), and the larger social context that demonstrates systemic inequalities or makes some identity groups more salient (the "macro" level pressures) (Doosje et al., 2016). This model was influenced by an earlier model developed by some of the same authors that argued that radicalization happened due to a confluence individual or motivational pressures, exposure and alignment to ideologies which met those needs, and a social or networking component by which a candidate was exposed to and incorporated into a specific group associated with some ideology (Kruglanski et al., 2014).

Using this basic framing, there are identified elements at the individual level that seem to be associated with an openness to radicalization. As predicted by the research on the self-concept, identity challenges appear to be a significant driver of radicalization. In the laboratory, experimental studies have shown that when people's self-concepts are challenged, they are more likely to identify strongly with groups they're associated with and in turn draw stronger distinctions between their group and out-groups (Sherman, Hogg, & Maitner, 2009). American conservatives show stronger identification with more extreme groups when their self-views are challenged (Gaffney, Rast, Hackett, & Hogg, 2014), and undergraduates who felt that centrally held self-views were threatened were more likely to endorse radical groups and radical action (Hogg, Meehan, & Farquharson, 2010). For people who were already strongly identified with a group (or "fused," using the term from identity fusion), challenges to personal self-views unrelated to group membership have been shown to increase reported commitment to extreme actions in support of the group (Swann et al., 2009; Swann & Buhrmester, 2015). Similarly, people with this level of identification are more likely to report willingness to self-sacrifice for the group under conditions which reduce cognitive processing capacity (Swann et al., 2009; Swann et al., 2014; Swann, Gómez, Huici, et al., 2010). This identification may be mediated in part by certainty: there is some evidence that for people who have strong and secure senses of identity, identity-related challenges don't cause the same reaction of extreme alignment with groups compared to people with strong but less certain identification (Rip, Vallerand, & Lafrenière, 2012).

Outside of the laboratory, there are strong identified links between identity and extremist behavior. As discussed above, people who are facing identity-related challenges appear to be most susceptible to radicalization. Literature on radicalization into Islamist groups finds that many recruits are people who are struggling to understand or define their Islamic identity in the context of the larger communities in which they live (Al Raffie, 2013). In particular, second-generation immigrants who feel unclear or uncertain connections both to their home and their heritage identities are more susceptible to radical messages (Lyons-Padilla, Gelfand, Mirahmadi, Farooq, & Van Egmond, 2015). A study of Al-Shabab members found that their religious identity as Muslims was central in many of their experiences with the group, and the author specifically argued that "These findings confirm that the interest of the collective—based on religion—serves as the most important component to a person's identity. For respondents, these two are interwoven in one.... any threat to the in-group will be interpreted as a threat to the individual." (Botha, 2014, p. 902). Studies of nationalist or white power extremists have found similar predictors: Simi, Bubolz, and Hardman (2013) argued that "identity discrepancies" caused when deeply held beliefs about the self weren't reinforced by society were a common experience among people joining far right terrorist groups. Analyses of online discussions among white power extremists shows that they are more likely to endorse violence as a response to perceived threats to group purity (such as racial intermarriage) rather than economic competition or other forms of group pressures (Glaser, Dixit, & Green, 2002). Similarly, despite the invocation of "economic anxiety" to explain radical movements, a study of hate-crime perpetrators found them to be no more concerned about economic issues than a control group, but significantly more concerned about threats to the perceived distinctiveness or purity of their group identities (Green, Abelson, & Garnett, 1999).

Although identity-related motivations appear central to extremism, it's not the case that anyone who is strongly affiliated with a specific collective identity is at risk of extremism. People who have certain and stable self-views appear less likely to respond to threats to identity with polarizing or exclusionary identification (Rip et al., 2012). Similarly, people with complex self-views that incorporate diverse social or personal identities are more resilient to challenges to their self-concept or self-esteem (Mussweiler, Gabriel, & Bodenhausen, 2000; Roccas, 2003). A study of Turkish migrants in Germany found that to the extent that migrants were able to develop a complex dual identification as Turkish or Muslim and German were less likely to develop radical or extremist orientations (Simon & Ruhs, 2008).

As discussed above, extremism as a psychological state is separate from a specific ideology or strategic decision to support violence, but creates a context in which it's easier to support violence. While identity issues appear to be significant in creating a predisposition to an extremist orientation, the actual move towards supporting violence appears to be more strongly linked to perceptions that the group is being mistreated by others (King & Taylor, 2011). A study of Muslims in Western Europe showed that people most at risk for radicalization into violent groups were those who both held their Islamic identity as central and important, and who were also aware of significant gaps in economic performance and political inclusion among European Muslims (Murshed & Pavan, 2011). This perception can come from direct exposure to these arguments through propaganda or news (Kirby, 2007). However, it is also the case that when considering the more meso level of predictors, social networks appear to be powerful elements of radicalization. One illustration of this comes from a study of Al-Shabab recruits in Kenya that found strong evidence for social networks as a part of radicalization, with 38% of their participants saying that friends were how they were introduced to the network (the largest single category), and 54% saying that they had in turn introduced new people to the group. Fully 71% of the sample joined Al-Shabab with friends rather than alone (Botha, 2014).

At the macro level, structural inequalities between different identity groups appear to make it easier to radicalize potential converts. In general, inequality between ethnic or identity groups is a significant predictor of intergroup tension and conflict (Cederman, Weidmann, & Gleditsch, 2011; Østby, Urdal, Tadjoeddin, Murshed, & Strand, 2011; Stewart, 2008). Specifically considering radicalization, a perception that the in-group is under threat is a significant part of most radicalizing messages and perceptions. The "14 words" of White Nationalists explicitly frame extremism as necessary for the defense of the in-group (ADL, n.d.), and Islamist propaganda often features themes of the oppression of Muslims internationally. A 2013 study of radicalization in the Netherlands found three major predictors of radicalization-identity-related uncertainty, a perception that the in-group was being treated unfairly, and a perception that the in-group was under threat (Doosje, Loseman, & van den Bos, 2013).

Collectively, this research would suggest that as predicted by research in self and identity, issues of the self-concept are central to radicalization and political extremism. Across multiple studies including both laboratory and field research, people are more likely to become radicalized when their self-concept is uncertain. In parallel, this research also demonstrates that uncertainty in and of itself is not sufficient: social and structural variables also predict increased radicalization. This generates some recommendations for work in preventing and countering violent extremism (P/CVE).

5.1 Recommendations for P/CVE Programming

The research on radicalization would suggest that identity-related issues are central to susceptibility to radicalization and the attractiveness of radical groups. A "core motives" approach to identity-related concerns would argue that people seek self-enhancement and self-certainty from their personal and social identities, and when those identities are challenged or undermined they will be more susceptible to alignment with radical or extremist groups. The empirical literature confirms this, but also underscores the importance of group ideology and the larger sociopolitical environment as conditioning this alignment. Someone who identifies strongly but uncertainly with a social identity that lacks extremist groups may be just as motivated to engage in self-sacrificing or dangerous behavior in the service of the group but may lack an ideological or sociopolitical context that encourages the form of that behavior to be violent.

This analysis then suggests that work in preventing or countering violent extremism could engage either with the core motivational elements creating predispositions towards joining groups. Of the two, psychological research would suggest that work on prevention should engage with the first element, while work on deradicalization should engage with the second. This is because it's in the selection and initial radicalization phase that individuals are searching for something which reaffirms challenged self-views, and it may not be the case that any specific group is necessary to meet those needs. On the other hand, once an individual has committed strongly to a specific group membership, changing or challenging that membership in an attempt to redirect their core social motivations will necessarily mean challenging the same self-certainty that drove participants to commit to the group in the first place.

Specific recommendations for programs on preventing or countering violent extremism derived from the identity research include the following:

1. Programs which reaffirm positive social and personal identities are preventative. To the extent that radicalization is a response to uncertain personal and social identities, any activity or program which affirms those identities is preventative against radicalization even if it doesn't directly engage radical messaging. If people feel that they are living out the self-views that they hold dearly, whether those self-views are related to their individual or social selves, they will need less external validation for these self-views. Providing potential converts alternate ways of living out positive self-views rather than extremist groups will potentially act as a preventive measure.

   When considering positive personal self-views, the research discussed above suggests that many converts to radical groups are looking for ways to act out personal self-views such as being brave, heroic, or otherwise doing work which has meaning. Atlantic reporter Graeme Wood has spent a significant amount of time in discussion with ISIS fighters, many of them recruited from developed countries. He argued that in those communities, in particular an attraction of ISIS was the draw of being directly involved in truly world-changing and important events that demanded sacrifice and struggle: "For certain true believers—the kind who long for epic good-versus-evil battles—visions of apocalyptic bloodbaths fulfill a deep psychological need… They believe that they are personally involved in struggles beyond their own lives, and that merely to be swept up in the drama, on the side of righteousness, is a privilege and a pleasure—especially when it is also a burden." (Wood, 2015). In many countries, day-to-day life may not provide many opportunities to live out these aspects of the self for most people. Programs which provide more prosocial opportunities for people to feel that they are contributing to the solution of larger social problems in their communities through service may have the additional effect of reducing the drivers of extremism. Similarly, in the case of social identities there is some evidence that for some people extremism is a response to challenged or uncertain social identities. In particular, many "homegrown" extremists in western societies are people who are second-generation immigrants who feel distance from both their parents' cultures and the cultures they have grown up in (Lyons-Padilla et al., 2015; Samata, 2018). In psychological terms, these people may have strongly held or important social identities that are unstable. For communities in which there are a large number of second-generation immigrants, programs which communicate the consistency or alignment between their social identity and the home culture's identity could be valuable: to the extent that people are receiving messages that it's impossible to be simultaneously (for example) Muslim and American, they are facing significant challenges to their self-views. Separately, programs which allow people to feel that they are more connected to ideologically nonviolent versions of their identity could have a preventive effect on extremism.

2. Messaging which associates violent groups with negative characteristics that are seen as positive to some are not preventative.

A drive for self-certainty supports behavior that reaffirms self-views even if those self-views are considered negative by society broadly (Swann, Pelham, & Krull, 1989). This is visible in radicalization as well, where elements of groups which may be seen by many analysts as self-evidently negative may at the same time be attractive to individuals who want to support self-views associated with that group membership. The Islamic State is noted as being skilled and aggressive in its use of social media, with this being a cornerstone of their attempts at recruitment and justification (Awan, 2017). Despite the fact that ISIS uses these videos explicitly to position themselves in the best light possible, these videos often feature gruesome violence, frequently against helpless people (Friis, 2015). While most people would interpret this violence as abhorrent—and indeed it has been described that way extensively in the coverage and political debate over ISIS (Friis, 2015)—in the context of the intended audience this violence is meant to be interpreted positively as both evidence of ISIS's power and also the powerful role of its fighters as "warriors" for the group (Farwell, 2014). Al-Shabaab has similarly released social media which included scenes of violence and casual cruelty off-putting to many but attractive to its core constituency (Menkhaus, 2013), and the Christchurch shooter's manifesto included a section in which he jokingly imagined the condemnation he would receive after the shooting and cast it as praise (Evans, 2019). To the extent that public messaging campaigns emphasize negative aspects of the group that play into the very self-views that potential group members feel uncertain about, these campaigns are likely to be ineffective at best or counterproductive at worst.

3. Conversely, messages which show the foolish or ludicrous elements of radical groups are more likely to be preventative.

To the extent that people join radical groups in a search for information that confirms or support deeply held self-views, it's likely that messages which undermine those self-views may be preventive. Specifically, as discussed above it's unlikely that messages that emphasize the severity, importance, or lethality of radical groups will be seen as unattractive to potential recruits. Instead, messages which present groups as ridiculous, farcical, or incompetent may be more effective: such messaging reinforces the existing uncertainty about self-views of competence or heroism.

There is some evidence for this. Famously, in 1946 the "Adventures of Superman" radio show featured a series of stories of Superman battling the "Clan of the Fiery Cross," a thinly fictionalized version of the Ku Klux Klan. The series used information from an infiltrator in the KKK, and broadcast the real secret passphrases of the KKK in a way that showed them as ridiculous, potentially contributing to a drop in the KKK's popularity (Bowers, 2012). More recently, a video journalist in Iraq was given footage ostensibly taken from a body-mounted camera of ISIS fighters. This video, which shows the chaos, frustration, and mistakes made by poorly trained ISIS fighters in combat, was briefly a pop-culture reference point mocking a fighter called "Abu Hajar" in the video for his many errors (Ames, 2016). The origin of this video has not been publicly verified, but whether it's an unedited natural recording or an edited piece of propaganda, it's significant in that it contributed to fragmenting the public vision of ISIS as competent, dangerous, and threatening (Lakomy, 2017). Such messaging may undermine the engagement of potential recruits willing to look lethal but unwilling to look incompetent.

4. Deradicalization strategies focused on changing identity are probably likely to fail, but changing the meaning of identities may be possible.

Considering the more significant challenge of deradicalization, the primary conclusion that comes from the psychological literature is that identity-related commitments are going to be hard to undermine. The same persistent social motives which lead people to significant acts in support of their self-views will vigorously defend these self-views against challenges from external actors. As such, attempts to change radical commitments should emphasize the continuity of the commitment to the group and the associated meaning that individuals have attached to it. Engagement around the specific ideology of the group, and in particular the identification of more attractive alternate ideologies that contain the same level of group commitment, may be necessary for deradicalization. This conclusion is an echo of what practitioners have already concluded. Consistent with the multiple pathways to radicalization, practitioners argue that "there is no one-size-fits-all approach" to deradicalization (Korn, 2016). However, there's some evidence that achieving change in formal commitments to groups or their messages may be much more challenging than achieving a change in willingness to use violence (Horgan & Braddock, 2010). The existing research does suggest that the primary successes come from approaches which don't attempt to directly counter identity-related commitment, but instead engage with the ideology attached to this that supports violence (Chowdhury & Krebs, 2010; Frey & Luechinger, 2008; Nasser-Eddine, Garnham, Agostino, & Caluya, 2011). In particular, these messages appear to be most effective when they come from peer figures rather than community leaders (Williams, Horgan, & Evans, 2016). This prediction is consistent with the predictions derived from psychological theory, in that the focus of this research has been on engaging with people who have already taken at least the initial step towards radicalization. Some limited research, specifically a 2017 study working with a sample of LTTE members, found that this approach was particularly effective when it included an emphasis on the individual self-views emphasizing personal significance (Webber et al., 2018).

6 Conclusion

An overwhelming consensus of the extant literature on the drivers of violent extremism is that there's no unified pathway to radicalization or support for violence (e.g. Lafree et al., 2018). It's clear that, as the Kruglanski et al. (2014) model describes it, that there are micro, meso, and macro factors that influence the pathways towards radicalization. Any approach to P/CVE that doesn't take this into account is not likely to succeed.

At the same time, there has been a relatively little focus on understanding the underlying psychology behind violent extremism, with most studies simply defining it in terms of its outcome as the willingness to use violence. This runs the risk of missing contributions to psychology more generally, in that extremism is a nearly unique phenomenon in the context of core social motives that should discourage the kind of behavior that extremism supports. More broadly, without understanding the core psychology of extremism there's a risk that P/CVE programs may be able to respond to specific threats by focusing on specific communities or messages, but miss the underlying drivers that could come out in new forms.

This chapter attempts to contribute to the discussion by providing an operational definition of extremism that is domain-neutral and not directly tied to support for violence, as well as a pathway that links this definition to support for violence. Based on the existing research on core social motives and extremism, we have also argued that while there are several elements that can predispose individuals towards an extremist orientation the state of extremism is ultimately tied to identity-related concerns. If this is true, then both PVE and deradicalization programs should consider these underlying motives in developing their theory of impact. The current empirical literature on the effectiveness of CVE programs and deradicalization programs is developing, but initial data do suggest that psychologically informed programs may be effective. Developing these approaches, and putting front-and-center a psychological motives-focused approach that emphasizes identity as a key driver of extremism, may be an important part of confronting violent extremism in the twenty-first century as well as improving understanding of extremist violence.

References

ADL. (n.d.). *14 words*. Retrieved April 29, 2019, from Anti-Defamation League website: https://www.adl.org/education/references/hate-symbols/14-words

Akhtar, S. (1999). Immigration and identity: Turmoil, treatment, and transformation. *Jason Aronson.*

Al Raffie, D. (2013). Social identity theory for investigating Islamic extremism in the diaspora. *Journal of Strategic Security, 6*(4), 67–91.

Allison, G. T. (1969). Conceptual models and the Cuban missile crisis. *American Political Science Review, 63*(3), 689–718.

Ames, J. (2016, April 28). *Abu Hajaar and that ISIS Video On Vice….* The Velvet Rocket. Retrieved from https://thevelvetrocket.com/2016/04/28/abu-hajaar-isis/

Aries, E., Olver, R. R., Blount, K., Christaldi, K., Fredman, S., & Lee, T. (1998). Race and gender as components of the working self-concept. *The Journal of Social Psychology, 138*(3), 277–290.

Army Enterprise Marketing. (2019, November 20). *U.S. Army's Marketing Campaign: "What's Your Warrior?"*. US Army Training and Doctrine Command. Retrieved from https://www.tradoc.army.mil/Publications-and-Resources/Article-Display/Article/2019551/us-armys-marketing-campaign-whats-your-warrior/\#:\~:text=%22What's%20Your%20Warrior%3F%22%20is,most%20powerful%20team%20on%20Earth

Atran, S. (2003). Genesis of suicide terrorism. *Science, 299*(5612), 1534–1539.

Awan, I. (2017). Cyber-extremism: Isis and the power of social media. *Society, 54*(2), 138–149. https://doi.org/10.1007/s12115-017-0114-0

Bakker, E., & De Graaf, B. (2011). Preventing lone wolf terrorism: Some CT approaches addressed. *Perspectives on Terrorism, 5*(5/6), 43–50.

Baumeister, R. F. (1999). *The self in social psychology*. Philadelphia, PA: Psychology Press.

Baumgartner, T., Götte, L., Gügler, R., & Fehr, E. (2012). The mentalizing network orchestrates the impact of parochial altruism on social norm enforcement. *Human brain mapping, 33*(6), 1452–1469.

Bernhard, H., Fehr, E., & Fischbacher, U. (2006). Third-party punishment within and across groups: An experimental study in Papua New Guinea. In *American Economic Review, Papers and Proceedings 92*(2), 217–221.

Besaw, C. (2018). *Altruistic punishment theory and inter-group violence*.

Bloom, M. M. (2004). Palestinian suicide bombing: Public support, market share, and outbidding. *Political Science Quarterly, 119*(1), 61–88.

Borum, R. (2011). Radicalization into violent extremism I: A review of social science theories. *Journal of Strategic Security, 4*(4), 7–36.

Botha, A. (2014). Political socialization and terrorist radicalization among individuals who joined Al-Shabaab in Kenya. *Studies in Conflict & Terrorism, 37*(11), 895–919.

Bowers, R. (2012). *Superman versus the Ku Klux Klan: The true story of how the iconic superhero battled the men of hate*. Washington, DC: National Geographic Society.

Bowles, S. (2006). Group competition, reproductive leveling, and the evolution of human altruism. *Science, 314*(5805), 1569–1572.

Brewer, M. B. (1991). The social self: On being the same and different at the same time. *Personality and Social Psychology Bulletin, 17*(5), 475–482.

Brewer, M. B. (2011). Optimal distinctiveness theory: Its history and development. In P. A. M. Van Lange, A. Kruglanski, & E. T. Higgins (Eds.), *Handbook of theories of social psychology* (Vol. 2, pp. 81–98). London, UK: Sage.

Burton-Chellew, M. N., Ross-Gillespie, A., & West, S. A. (2010). Cooperation in humans: competition between groups and proximate emotions. *Evolution and Human Behavior, 31*(2), 104–108.

Canetti, D., & Pedahzur, A. (2002). The effects of contextual and psychological variables on extreme right-wing sentiments. *Social Behavior & Personality, 30*(4).

Carter, D. B. (2016). Provocation and the strategy of terrorist and guerrilla attacks. *International Organization, 70*(1), 133–173. https://doi.org/10.1017/S0020818315000351

Cederman, L.-E., Weidmann, N. B., & Gleditsch, K. S. (2011). Horizontal inequalities and ethnonationalist civil war: A global comparison. *American Political Science Review, 105*(3), 478–495. https://doi.org/10.1017/S0003055411000207

Choi, J. K., & Bowles, S. (2007). The coevolution of parochial altruism and war. *Science, 318*(5850), 636–640.

Chowdhury, A., & Krebs, R. R. (2010). Talking about terror: Counterterrorist campaigns and the logic of representation. *European Journal of International Relations, 16*(1), 125–150. https://doi.org/10.1177/1354066109352917

Cohen, K., Johansson, F., Kaati, L., & Mork, J. C. (2014). Detecting linguistic markers for radical violence in social media. *Terrorism and Political Violence, 26*(1), 246–256.

Conrad, J., & Greene, K. (2015). Competition, differentiation, and the severity of terrorist attacks. *The Journal of Politics, 77*(2), 546–561.

Crenshaw, M. (1981). The causes of terrorism. *Comparative Politics, 13*(4), 379–399.

Crenshaw, M. (2000). The psychology of terrorism: An agenda for the 21st century. *Political Psychology, 21*(2), 405–420.

Decety, J., & Sommerville, J. A. (2003). Shared representations between self and other: A social cognitive neuroscience view. *Trends in Cognitive Sciences, 7*(12), 527–533. https://doi.org/10.1016/j.tics.2003.10.004

De Quervain, D. J., Fischbacher, U., Treyer, V., & Schellhammer, M. (2004). The neural basis of altruistic punishment. *Science, 305*(5688), 1254.

Doosje, B., Loseman, A., & van den Bos, K. (2013). Determinants of radicalization of Islamic Youth in the Netherlands: Personal uncertainty, perceived injustice, and perceived group threat. *Journal of Social Issues, 69*(3), 586–604. https://doi.org/10.1111/josi.12030

Doosje, B., Moghaddam, F. M., Kruglanski, A. W., De Wolf, A., Mann, L., & Feddes, A. R. (2016). Terrorism, radicalization and de-radicalization. *Current Opinion in Psychology, 11*, 79–84.

Evans, R. (2019, March 15). *Shitposting, inspirational terrorism, and the Christchurch mosque massacre.* Retrieved April 23, 2019, from Bellingcat website: https://www.bellingcat.com/news/rest-of-world/2019/03/15/shitposting-inspirational-terrorism-and-the-christchurch-mosque-massacre/

Farwell, J. P. (2014). The media strategy of ISIS. *Survival, 56*(6), 49–55. https://doi.org/10.1080/00396338.2014.985436

Feddes, A. R., Mann, L., & Doosje, B. (2015). Increasing self-esteem and empathy to prevent violent radicalization: a longitudinal quantitative evaluation of a resilience training focused on adolescents with a dual identity. *Journal of Applied Social Psychology, 45*(7), 400–411.

Federal Bureau of Investigations. (n.d.-a). *What is violent extremism?* Retrieved June 10, 2020, from the FBI website: https://www.fbi.gov/cve508/teen-website/what-is-violent-extremism

Federal Bureau of Investigations. (n.d.-b). *What are known violent extremist groups?* Retrieved June 10, 2020, from FBI website: https://www.fbi.gov/cve508/teen-website/what-are-known-violent-extremist-groups

Fehr, E., & Gächter, S. (2002). Altruistic punishment in humans. *Nature, 415*(6868), 137–140.

Fiske, S. T. (2007). Core social motivations: Views from the couch, consciousness, classroom, computers, and collectives. In J. Y. Shah & W. Gardener (Eds.), *Handbook of motivation science* (pp. 3–22). New York, NY: Guilford Press.

Fiske, S. T. (2009). *Social beings: Core motives in social psychology.* New York, NY: Wiley.

Fiske, A. P., & Rai, T. S. (2014). *Virtuous violence: Hurting and killing to create, sustain, end, and honor social relationships.* Cambridge University Press.

Fiske, S. T., & Taylor, S. E. (1991). *Social cognition.* New York, NY: McGraw-Hill.

Freedman, L. (2007). Terrorism as a Strategy. *Government and Opposition, 42*(3), 314–339.

Frey, B. S., & Luechinger, S. (2008). Three strategies to deal with terrorism. *Economic Papers, 27*(2), 107–114.

Friis, S. M. (2015). 'Beyond anything we have ever seen': Beheading videos and the visibility of violence in the war against ISIS. *International Affairs, 91*(4), 725–746.

Gaffney, A. M., Rast, D. E., III, Hackett, J. D., & Hogg, M. A. (2014). Further to the right: Uncertainty, political polarization and the American "Tea Party" movement. *Social Influence, 9*(4), 272–288. https://doi.org/10.1080/15534510.2013.842495

Gintis, H. (2014). *The Bounds of Reason: Game Theory and the Unification of the Behavioral Sciences-Revised Edition.* Princeton University Press.

Glaser, J., Dixit, J., & Green, D. P. (2002). Studying hate crime with the internet: What makes racists advocate racial violence? *Journal of Social Issues, 58*(1), 177–193. https://doi.org/10.1111/1540-4560.00255

Green, D. P., Abelson, R. P., & Garnett, M. (1999). The distinctive political views of hate-crime perpetrators and white supremacists. In D. A. Prentice & D. T. Miller (Eds.), *Cultural divides:*

Understanding and overcoming group conflict (pp. 429–464). New York, NY: Russell Sage Foundation.

Hacker, F. J., & Hacker, F. (1976). *Crusaders, criminals, crazies: Terror and terrorism in our time*. New York: Norton.

Hayes, B. C., & McAllister, I. (2001). Sowing dragon's teeth: Public support for political violence and paramilitarism in Northern Ireland. *Political Studies, 49*(5), 901–922. https://doi.org/10.1111/1467-9248.00346

Henck, N. (2007). *Subcommander marcos: The man and the mask*. Durham, NC: Duke University Press.

Henrich, J., McElrath, R., Barr, A., Ensminger, J., Barrett, C., Bolyantz, A., … Zilker, J. (2006). Costly punishment across human societies. *Science, 312*, 1767–1770.

Hoffman, B. (1998). *Inside terrorism*. Columbia university press.

Hoffman, B. (2019). Al Qaeda, Trends in Terrorism, and Future. Transnational Terrorism, 31.

Hofmann, C., & Schneckener, U. (2011). Engaging non-state armed actors in state-and peace-building: options and strategies. *International Review of the Red Cross, 93*, 603.

Hogg, M. A. (2014). From uncertainty to extremism: Social categorization and identity processes. *Current Directions in Psychological Science, 23*(5), 338–342.

Hogg, M. A., Meehan, C., & Farquharson, J. (2010). The solace of radicalism: Self-uncertainty and group identification in the face of threat. *Journal of Experimental Social Psychology, 46*(6), 1061–1066.

Hogg, M. A., & Terry, D. J. (2000). Social identity and self-categorization processes in organizational contexts. *The Academy of Management Review, 25*(1), 121–140. https://doi.org/10.2307/259266

Hogg, M. A., & Turner, J. C. (1987). Intergroup behaviour, self-stereotyping and the salience of social categories. *British Journal of Social Psychology, 26*(4), 325–340. https://doi.org/10.1111/j.2044-8309.1987.tb00795.x

Horgan, J. (2008). From profiles to pathways and roots to routes: Perspectives from psychology on radicalization into terrorism. *The Annals of the American Academy of Political and Social Science, 618*(1), 80–94.

Horgan, J., & Braddock, K. (2010). Rehabilitating the terrorists?: Challenges in assessing the effectiveness of de-radicalization programs. *Terrorism and Political Violence, 22*(2), 267–291. https://doi.org/10.1080/09546551003594748

James, W. (1890). *The principles of psychology*. New York, NY: Holt.

Kalmoe, N. P. (2014). Fueling the fire: Violent metaphors, trait aggression, and support for political violence. *Political Communication, 31*(4), 545–563. https://doi.org/10.1080/10584609.2013.852642

Kaplan, J., Lööw, H., & Malkki, L. (2014). Introduction to the special issue on lone wolf and autonomous cell terrorism. *Terrorism and Political Violence, 26*(1), 1–12.

Kalyvas, S. N. (2006). The logic of violence in civil war. Cambridge University Press.

King, M., & Taylor, D. M. (2011). The radicalization of homegrown jihadists: A review of theoretical models and social psychological evidence. *Terrorism and Political Violence, 23*(4), 602–622. https://doi.org/10.1080/09546553.2011.587064

Kirby, A. (2007). The London bombers as "self-starters": A case study in indigenous radicalization and the emergence of autonomous cliques. *Studies in Conflict & Terrorism, 30*(5), 415–428. https://doi.org/10.1080/10576100701258619

Korn, J. (2016). European CVE strategies from a practitioner's perspective. *The Annals of the American Academy of Political and Social Science, 668*(1), 180–197. https://doi.org/10.1177/0002716216671888

Kruglanski, A. W., Gelfand, M. J., Bélanger, J. J., Sheveland, A., Hetiarachchi, M., & Gunaratna, R. (2014). The psychology of radicalization and deradicalization: How significance quest impacts violent extremism. *Political Psychology, 35*, 69–93.

Kruglanski, A. W., Jasko, K., Chernikova, M., Dugas, M., & Webber, D. (2017). To the fringe and back: Violent extremism and the psychology of deviance. *American Psychologist, 72*(3), 217.

Kydd, A. H., & Walter, B. F. (2006). The strategies of terrorism. *International Security, 31*(1), 49–80.

Lafree, G., Jensen, M. A., James, P. A., & Safer-Lichtenstein, A. (2018). Correlates of violent political extremism in the United States. *Criminology, 56*(2), 233–268. https://doi.org/10.1111/1745-9125.12169

Lakomy, M. (2017). Cracks in the online "caliphate": How the Islamic state is losing ground in the battle for cyberspace. *Perspectives on Terrorism, 11*(3), 40–53.

Laqueur, W. (2000). *The new terrorism: Fanaticism and the arms of mass destruction.* Oxford University Press on Demand.

Lee, A. (2011). Who becomes a terrorist? Poverty, education, and the origins of political violence. World Politics, 203–245.

Leonardelli, G. J., Pickett, C. L., & Brewer, M. B. (2010). Optimal distinctiveness theory: A framework for social identity, social cognition, and intergroup relations. In M. P. Zanna & J. M. Olson (Eds.), *Advances in experimental social psychology* (Vol. 43, pp. 63–113). San Diego, CA: Academic Press. https://doi.org/10.1016/S0065-2601(10)43002-6

Linville, P. W. (1985). Self-complexity and affective extremity: Don't put all of your eggs in one cognitive basket. *Social Cognition, 3*(1), 94–120.

Linville, P. W. (1987). Self-complexity as a cognitive buffer against stress-related illness and depression. *Journal of Personality and Social Psychology, 52*(4), 663.

List, C., & Spiekermann, K. (2013). Methodological individualism and holism in political science: A reconciliation. *American Political Science Review*, 629–643.

Lyons-Padilla, S., Gelfand, M. J., Mirahmadi, H., Farooq, M., & Van Egmond, M. (2015). Belonging nowhere: Marginalization & radicalization risk among Muslim immigrants. *Behavioral Science & Policy, 1*(2), 1–12.

Markus, H., & Kunda, Z. (1986). Stability and malleability of the self-concept. *Journal of Personality and Social Psychology, 51*(4), 858.

Markus, H., & Wurf, E. (1987). The dynamic self-concept: A social psychological perspective. *Annual Review of Psychology, 38*(1), 299–337.

McCartan, L. M., Masselli, A., Rey, M., & Rusnak, D. (2008). The logic of terrorist target choice: An examination of Chechen rebel bombings from 1997–2003. *Studies in Conflict & Terrorism, 31*(1), 60–79.

McConnell, A. R. (2011). The multiple self-aspects framework: Self-concept representation and its implications. *Personality and Social Psychology Review, 15*(1), 3–27.

McCormick, G. H. (2003). Terrorist decision making. *Annual Review of Political Science, 6*(1), 473–507.

Menkhaus, K. (2013). Al-Shabaab and social media: A double-edged sword. *Brown Journal of World Affairs, 20*, 309.

Merari, A. (1993). Terrorism as a Strategy of Insurgency. *Terrorism and political violence, 5*(4), 213–251.

Montague, P. R., & Lohrenz, T. (2007). To detect and correct: norm violations and their enforcement. *Neuron, 56*(1), 14–18.

Murshed, S. M., & Pavan, S. (2011). Identity and Islamic radicalization in Western Europe. *Civil Wars, 13*(3), 259–279. https://doi.org/10.1080/13698249.2011.600000

Mussweiler, T., Gabriel, S., & Bodenhausen, G. V. (2000). Shifting social identities as a strategy for deflecting threatening social comparisons. *Journal of Personality and Social Psychology, 79*(3), 398.

Nasser-Eddine, M., Garnham, B., Agostino, K., & Caluya, G. (2011). *Countering Violent Extremism (CVE) literature review* (No. DSTO-TR-2522). Counter Terrorism and Security Technology Centre, Defence Science and Technology Organisation, Edinburgh, Australia.

Nelissen, R., & Zeelenberg, M. (2009). When guilt evokes self-punishment: evidence for the existence of a Dobby Effect. *Emotion, 9*(1), 118.

Neumayer, E., & Plümper, T. (2009). International terrorism and the clash of civilizations. *British Journal of Political Science, 39*(4), 711–734. Retrieved from JSTOR.

Nemeth, S. (2014). The effect of competition on terrorist group operations. *Journal of Conflict Resolution, 58*(2), 336–362.

Østby, G., Urdal, H., Tadjoeddin, M. Z., Murshed, S. M., & Strand, H. (2011). Population pressure, horizontal inequality and political violence: A disaggregated study of Indonesian provinces, 1990–2003. *The Journal of Development Studies, 47*(3), 377–398. https://doi.org/10.1080/00 220388.2010.506911

Pape, R. (2006). *Dying to win: The strategic logic of suicide terrorism* (Reprint edition). New York, NY: Random House Trade Paperbacks.

Pettersson, T., & Eck, K. (2018). Organized violence, 1989–2017. *Journal of Peace Research, 55*(4), 535–547.

Polo, S. M., & Gleditsch, K. S. (2016). Twisting arms and sending messages: Terrorist tactics in civil war. *Journal of Peace Research, 53*(6), 815–829. https://doi.org/10.1177/0022343316667999

Post, J. M. (1990). Terrorist psycho-logic: Terrorist behavior as a product of psychological forces. In W. Reich (Ed.), *Woodrow Wilson Center series. Origins of terrorism: Psychologies, ideologies, theologies, states of mind* (p. 25–40). Cambridge University Press; Woodrow Wilson International Center for Scholars.

Post, J., Sprinzak, E., & Denny, L. (2003). The terrorists in their own words: Interviews with 35 incarcerated Middle Eastern terrorists. *Terrorism and Political Violence, 15*(1), 171–184.

Post, J. M. (2007). *The mind of the terrorist: The psychology of terrorism from the IRA to al-Qaeda*. New York, NY: St. Martin's Press.

Postmes, T., Baray, G., Haslam, S. A., Morton, T. A., & Swaab, R. I. (2006). The dynamics of personal and social identity formation. In T. Postmes & T. Jetten (Eds.), *Individuality and the group: Advances in social identity*. London, UK: Sage.

Rapoport, D. C. (2004). The four waves of modern terrorism. In A. K. Cronin & J. Ludes (Eds.), *Attacking terrorism: Elements of a grand strategy* (pp. 46–73). Washington, DC: Georgetown University Press.

Rasch, W. (1979). Psychological dimensions of political terrorism in the Federal Republic of Germany. *International journal of law and psychiatry, 2*(1), 79–85.

Rip, B., Vallerand, R. J., & Lafrenière, M.-A. K. (2012). Passion for a cause, passion for a creed: On ideological passion, identity threat, and extremism. *Journal of Personality, 80*(3), 573–602.

Roccas, S. (2003). The effects of status on identification with multiple groups. *European Journal of Social Psychology, 33*(3), 351–366.

Rubin, M., & Hewstone, M. (1998). Social identity theory's self-esteem hypothesis: A review and some suggestions for clarification. *Personality and Social Psychology Review, 2*(1), 40–62.

Rusch, H. (2014). The evolutionary interplay of intergroup conflict and altruism in humans: a review of parochial altruism theory and prospects for its extension. *Proceedings of the Royal Society B: Biological Sciences, 281*(1794), 20141539.

Samata, S. (2018). Language, exclusion and violent jihad: Are they related? *International Journal of Bilingual Education and Bilingualism, 21*(6), 680–689. https://doi.org/10.1080/13670050. 2016.1208143

Santifort, C., Sandler, T., & Brandt, P. T. (2013). Terrorist attack and target diversity: Changepoints and their drivers. *Journal of Peace Research, 50*(1), 75–90.

Sandler, T., Tschirhart, J. T., & Cauley, J. (1983). A theoretical analysis of transnational terrorism. *The American Political Science Review*, 36–54.

Sanfey, A. G., Rilling, J. K., Aronson, J. A., Nystrom, L. E., & Cohen, J. D. (2003). The neural basis of economic decision-making in the ultimatum game. *Science, 300*(5626), 1755–1758.

Sedgwick, M. (2010). The concept of radicalization as a source of confusion. *Terrorism and Political Violence, 22*(4), 479–494. https://doi.org/10.1080/09546553.2010.491009

Seyle, C., & Swann, W. B. (2007). Being oneself in the workplace: Self-verification and identity in organizational contexts. In C. A. Bartel, S. Blader, & A. Wrzesniewski (Eds.), *Identity and the modern organization* (pp. 201–222). Mahwah, NJ: Erlbaum.

Seyle, D. C. (2007). *Identity fusion and the psychology of political extremism* (Dissertation). University of Texas, Austin, TX.

Sherman, D. K., Hogg, M. A., & Maitner, A. T. (2009). Perceived polarization: Reconciling ingroup and intergroup perceptions under uncertainty. *Group Processes & Intergroup Relations, 12*(1), 95–109.

Sidanius, J. (1985). Cognitive functioning and sociopolitical ideology revisited. *Political Psychology*, 637–661.

Silber, M. D., Bhatt, A., & Analysts, S. I. (2007). *Radicalization in the West: The homegrown threat* (pp. 1–90). New York: Police Department.

Simi, P., Bubolz, B. F., & Hardman, A. (2013). Military experience, identity discrepancies, and far right terrorism: An exploratory analysis. *Studies in Conflict & Terrorism, 36*(8), 654–671. https://doi.org/10.1080/1057610X.2013.802976

Simon, B., & Ruhs, D. (2008). Identity and politicization among Turkish migrants in Germany: The role of dual identification. *Journal of Personality and Social Psychology, 95*(6), 1354–1366. https://doi.org/10.1037/a0012630

Singer, T., Critchley, H. D., & Preuschoff, K. (2009). A common role of insula in feelings, empathy and uncertainty. *Trends in cognitive sciences, 13*(8), 334–340.

Smith, A. (2004). Summary of research on suicide terrorism. In *Suicide Terrorism Conference*. United States Department of Justice, Washington, DC.

Spaaij, R. (2010). The enigma of lone wolf terrorism: An assessment. *Studies in Conflict & Terrorism, 33*(9), 854–870.

Stewart, F. (2008). *Horizontal inequalities & conflict: Understanding group violence in multiethnic societies*. London, UK: Palgrave Macmillan.

Strobel, A., Zimmermann, J., Schmitz, A., Reuter, M., Lis, S., Windmann, S., & Kirsch, P. (2011). Beyond revenge: neural and genetic bases of altruistic punishment. *Neuroimage, 54*(1), 671–680.

Swann, W. B. (1984). Quest for accuracy in person perception: A matter of pragmatics. *Psychological Review, 91*(4), 457.

Swann, W. B., & Buhrmester, M. D. (2015). Identity fusion. *Current Directions in Psychological Science, 24*(1), 52–57.

Swann, W. B., Gómez, Á., Buhrmester, M. D., López-Rodríguez, L., Jiménez, J., & Vázquez, A. (2014). Contemplating the ultimate sacrifice: Identity fusion channels pro-group affect, cognition, and moral decision making. *Journal of Personality and Social Psychology, 106*(5), 713.

Swann, W. B., Gómez, Á., Dovidio, J. F., Hart, S., & Jetten, J. (2010). Dying and killing for one's group: Identity fusion moderates responses to intergroup versions of the trolley problem. *Psychological Science, 21*(8), 1176–1183.

Swann, W. B., Gómez, A., Huici, C., Morales, J., & Hixon, J. G. (2010). Identity fusion and self-sacrifice: Arousal as a catalyst of pro-group fighting, dying, and helping behavior. *Journal of Personality and Social Psychology, 99*(5), 824.

Swann, W. B., Gómez, Á., Seyle, D. C., Francisco, J., & Huici, C. (2009). Identity fusion: The interplay of personal and social identities in extreme group behavior. *Journal of Personality and Social Psychology, 96*(5), 995–1011. https://doi.org/10.1037/a0013668

Swann, W. B., Pelham, B. W., & Krull, D. S. (1989). Agreeable fancy or disagreeable truth? Reconciling self-enhancement and self-verification. *Journal of Personality and Social Psychology, 57*(5), 782.

Swann, W. B., Rentfrow, P. J., & Guinn, J. S. (2003). Self-verification: The search for coherence. In M. R. Leary & J. P. Tangney (Eds.), *Handbook of self and identity* (pp. 367–383). New York, NY: The Guilford Press.

Swann, W. B., & Seyle, C. (2005). Personality psychology's comeback and its emerging symbiosis with social psychology. *Personality and Social Psychology Bulletin, 31*(2), 155–165. https://doi.org/10.1177/0146167204271591

Tezcür, G. M., & Besaw, C. (2020). Jihadist waves: Syria, the Islamic State, and the changing nature of foreign fighters. *Conflict Management and Peace Science, 37*(2), 215–231.

Trafimow, D., Triandis, H. C., & Goto, S. G. (1991). Some tests of the distinction between the private self and the collective self. *Journal of Personality and Social Psychology, 60*(5), 649.

Tullock, G. (1971). The paradox of revolution. *Public Choice, 11*(1), 89–99.

Turner, J. C. (1985). Social categorization and the self-concept: A social cognitive theory of group behavior. In E. J. Lawler (Ed.), *Advances in group processes: Theory and research* (Vol. 2, pp. 77–122). Greenwich, CT: JAI Press.

Turner, J. C., Hogg, M. A., Turner, P. J., & Smith, P. M. (1984). Failure and defeat as determinants of group cohesiveness. *British Journal of Social Psychology, 23*(2), 97–111.

Turner, J. C., & Reynolds, K. J. (2011). Self-categorization theory. In P. A. M. V. Lange, A. W. Kruglanski, & E. T. Higgins (Eds.), *Handbook of theories of social psychology: Volume Two* (pp. 399–414). London, UK: Sage.

Valentino, B. A. (2014). Why we kill: The political science of political violence against civilians. *Annual Review of Political Science, 17*, 89–103.

Vanderwal, T., Hunyadi, E., Grupe, D. W., Connors, C. M., & Schultz, R. T. (2008). Self, mother and abstract other: An fMRI study of reflective social processing. *NeuroImage, 41*(4), 1437–1446. https://doi.org/10.1016/j.neuroimage.2008.03.058

Victoroff, J. (2005). The mind of the terrorist: A review and critique of psychological approaches. *Journal of Conflict resolution, 49*(1), 3–42.

Von Neumann, J., & Morgenstern, O. (1944). *Theory of games and economic behavior*. Princeton, NJ: Princeton University Press.

Walter, B. F. (2017). The extremist's advantage in civil wars. *International Security, 42*(2), 7–39.

Webber, D., Chernikova, M., Kruglanski, A. W., Gelfand, M. J., Hettiarachchi, M., Gunaratna, R., … Belanger, J. J. (2018). Deradicalizing detained terrorists. *Political Psychology, 39*(3), 539–556. https://doi.org/10.1111/pops.12428

Weinstein, J. M. (2006). *Inside rebellion: The politics of insurgent violence*. Cambridge University Press.

Whitehouse, H. (2018). Dying for the group: Towards a general theory of extreme self-sacrifice. *Behavioral and Brain Sciences, 41*, 1–64. https://doi.org/10.1017/S0140525X18000249

Williams, M., Horgan, J., & Evans, W. (2016). Evaluation of a multi-faceted, U.S. community-based, muslim-Led CVE Program.

Wood, G. (2015, March). *What ISIS really wants*. The Atlantic. Retrieved from https://www.the-atlantic.com/magazine/archive/2015/03/what-isis-really-wants/384980/

Zaidise, E., Canetti-Nisim, D., & Pedahzur, A. (2007). Politics of god or politics of man? The role of religion and deprivation in predicting support for political violence in Israel. *Political Studies, 55*(3), 499–521. https://doi.org/10.1111/j.1467-9248.2007.00673.x

The Use of Love and Hate in Extremist Groups

Katherine V. Aumer and Michael A. Erickson

> *To fear the L*ORD *is to hate evil;I hate pride and arrogance,evil behavior and perverse speech.*
> *— Proverbs 8:13*

Hate and love have often been viewed as polar opposites. Historically, researchers have viewed hate as a destructive and hostile emotion (Royzman, McCauley, & Rozin, 2005). Oatley, Keltner, and Jenkins (2006) even went so far as to posit that hate is "our biggest handicap as a social species" (p. 44). Philosophers and psychologists have continuously debated hate's categorization and characteristics. Rempel and colleagues have examined people's explanations for interpersonal scenarios and classified hate as a motivation (e.g., Rempel & Burris, 2005; Rempel, Burris, & Fathi, 2019). Others, using more explicit criteria and prototype analyses, categorized hate as an emotion (Fitness & Fletcher, 1993; Sternberg, 2003). Yet hate could also be an attitude (Ekman, 1992) or a syndrome (Shand, 1920). When considering the consequences of hate, Descartes (1694/1989) argued that hate causes a kind of withdrawal, while Aristotle contended that hate initiates attack (Aristotle, trans., 1954). Categorical incongruencies aside, there is a general repugnance for hate shared by both laypersons and scholars. The presumption that hate is bad is not without merit. Sternberg (2003) argued that hate is at the root of war, ethnic cleansing, and evil. Halperin, Russell, Dweck, and Gross (2011) demonstrated that Israelis with high levels of hate and anger are less likely to compromise with Palestinians on upcoming peace negotiations. U.S. Federal law contains a special classification of crime: "hate crimes," that are considered especially egregious and opprobrious, and that usually result in more severe penalties (Iganski & Lagou, 2015). People tend

K. V. Aumer (✉)
University of Hawai'i–West O'ahu, Kapolei, Hawaii, USA
e-mail: kaumer@hawaii.edu

M. A. Erickson
Hawaii Pacific University, Honolulu, Hawaii, USA

© Springer Nature Switzerland AG 2020
K. V. Aumer (ed.), *The Psychology of Extremism*,
https://doi.org/10.1007/978-3-030-59698-9_4

83

not to have the same disdain, moral repugnance, or severity of sanction for "crimes of passion" or for "white-collar crimes" although both may and can be committed with hate. Even in common discourse, hate is consistently denounced. For example, websites like hateiswrong.org declare that, "Hate in any form is wrong" (Hate is wrong, 2020). Political leaders such as Nelson Mandela and Barack Obama tweet laments about hate's abhorrent unnatural source with declarations such as, "People must learn to hate…" (Obama, 2017). Regardless of whether hate is an emotion, an attitude, or a motivation, scholars and laypersons seem to agree that it is a bad thing. A rare exception to this can be seen in Proverbs 8:13 (New International Version), where hate is advocated to be a wise response when targeted at certain adverse qualities or behaviors.

In contrast, love is seen much more positively. Although the study of love has not been without controversy (e.g., Hatfield, 2006), love is generally viewed positively by both laypersons and scholars. There are numerous songs, poems, dramas, and stories written and dedicated to love and all its panacea-like qualities. "Make love, not war" a common 1960s civil rights phrase ("Make love, not war,", n.d.), and "All You Need Is Love," by the Beatles (Lennon-McCartney, 1967) are significant tributes to the belief in the power and goodness of love. The importance and belief in the power of love is not only recognized in popular culture, but is heralded and supported by scholars who argue that it plays a fundamental role in psychological well-being (Erikson, 1963; Maslow, 1954; Rogers, 1961). The idea that hate is bad and love is good seems to have widespread support.

Yet, by applying a moral judgment to an emotion, researchers may lose objectivity in their efforts to study its nature, characteristics, and consequences. By categorizing hate as bad or negative researchers may fall victim to confirmation bias by tending to focus only on information that supports their view of hate as "bad." Similarly, by categorizing love as good or positive, researchers may only search for evidence of its halo-like qualities, ignoring its negative consequences. To be clear, it is important to recognize the dangers of hate. People should not be hated for the color of their skin, for their gender, or for their religion. Similarly, it is important that people entrust their love to those who support and care for them: their families, friends, and significant others. Nevertheless, there are situations in which people's love, like their hate, is not beneficial. For example, maintaining one's love for, and relationships with, abusive spouses, duplicitous friends, or people who are harmful should not be condoned. There are numerous cases of domestic violence, murder of significant others or family members, and acts of betrayal between people who love and care for each other (National Coalition Against Domestic Violence, 2020) that rip apart families and even start wars (Homer trans., 1996). How many of these terrible situations and atrocities could have been prevented if people had ceased loving people they should not have? If there are people in one's life that one should and should *not* love and there are people in one's life one should *not* hate, is it possible then, as Proverbs 8:13 suggests, that there are people and things in one's life that one *should* hate? Might hate have a purpose? Is it possible that hate is not just some flippant four-letter word that should be avoided, but that it helps people navigate their social world not only to help with survival but also in creating prosperous and productive social environments? This chapter is dedicated to better understanding hate and love and their respective roles in people's lives in the hope of finding ways to better control them. Although we do not disagree that hate has negative consequences and love positive consequences, we undertake this analysis by removing the value-laden judgments that seem to saturate the study of hate and love. By withdrawing from the cultural and social tendency to conceptualize hate as a bad and unnatural influence, and love as a good and organic force, we hope to learn more about controlling and being mindful of these emotions. In this chapter we:

1. Examine how hate is defined and characterized by both laypersons and scholars.
2. Present studies that show how hate and love can bring people together and enhance intimacy.
3. Discuss how both love and hate can be used to help foster extremism.

We conclude with a discussion of the ways in which a more explicit consideration of hate can help people learn and control hate in the future.

1   Conceptualization of Hate

Hate has been primarily studied as an intergroup emotion while love has been studied as an interpersonal emotion. Much of the current research on hate focuses on prejudice and discrimination with the underlying assumption being that hate is primarily felt toward groups of people while love is felt toward individuals. Interestingly, hate is often seen by emotions researchers as the polar opposite of love and that the two cannot co-occur: if one loves someone, one cannot hate them and if one hates someone, one cannot love them. Although some research has addressed the experience of ambivalence: loving and hating someone at the same time, much of this literature is located in the psychoanalytic and psychodynamic literature and has little empirical evidence and is difficult to measure given current attitudinal research standards (Gardner, 1987). Love has been studied continuously in social psychology since the late 1960s (Berscheid & Hatfield, 1969; Sternberg, 1986). The study of hate, however, has been much more recent. In order to better understand how people conceptualize hate, whether hate is really only an intergroup emotion, and whether hate can be experienced with love, we describe a series of studies here.

To better understand the layperson's perspective of hate, Aumer-Ryan and Hatfield (2007) conducted a study that asked people three questions: (1) What does it mean to hate someone? (2) Who do you hate right now? And (3) Why do you hate this person? Over 700 people responded to this questionnaire. Their answers to the first question: "what does it mean to hate someone?" revealed four main themes: (1) extreme dislike, (2) wanting the person to die or be eliminated from their lives, (3) extreme anger, and (4) extreme disgust. These responses revealed that people conceptualize hate as a complex emotion that involves not just one kind of motivation or attitude but a combination of feelings, attitudes, and motivations. Since this study, more research has found further support for the complexity and uniqueness of hate. Rempel and Burris (2005) have found empirical support in several studies that hate can be conceived of differently from most emotions by its primary goal to eliminate or hurt the target of hate. Sternberg has shown the theoretical importance of anger and disgust as components of hate, and has provided a questionnaire based on his theory, though this work was primarily aimed at hate toward groups of people (Sternberg, 2003). Additionally, Roseman and colleagues have done extensive research to also distinguish hate from other emotions like jealousy, anger, and contempt, and have shown how these emotions can overlap. Additionally, they found key areas in the emotions' expression, motivation, and phenomenology that distinguished them from hate (Fischer & Roseman, 2007; Roseman & Steele, 2018). Importantly, what this research has shown is that hate is an emotion with various characteristics: dislike, disgust, anger, and the desire to destroy and hurt someone and that this combination of feelings and motivations is essential to the understanding of hate. For the purpose of our research, we define hate as an emotion in which one sees the target as a threat, consistently thinks negatively of the target, feels repulsed by the target, and wants the target to be gone or have bad things happen to them.

Based on this preliminary understanding of participants' experience of hate, we examined their answers to the question, "Who do you hate now?" We wondered whether their hate would be primarily aimed at groups of people: racial groups, religious groups, or even sports teams. However, what we found did not support the idea that hate is primarily felt toward groups of people. Figure 1 shows that most participants named friends, friends of friends, exes, coworkers, and family members

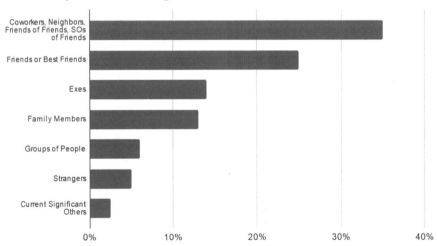

Fig. 1 From Aumer-Ryan and Hatfield (2007), where participants ($n = 433$) identified their targets of hate. Participants were most likely to identify those who they have spent a considerable time with, been close with intimately or emotionally, or knew well

as people they currently hate (Aumer-Ryan & Hatfield, 2007). We have since replicated this finding and have consistently found that these relationships are named (Aumer, 2019; Aumer et al., 2016; Aumer & Bahn, 2016; Aumer & Krebs-Bahn, 2019). What is interesting about these findings is that much research on hate focuses on an intergroup emotional response aimed at large groups of people or possibly aimed at an individual *because* of the social group that this person belongs to or identifies with. However, what we found is that most of the people named as targets of hate were far more intimate to participants than unspecified members of a social group. Friends, friends of friends, exes, coworkers, and family members are people we tend to spend time with, care about, and even love or have loved. These people tend to know us well, or have spent enough time with us to develop an intimate relationship with us. In many ways then, it is not surprising that the people who know us best, may know the best ways to hurt us.

To better understand why participants hated these people we coded the responses to the questions: "Why do you hate this person?" We found three main themes in the participant's answers: (1) betrayal/failed expectations, (2) the person had hurt or harmed them, and (3) something inherently wrong with the person's personality or character. These findings suggest that the hate people feel toward their targets is not arbitrary, but often follows substantial violations of expectations of acceptable behavior. For example, one participant said the following about her ex-boyfriend: "I hated him because he had cheated on me when I was so totally in love with him. I felt like he took my innocence from me" (Aumer-Ryan & Hatfield, 2007). In this example, the young woman's statement expressed her hate for a man that had violated what she considered to be a basic norm: fidelity. Not only did he violate rules of monogamy, he also took something she valued: her innocence. He betrayed her, violated social norms, and the hurt was significant enough that the desire to avoid future harm would be likely. Whether or not he would or even could harm her again, was not certain. However, as this example demonstrates, hate may be triggered when one has experienced a significant amount of hurt and anticipates a significant threat in the future.

We suggest that the hate people feel may be something that helps them identify threats to themselves and the people they love. A person who demonstrates a pattern of hurting or harming someone or has hurt or harmed someone significantly, has violated important relationship expectations, appears to be inherently evil, or has some deviant character flaw should reasonably be seen as a current and future threat to one's well-being. In this case, it seems reasonable to conclude that if hate is a kind of emotion that motivates people to hurt or remove someone in our lives and these people they hate are those who know them well and have means to hurt them badly, then hating these people who threaten them may be the most efficient way of dealing with this social problem. Recent research by Roseman and Steele (2018) supports this reasoning. Their research has shown that unlike other emotions such as anger, disgust, contempt, or dislike, the goal of hate is to incapacitate the threat. Incapacitation can be done by avoidance, harming, or in most extreme circumstances killing the individual or people who are perceived to be the source of that threat. This has led other researchers to argue that hate is a self-protective emotion that is elicited specifically when someone is seen as a threat (Aumer & Bahn, 2016; Fischer, Halperin, Canetti, & Jasini, 2018; Shapiro, 2016). The threat may be real, perceived, or imagined, however, because the goal of hate is specifically aimed at incapacitating the person who is a threat, hate is a powerful and efficient emotion to address the problem. Although hate may not be socially acceptable (at least in many societies), it may be the best emotional response to help people know that someone could hurt them and should no longer be a part of their lives. If a coworker has sabotaged someone routinely and makes their life at work difficult, then hating that coworker may help them remove themself from that person's influence and control. The idea that hate may be useful in preventing future strife is not original. In Proverbs, Solomon asks God for wisdom, and the primary theme of this book is how to live an effective life. A personified "Wisdom" speaks to the reader and informs him (the intended reader seems to be specifically male) that there are many temptations and threats to living a good life and in response to those temptations and threats, God hates them (Proverbs 6:16–19 and 8:13). God hates pride, arrogance, evil behavior, perverse speech, haughty eyes, a lying tongue, and many other things that cause one to deviate from the path of righteousness. From Proverbs, it appears that hate is not just a natural emotion, but a wise emotion to feel when trying to lead a just life.

Hate, however, may serve another function besides identification and elimination of the threats. We provide a personal example from Katherine Aumer's childhood here to illustrate.

> I grew up in a midwestern town where the residents were primarily White. Being half White and Asian myself, this did not bother me. However, it seemed to bother a lot of White people who felt that my existence was annoying, if not intolerable. Routinely, like any young kid, I was picked on for various reasons: the kind of clothes I wore, the kind of laugh I had, my apparent brown-nosing with my teachers, but I was also picked on for reasons that seemed far less controllable. My squinty eyes were the foundation for a variety of jokes and rhymes that somehow ended in "dirty knees," and these kids found it very easy to tell me often that I needed to: "Go back to where you came from." This confused me as a kid, because they often said this to me at school or near my home—in other words, where I was from. When experiencing these instances of racism, I noticed that the people who picked on me and hated me for being part Asian were all very close to one another. They seemed to get along and their mockery of me seemed to fuel, inspire, and solidify their bonds. Similarly, the people who were my friends, those who did support and defend me, were people who I really liked and who liked me, and having a common enemy helped bring us together.

Of course, many people have similar stories in their lives and such instances can make one wonder if the hate people feel is not just something that can help them identify and eliminate threats in their lives, but hate (both shared and as the target of it) can also help people form coalitions and bond with people who share their hate?

2   Interpersonal Bonding Through Hate and Love

Interpersonal bonds can be initiated and maintained in a variety of ways. Sharing similar qualities with a friend or family member or romantic partner is often cited as a common way in which relationships develop and thrive. Similarity of features like physical attractiveness (Berscheid, Dion, Walster, & Walster, 1971), level of intelligence (Watson et al., 2004), economic status (Byrne, Clore, & Worchel, 1966), and political orientation (Buss & Barnes, 1986) have all been found to be important shared qualities when initiating and maintaining positive interpersonal relationships. Similarly, shared attitudes have also been found to be an important part of interpersonal relationships (Byrne, 1971; Miller & Geller, 1972; Jamieson, Lydon, & Zanna, 1987; Lydon, Jamieson, & Zanna, 1988). There are many reasons why similarities are so important in the initiation and maintenance of relationships. Shared physical attractiveness can itself be rewarding and help to maintain the social benefits and accustomed lifestyle that people with similar attractiveness experience (Sigall & Landy, 1973). Similarly, having shared levels of intelligence with a friend, family member, or romantic partner enhances communication and understanding (Watson et al., 2004). In essence, having shared traits with friends, family members, and romantic partners simplifies relationships. It could be very disappointing if every time someone went out with a friend or family member we could not agree upon the kind of food, entertainment, or mode of transportation we preferred.

Attitudes are an especially important part of relationships, because attitudes often reflect people's identity, status, and feelings about themselves. Heider (1946, 1958) showed that participants could often predict the degree to which two people were likely to develop a friendship based on the "balance" of their attitudes. For example, if two people shared either a positive or a negative attitude toward an object, their attitudes would be considered to be "balanced" and therefore much more likely to form a friendship. If you and your friend both like chocolate or both dislike a political candidate, then your attitudes would be considered balanced and you would both be much more likely to form a friendship. However, if such a relationship were to be "unbalanced" (e.g., you like chocolate and your friend dislikes chocolate or you dislike a political candidate and your friend likes the political candidate) then you would be less likely to form or maintain that friendship. The "balance" in people's attitudes that Heider references is important to the development and maintenance of friendships and is rooted in cognitive consistency. Cognitive consistency is the motive and desire to maintain one's values and beliefs over time, and when people either do something or believe in something that is not consistent with their values or behaviors, dissonance is created. Festinger (1957) argued that when this anxiety or dissonance occurs, people try to lessen their anxiety by either changing their beliefs to align with their behavior or their behavior to align with their beliefs. According to Hedier, when it comes to relationships, having balanced attitudes with potential friends and partners maintains cognitive consistency and avoids the anxiety and angst people feel with cognitive dissonance.

Several studies have confirmed the importance of similar and balanced attitudes for the formation, maintenance, and satisfaction in relationships (Berscheid & Hatfield, 1969; Byrne, 1971; Byrne, London, & Reeves, 1968).

It may seem intuitive that having shared positive attitudes would be conducive to initiating and maintaining a relationship. After all, positivity in general seems to be more appreciated and valued than negativity (Folkes & Sears, 1977). Expressing positive evaluations or attitudes about a given subject or person may promote perceptions of warmth and sociability which are important in initial impression formation (Asch, 1946; Kelley, 1950). Additionally, when people express and share those positive attitudes balance is created and similarity is established. However, Bosson et al. (2006) proposed that a balance system consisting of negative attitudes would be more effective at creating closeness and familiarity than a balance system consisting of positive attitudes. In one study, participants listened to a taped interaction between two fictitious characters: Brad and a potential date. While listening to the taped conversation, participants generated novel positive and negative attitudes about Brad and rated how strongly they held each attitude. Later, participants learned they would be interacting with a stranger who had also listened to the same conversation and either shared some of their positive or negative attitudes of Brad. Participants got to rate their liking and closeness toward this stranger given their shared positive or negative attitudes. Interestingly, liking and closeness toward the stranger was impacted by both the valence of the attitude (i.e., positive vs. negative) and the strength of the attitude. Specifically, attitude strength moderated the relationship between valence of the attitude and closeness. When participants shared a strong positive or negative attitude with the stranger, participants reported high levels of closeness. However, when the attitude was weak, participants felt closer toward the stranger if that shared weak attitude was negative, rather than positive (see Fig. 2). These findings have two important implications: (1) the increase in

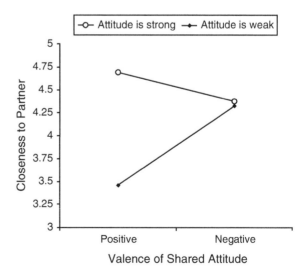

Fig. 2 From Bosson et al. (2006). Participants reported closeness to partners is impacted by both their shared attitude strength and valence. Shared strong positive or negative attitudes result in high closeness scores; however, weak attitude scores result in high closeness scores, only when the attitude is negative

reported closeness to strangers when they shared either strong positive or strong negative attitudes supports Heider's balance theory and suggests that positivity may not be the only important factor in establishing and maintaining relationships, and (2) sharing negative attitudes with someone, whether those negative attitudes are weakly or strongly held, seems to create a closeness and familiarity with that person that positive attitudes can only do when they are strongly held. To put another way, Mary is likely to feel close to a stranger if they both strongly like the new presidential candidate or both strongly dislike the current president. Similarly, Mary is likely to feel close to a stranger if they both weakly dislike Hitler, but not if they both weakly like Tom Cruise. The findings of Bosson and her colleagues suggest that negative attitudes themselves may be special in the formation of friendships. Could this same relationship be extended if not found with hate? May people, like kids on a playground picking on a half White and Asian girl, find themselves closer to those who also share their hate for her or the people they hate?

A series of studies was conducted to better understand how hate may play a role in our intimate relationships (Aumer, 2019). In the first study, participants obtained through Amazon's Mechanical Turk were asked to name someone they hated and then someone they loved. Participants in this study named a variety of targets of hate that supported findings from past studies (Aumer-Ryan & Hatfield, 2007): friends of friends, exes, coworkers, and family members. Additionally, however, they also routinely reported Donald Trump and Satan, as well as a variety of people they loved as well as hated, such as significant others and family members. Participants were then asked to name four separate friends who were not family members: one who shared the hate the participant had for the target of hate, one who did *not* share the hate the participant had for the target of hate, one who shared the love the participant had for the target of love, and one who did *not* share the love the participant had for the target of love. We then asked participants to rate how intimate they felt with each of these friends. As can be seen in Fig. 3, participants tended to feel much

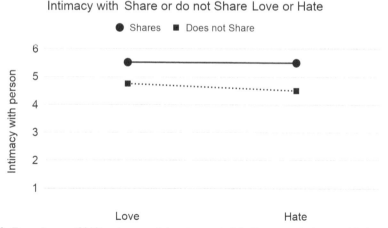

Fig. 3 From Aumer (2019), where participants reported feeling more intimate with those that shared their love and hate for a targeted individual than with those that did not share their love or hate

closer to people who either shared their hate or love for a person than those who did not share their hate or love. We did a series of studies in this paper (Aumer, 2019) that found similar results: people felt more intimate with those that shared their love or hate than did not. In one of these studies we asked half of the participants to identify *groups* of people they love and the other half to name groups of people they hate. Those who were asked to name a group they hated were asked to "name a group that really bothers you and that you wish were eliminated from your life." Participants named a variety of groups including "rapists," "child-molestors," and "drug addicts." The other half of the participants were asked to name a group of people that they love, who "really makes you happy and you wish were more a part of your life." Participants named a variety of groups including "philanthropists," "nerds," or "grandmas." We then asked half of the participants, like in our previous studies, to name a friend that shares their hate for that group and another friend who does not share their hate for that group and for the other half of the participants to name a friend who shares their love for that group and a friend who does not share their love for that group. We then asked participants to rate how intimate they felt with each of these friends. In line with the other studies reported by Aumer (2019), we found that participants felt more intimate and close with those that shared their hate and love than those who did not.

Bossons' (2006) and Aumer's (2019) studies demonstrate that the effect of similarity on the intimacy of our relationships extends beyond just superficial characteristics like attractiveness and attitudes, but into people's values and emotions. Hate and love are often emotions people have toward others who have a significant influence and purpose in their lives. People do not just love or hate anyone, but as the previous section demonstrates their love and especially their hate is often aimed at those that know them well and have the means to best help or hurt them. When someone has a vested hatred toward someone else, that person has been identified as someone who can potentially cause harm, and that hate may help the person or their influence be eliminated from one's life. As these studies show, hate serves not only as a detection system for threat but also as a means to find and feel closer to those that also see one's targets of hate as threats. Those who share in a person's feelings that someone is a common enemy becomes that person's friend and may be able to help them eliminate that threat as well.

3   The Role of Love and Hate in Extremism

Both hate and love can be seen as "extreme" emotions. Extreme can be defined as "exceeding the ordinary, usual, or expected" (Merriam-Webster, n.d., Definition 1c). From that definition, it seems appropriate to categorize hate as an extreme emotion, because hate is not an ordinary or expected feeling to have for people when we meet them. Most of our research on hate (e.g., Aumer-Ryan & Hatfield, 2007), as well as the research by others (e.g., Rempel & Burris, 2005) has shown that between 20 and 30% of people either do not experience or deny experiencing hate. That being said, statistical normality does not dictate normalcy and although hate may itself be extreme, it does not mean that anyone who experiences hate would be considered an extremist. The essence of extremism in the field of psychology does not lie in the unusualness or strangeness in one's feelings or desires, but in the extent to which one is willing to sacrifice, fight, and cross social and physical boundaries to achieve an identity and significance within a group.

Kruglanski, Jasko, Chernikova, Dugas, and Webber (2017) have defined extremism in relation to an imbalance of motivational goals and "a willful deviation from the norms of conduct in a given context or situation" (p. 218). Kruglanski and his colleagues argue that most people tend to exhibit moderate behaviors which allows them to achieve their basic psychological and physical needs (e.g., Maslow, 1943). For example, I may have a great need for esteem and to be admired and one of those ways to achieve that need may be to crush my opponents in war or dissolve a corrupt working environment by destroying my boss's career. However, my need for bodily safety and a paying job may attenuate that goal and moderate my behavior so I can survive. An imbalance of motivational goals is likely to occur when the desire to be significant outweighs other, more substantial basic goals. Significance can have all sorts of meanings to an individual, but according to Kruglanski, Chen, Dechesne, Fishman, Orehek (2009), Kruglanski et al. (2013, 2014), it would be "to matter, to be someone, to merit respect" (Kruglanski et al., 2017, pp. 221–222). The shift from focusing on one's basic or common needs to suppressing them so that one can obtain significance is an important element of extremism. This definition is reflected and bolstered in Seyle and Besaw's chapter in this book, who define extremism as a psychological alignment with a group that is seen as having moral weight, being absolutely correct, and under threat where one is committed to the group's goals (Seyle, 2007). In both definitions (Kruglanski et al., 2017; Seyle, 2007), the needs of the individual become aligned with the group's goals and by helping achieve the goals of the group, one can then merit respect and be significant. The need to belong and the need to feel significant may be the driving force behind joining extremist groups, but as Seyle and Besaw also discuss in their chapter, so is having certain emotions. In contrast to Seyle and Besaw's focus on anger, the rest of this chapter discusses the critical role of hate and love in extremism.

As stated in Seyle's (2007) definition of extremism, members who join extremist groups see their group as actively under threat. Because hate has a self-protective function, people who are part of an extremist group are likely to see themselves and their group as under threat, and should therefore be inclined to feel hate toward those that have threatened them or their group. The threat may be presented explicitly by members of another group, or it could be indirect, even merely suspected, based on the perception of some usurpation of power, control, or dominance from some other group. The threat toward one's group may not even be witnessed firsthand or directed at the individual. The threat could be indirect, something seen online or through other media sources. What is important is that a group member perceives a threat that leads them to feel the need to protect themselves and their group that they now feel is under threat. Once that feeling of threat is perceived, the group member is likely to start to develop concomitant feelings of hatred toward the threat.

Richeson and Craig (Craig & Richeson, 2014; Richeson & Craig, 2011) provided evidence that the perception of threat can impact attitudes and emotions. In their studies, they examine how people react to a majority–minority shift in the United States (U.S.). The majority–minority shift in the U.S. is a demographic change from a population in which the majority of people identify as White to one in which the majority identifies as People of Color (POC), as forecast by the U.S. Census Bureau (2012). Consideration of a majority–minority shift has different threat implications depending on one's racial identification. The awareness that White Americans will no longer be represented as a numerical majority in the U.S. has different implications for different racial groups. On the one hand, this shift could be perceived by everyone as a positive outgrowth of the growing diversity of the nation. For minorities, this could have complicated implications depending on one's racial group membership and status. However, for many White Americans whose status has been typically high and whose numerical majority has been maintained for centuries, this shift could be perceived as a threat. Status change can lead to a host of anxieties and fears, especially if the status change is one from a relatively high status to one that is of an unknown or possibly lower status. Additionally, when many White Americans become aware of the majority–minority shift, they may imagine their status becoming occupied or crowded out by POC. Considering those White Americans who have a strong desire to be significant and who strive to belong and have a strong identity, as described by Kruglanski et al. (2017), this knowledge of a majority–minority shift may be perceived as exceptionally threatening and may implicitly encourage them to find a group in which they can find comfort and safety.

Extremist groups may be able to provide this comfort and safety to those who find themselves lost, without identity, and without significance. Extremist groups provide followers with information that can be biased or false. This, however, can help a person feel special, connected, and part of an exclusive and possibly secretive group. Extremist groups can be formed around a person and/or ideology, but an important element of recruiting for an extremist group is that it helps fill that need for identification and achievement. We note that there can be many different pathways to joining extremist groups and what we propose does not encompass everyone's situation, but this theory is drawn from a variety of research and sources that have found similar themes. We propose that love and hate are used by many extremist groups in three steps:

1. Establishing love for values and for certain people.
2. The recognition that these values and people are under threat.
3. The encouragement to use hate to help eliminate these threats.

By using and exploiting love and hate in these three steps, extremist groups help members fulfill their need to find recognition, identification, and importance.

3.1 Establishing Love

The love for certain values, people, and history is the foundation for many extremist groups. The "Birth of a Nation" (Griffith, 1915) helped the second Klan (which spanned from 1915–1944) form a stronghold in the midwestern and western states by espousing values that concerned the protection of White womanhood, family values, and the "purity" of Americanism. Without a love for these values and people, it would be difficult for a member to identify with the Klan. By loving these values, a person finds a beginning to their identity and a possible membership. The Ku Klux Klan is just one extremist group, but many extremist groups use similar values to help current and future members find something to love and devote themselves to: Christian values (Aryan Nations), brotherhood (Aryan Brotherhood), protection of children (American College of Pediatricians), traditional moral values (American Family Association and Family Research Council), and Black and heterosexual justice (Nation of Islam) (Southern Poverty Law Center, 2020a, 2020b, 2020c, 2020d). All these values sound positive and many people would probably endorse at least some of them and even stand up for them. Some may argue that these values are just obfuscating these groups' real agendas. Nevertheless, these groups have used their values to brand their identity, and whether or not that branding actually reflects the true goals of the group, it does not mean that the love these members have for these values is not real.

In addition to using one's love for certain espoused values or goals to attract members to an extremist group, many recruiters may also use a person's love for their family members and friends to help attract members. Many recruits for extremist or terrorist groups are attracted shortly after they have lost a loved one or when a loved one has been or is perceived to have been harmed or hurt. McCauley and Moskalenko (2008) describe how people can become radicalized after having lost a loved one through the exploitation of their pain. An extremist organization may take advantage of the situation to help people who have suffered a loss find retribution and justice. Additionally, recruits for extremist groups may come out of loyalty for someone who they loved. If a loved one joins an extremist group and one wants to be part of that person's life, it may seem practical and even essential to uphold that social bond by joining the extremist group to show support for the loved one (Borum, 2011; McCauley & Moskalenko, 2008). Love, for the group's values or for the members involved, helps extremist groups find loyal and active members.

3.2 The Recognition of a Threat

Historically, extremist groups have had a variety of reasons for their formation. The Aryan Brotherhood formed along with other race-based prison gangs in the San Quentin State Prison when the prison system became desegregated (Southern

Poverty Law Center, 2020a, 2020b, 2020c, 2020d). The Aryan Brotherhood saw themselves and their "White brothers" as victims of their White identification in a prison system. The American College of Pediatricians started when the American Academy of Pediatricians allowed for and endorsed same-sex adoption, threatening conservative family values (Southern Poverty Law Center, 2020a, 2020b, 2020c, 2020d). A small faction of the conservative pediatricians split from the American Academy of Pediatricians to start their own group that they believed upheld their conservative values. These examples seem to justify at least the *feelings* of threat these members may have had. Whether or not White men and conservative family values were actually under threat by any outside observer is difficult to discern. Nevertheless, it is understandable how one could see these policy changes as threatening to the beliefs and values these people cherished and loved. The threat they perceive need not be real or even clear, but the idea of a threat needs to become marketed and publicized.

At the time of writing this chapter, we are currently at home undergoing "stay-at-home" measures by the governor of Hawaii and the mayor of Honolulu to help avoid the spread of COVID-19. The virus appears to be a very legitimate concern, and most people in Hawaii have complied as rates in Hawaii are one of the lowest in any state (Hawaii Free Press, 2020). However, there have been social media posts from a certain group of people called: "Reopen Hawaii" that are trying to spotlight the idea of a more sinister threat: a threat to personal and state's rights. On these social media posts, people are told that these "stay-at-home" measures are ways in which the government is trying to eliminate freedoms and liberty, that people need to get "our freedom back" (see Fig. 4). These posts propose that if one loves or values freedom then one will want to reopen Hawaii during this pandemic. This argument seems to have failed for many, as Hawaii's compliance with the stay-at-home order has been one of the best in the country (Caring.com, 2020). What remains evident is that the idea of the threat is real, and for those willing to entertain the idea, they could find themselves engaged in protests and finding themselves driven by a purpose to help save cherished freedom and liberty. "Reopen Hawaii's" idea that the "real" threat is not the virus, but the government, can be a very charming proposition to groups that prioritize personal liberty and values. We are not saying "Reopen Hawaii" is an actual extremist group or even a group based in Hawaii. (Many writers have questioned the authenticity of these groups, including Ambinder, 2020.) However, like many extremist groups, this group is trying to spread the idea of a threat, and this idea can be attractive to those who want to find evidence to support the threats they may already imagine or fear to be there. Once one is willing to believe in the idea of the threat, then the group can help direct behavior on how to handle the threat and save what is loved.

Fig. 4 From the "Re-Open Hawaii" Facebook post on April 27th, 2020

3.3 Encouraging the Use of Hate

The final step in helping to recruit and maintain members in an extremist group is to help them see that the way to resolve the threat against the things they love is through hate. Hate may not always be explicitly mentioned or identified, because it can be politically or socially inappropriate. However, hate, as defined earlier in this chapter, is an emotion in which one consistently thinks of a person negatively, feels repulsed by them, and wants them to be gone or have bad things happen to them. This definition can be extended to groups. The Southern Poverty Law Center defines hate groups and extremist groups as having "beliefs or practices that attack or malign an entire class of people, typically for their immutable characteristics"

(Southern Poverty Law Center, 2020a, 2020b, 2020c, 2020d). Whoever the target may be, extremist groups help their members by identifying them as the source of the threat and enlisting the members with the promise of a mission that will help them feel important and significant. The mission may be something as simple as creating online movements, staging and organizing protests, or helping with the group's next meeting. The mission may also be more violent or disturbing like intimidating, hurting, or murdering out-group members who are thought to be a threat. Whatever the mission, it is through the use of hate that helps the person feel their membership and identification with the group. Hating politicians or minority groups can be conceived as a good thing, because these people are threatening the good: the values, the people that the group member loves. For group members, thinking bad things about these people, feeling repulsed by them, and wanting bad things to happen to them becomes an honorable duty.

Moreover, because shared hate can help people feel closer (Aumer, 2019), the bond one develops with others in an extremist group can help members find not just duty or a mission, but a family. Because hate is viewed negatively and is somewhat taboo, it may feel invigorating for a person to feel like they are breaking social norms with another person by declaring their hatred explicitly without being shunned by those around them. Finding a group whose members share attitudes as well as hatred for a target can help the members feel less alone and more connected. It may be tangential to a member that they have joined a group that is viewed as an extremist group, or a hate group, or even a terrorist organization, because now the person can feel more comfortable or vulnerable with those who understand them and their situation. Hate becomes a very realistic and provocative answer to someone who desires to have purpose, importance, and significance in this world, because it does not just supply them with a resolution to a threat, but also protection and social connection.

4 Conclusion

The conceptualization of hate, regardless of whether it is thought of as an emotion, attitude, or motivation, is typically negative (Oatley et al., 2006; Royzman et al., 2005). Love on the other hand, has been viewed as positive (Erikson, 1963; Maslow, 1954; Rogers, 1961). Although we agree with scholars and laypersons that love is a positive and hate a destructive emotion, that does not mean that hate should be avoided as a topic of study or be conceived of as something without purpose or function. Like love, hate should be studied and examined to better understand how it functions in people's lives and to identify ways to help control its exploitation and impact. This chapter has three main goals:

1. Examine how hate is defined and characterized by both laypersons and scholars.
2. Present studies that show how hate and love can bring people together and enhance intimacy.

3. Discuss how both love and hate can be used to help foster extremism.

As previously defined, hate is an emotion in which one consistently thinks negatively of a person, feels repulsed by the individual, and wants the person to be gone or have bad things happen to them. Hate is elicited by a perceived threat in one's life and helps them focus on eliminating that threat in their lives. The threat does not have to be explicit or direct, but importantly the threat is perceived by the person to be real. Additionally, hate can also help form coalitions and help unite people to help eliminate that threat. With the use of both love and hate extremist groups can recruit and maintain members in a three step process:

1. Establishing love for values and certain people.
2. The recognition that these values and people are under threat.
3. The encouragement to use hate to help eliminate these threats.

Extremist groups help people seeking identity and significance who want to find purpose and meaning in their lives (Kruglanski et al., 2009, 2013, 2014; Seyle, 2007). Extremism is not just an extreme experience of emotion or behavior, but it involves a complexity of identification, feelings of importance, and the use of emotion. By studying hate, we can learn more about its purpose, function, and how it can be used to manipulate people. We do not encourage the use of hate. However, denying that it occurs, avoiding the use of the word, or pretending to ignore it will not end the hate that people experience. By acknowledging that hate is a normal part of the human experience and by devoting time and energy into its examination, we can learn more how hate shapes life. In this chapter, we have described how hate is often instigated when a person feels a threat toward something they love or cherish. People obviously cannot eliminate all possible threats, but maybe there are ways to help alleviate threats by changing perception, creating distance, or providing non-threatening experiences with targets of hate. Additionally, we demonstrated that shared hate can bring people together as well as helping to form social bonds. Can we find ways to examine those bonds? For example, does it create and bolster bias amongst group members, and can those bonds be used to help eliminate hate when one member has a change of heart? Finally, we discussed how both love and hate can be used to pull people into extremist organizations. This information can be used to help empower people and prevent them from succumbing too easily to this attraction. By being aware of how powerful both love and hate can be and how susceptible people can be to the biases they create, people may be able to redirect life choices.

As Proverbs 8:13 (New International Version) suggests, hate may be used to help us overcome what we see as evil, but it can also be used by any group or organization as a way to create identification and camaraderie. Hate and love may not necessarily be polar opposites, but they seem to work together in directing how people behave and think about the people and things they value. Going forward, acknowledging hate's presence and influence in our lives, studying it without the bias of its reputation, may help us be more mindful of its presence and enable us to better control hate when it does occur.

References

Ambinder, M. (2020, April 24). Reopen protest movement created, boosted by fake grassroots tactics. *The conversation.* Retrieved from https://theconversation.com/reopen-protest-movement-created-boosted-by-fake-grassroots-tactics-137027

Aristotle. (1954). *The rhetoric and the poetics of Aristotle* (W. R. Roberts, Trans.). Modern Library (Original work written ca. 340 B.C.)

Asch, S. E. (1946). Forming impressions of personality. *The Journal of Abnormal and Social Psychology, 41*(3), 258.

Aumer, K. (2019, May). *Shared hate bringing people together.* Paper presented at the Annual Convention of the Association for Psychological Science in Washington, D.C. Symposium Speaker and Chair.

Aumer, K., & Bahn, A. C. K. (2016). Hate in intimate relationships as a self-protective emotion. In *The psychology of love and hate in intimate relationships* (pp. 131–151). New York, NY: Springer.

Aumer, K., Bahn, A. C. K., Janicki, C., Guzman, N., Pierson, N., Strand, S. E., & Totlund, H. (2016). Can't let it go: Hate in interpersonal relationships. *Journal of Relationships Research, 7*(2), 15–23. https://doi.org/10.1017/jrr.2016

Aumer, K., & Krebs-Bahn, A. (2019, July). *Eliminating hate: What we think works vs. what does work.* Paper presented at the International Society for Research on Emotions, Amsterdam, The Netherlands.

Aumer-Ryan, K., & Hatfield, E. C. (2007). The design of everyday hate: A qualitative and quantitative analysis. *Interpersona: An International Journal on Personal Relationships, 1*(2), 143–172.

Berscheid, E., Dion, K., Walster, E., & Walster, G. W. (1971). Physical attractiveness and dating choice: A test of the matching hypothesis. *Journal of Experimental Social Psychology, 7*(2), 173–189.

Berscheid, E., & Hatfield, E. (1969). *Interpersonal attraction.* New York, NY: Addison-Wesley.

Borum, R. (2011). Radicalization into violent extremism I: A review of social science theories. *Journal of Strategic Security, 4*(4), 7–36.

Bosson, J. K., Johnson, A. B., Niederhoffer, K., & Swann Jr, W. B. (2006). Interpersonal chemistry through negativity: Bonding by sharing negative attitudes about others. *Personal Relationships, 13*(2), 135–150.

Buss, D. M., & Barnes, M. (1986). Preferences in human mate selection. *Journal of Personality and Social Psychology, 50*(3), 559–570.

Byrne, D., Clore, G. L., Jr., & Worchel, P. (1966). Effect of economic similarity-dissimilarity on interpersonal attraction. *Journal of Personality and Social Psychology, 4*(2), 220–224.

Byrne, D., London, O., & Reeves, K. (1968). The effects of physical attractiveness, sex, and attitude similarity on interpersonal attraction. *Journal of Personality, 36*(2), 259–271.

Byrne, D. E. (1971). *The attraction paradigm* (Vol. 462). New York, NY: Academic Press.

Caring.com. (2020, May 19). *Safest states for seniors during COVID-19.* Caring.com. Retrieved from https://www.caring.com/coronavirus/best-states-for-seniors-during-covid-19#key-findings

Craig, M. A., & Richeson, J. A. (2014). More diverse yet less tolerant? How the increasingly diverse racial landscape affects white Americans' racial attitudes. *Personality and Social Psychology Bulletin, 40*(6), 750–761.

Descartes, R. (1989). *On the passions of the soul* (S. Voss, Trans.). Hackett. (Original work published 1694).

Ekman, P. (1992). An argument for basic emotions. *Cognition and Emotion, 6*, 169–200.

Erikson, E. H. (1963). *Childhood and society* (2nd ed.). New York, NY: W. W. Norton & Company.

Festinger, L. (1957). *A theory of cognitive dissonance* (Vol. 2). Stanford University Press.

Fischer, A., Halperin, E., Canetti, D., & Jasini, A. (2018). Why we hate. *Emotion Review, 10*(4), 309–320.

Fischer, A. H., & Roseman, I. J. (2007). Beat them or ban them: The characteristics and social functions of anger and contempt. *Journal of Personality and Social Psychology, 93*(1), 103–115.

Fitness, J., & Fletcher, G. J. O. (1993). Love, hate, anger, and jealousy in close relationships: A prototype and cognitive appraisal analysis. *Journal of Personality and Social Psychology, 65*, 942–958.

Folkes, V. S., & Sears, D. O. (1977). Does everybody like a liker? *Journal of Experimental Social Psychology, 13*, 505–519.

Gardner, P. L. (1987). Measuring ambivalence to science. *Journal of Research in Science Teaching, 24*(3), 241–247.

Griffith, D. W. (1915). *Birth of a Nation. [Motion Picture]*. Los Angeles, CA: David. W. Griffith Corp.

Halperin, E., Russell, A., Dweck, C., & Gross, J. J. (2011). Anger, hatred, and the quest for peace: Anger can be constructive in the absence of hatred. *Journal of Conflict Resolution, 55*(2), 274–291.

Hate is wrong. (2020). *Hate is wrong*. Retrieved May 21, 2020, from https://hateiswrong.org/

Hatfield, E. (2006, June 1). *The golden fleece award: Love's labours almost lost*. Association for Psychological Science. Retrieved from https://www.psychologicalscience.org/observer/the-golden-fleece-award-loves-labours-almost-lost

Hawaii Free Press. (2020, May 28). *Hawaii safest state for seniors during COVID-19*. Hawaii Free Press. Retrieved from http://www.hawaiifreepress.com/ArticlesMain/tabid/56/ID/25649/Hawaii-Safest-State-for-Seniors-During-COVID-19.aspx

Heider, F. (1946). Attitudes and cognitive organization. *The Journal of Psychology, 21*(1), 107–112.

Heider, F. (1958). *The psychology of interpersonal relations*. New York: Wiley.

Homer. (1996, Trans.). *The odyssey* (R. Fagles, Trans.). Viking.

Iganski, P., & Lagou, S. (2015). Hate crimes hurt some more than others: Implications for the just sentencing of offenders. *Journal of Interpersonal Violence, 30*(10), 1696–1718.

Jamieson, D. W., Lydon, J. E., & Zanna, M. P. (1987). Attitude and activity preference similarity: Differential bases of interpersonal attraction for low and high self-monitors. *Journal of Personality and Social Psychology, 53*(6), 1052.

Kelley, H. H. (1950). The warm-cold variable in first impressions of persons. *Journal of Personality, 18*, 431–43.

Kruglanski, A. W., Bélanger, J. J., Gelfand, M., Gunaratna, R., Hettiarachchi, M., Reinares, F., … Sharvit, K. (2013). Terrorism—A (self) love story: Redirecting the significance quest can end violence. *American Psychologist, 68*(7), 559–575.

Kruglanski, A. W., Chen, X., Dechesne, M., Fishman, S., & Orehek, E. (2009). Fully committed: Suicide bombers' motivation and the quest for personal significance. *Political Psychology, 30*(3), 331–357.

Kruglanski, A. W., Gelfand, M. J., Bélanger, J. J., Sheveland, A., Hetiarachchi, M., & Gunaratna, R. (2014). The psychology of radicalization and deradicalization: How significance quest impacts violent extremism. *Political Psychology, 35*, 69–93.

Kruglanski, A. W., Jasko, K., Chernikova, M., Dugas, M., & Webber, D. (2017). To the fringe and back: Violent extremism and the psychology of deviance. In *The motivated mind* (pp. 344–366). Abingdon, UK: Routledge.

Lennon-McCartney. (1967). All you need is love. Non-album single [MP3]. Olympic Sound and EMI.

Lydon, J. E., Jamieson, D. W., & Zanna, M. P. (1988). Interpersonal similarity and the social and intellectual dimensions of first impressions. *Social cognition, 6*(4), 269–286.

Make love, not war. (n.d.). *Wikipedia*. Retrieved May 21, 2020, from https://en.wikipedia.org/wiki/Make_love,_not_war

Maslow, A. H. (1943). A theory of human motivation. *Psychological Review, 50*(4), 370–396.

Maslow, A. H. (1954). The instinctoid nature of basic needs. *Journal of Personality, 22*, 326–347.

McCauley, C., & Moskalenko, S. (2008). Mechanisms of political radicalization: Pathways toward terrorism. *Terrorism and Political Violence, 20*(3), 415–433.

Merriam-Webster. (n.d.). *Extreme. Merriam-Webster.com dictionary*. Retrieved August 7, 2019, from https://www.merriam-webster.com/dictionary/extreme

Miller, H., & Geller, D. (1972). Structural balance in dyads. *Journal of Personality and Social Psychology, 21*(2), 135.

National Coalition Against Domestic Violence. (2020). *Domestic violence*. Retrieved from https://assets.speakcdn.com/assets/2497/domestic_violence2.pdf

Oatley, K., Keltner, D., & Jenkins, J. M. (2006). *Understanding emotions*. Hoboken, NJ: Blackwell Publishing.

Obama, B. [@BarackObama]. (2017, August 12). *"People must learn to hate, and if they can learn to hate, they can be taught to love..." [Tweet]*. Twitter. Retrieved from https://twitter.com/BarackObama/status/896523304873238528

Rempel, J. K., & Burris, C. T. (2005). Let me count the ways: An integrative theory of love and hate. *Personal Relationships, 12*(2), 297–313.

Rempel, J. K., Burris, C. T., & Fathi, D. (2019). Hate: Evidence for a motivational conceptualization. *Motivation and Emotion, 43*, 179–190.

Richeson, J. A., & Craig, M. A. (2011). Intra-minority intergroup relations in the twenty-first century. *Daedalus, 140*(2), 166–175.

Rogers, C. R. (1961). *On becoming a person: A psychotherapists view of psychotherapy*. Boston, MA: Houghton Mifflin.

Roseman, I. J., & Steele, A. K. (2018). Concluding commentary: Schadenfreude, gluckschmerz, jealousy, and hate—What (and when, and why) are the emotions? *Emotion Review, 10*(4), 327–340.

Royzman, E. B., McCauley, C., & Rozin, P. (2005). From Plato to Putnam: Four ways to think about hate. In R. J. Sternberg (Ed.), *The psychology of hate* (pp. 3–35). Washington, DC: American Psychological Association.

Seyle, D. C. (2007). *Identity fusion and the psychology of political extremism* (Dissertation). University of Texas, Austin, TX.

Shand, A. F. (1920). *The foundations of character* (2nd ed.). London, UK: Macmillan.

Shapiro, J. L. (2016). We hate what we fear: Interpersonal hate from a clinical perspective. In K. Aumer (Ed.), *The psychology of love and hate in intimate relationships*. New York, NY: Springer.

Sigall, H., & Landy, D. (1973). Radiating beauty: Effects of having a physically attractive partner on person perception. *Journal of Personality and Social Psychology, 28*(2), 218–224.

Southern Poverty Law Center. (2020a, May 18). *American College of Pediatricians*. Retrieved from https://www.splcenter.org/fighting-hate/extremist-files/group/american-college-pediatricians

Southern Poverty Law Center. (2020b, May 18). *Aryan Brotherhood*. Retrieved from https://www.splcenter.org/fighting-hate/extremist-files/group/aryan-brotherhood

Southern Poverty Law Center. (2020c, May 18). *Groups*. (2020). Retrieved from https://www.splcenter.org/fighting-hate/extremist-files/groups

Southern Poverty Law Center. (2020d, May 18). *What is a hate group?* (2020). Retrieved from https://www.splcenter.org/20200318/frequently-asked-questions-about-hate-groups#hate%20group

Sternberg, R. J. (1986). A triangular theory of love. *Psychological Review, 93*(2), 119–135.

Sternberg, R. J. (2003). A duplex theory of hate: Development and application to terrorism, massacres, and genocide. *Review of General Psychology, 7*(3), 299–328.

U.S. Census Bureau. (2012, May 17). *Most children younger than 1 are minorities*. Washington, DC: U.S. Census Bureau. Retrieved from https://www.census.gov/newsroom/releases/archives/population/cb12-90.html

Watson, D., Klohnen, E. C., Casillas, A., Nus Simms, E., Haig, J., & Berry, D. S. (2004). Match makers and deal breakers: Analyses of assortative mating in newlywed couples. *Journal of Personality, 72*(5), 1029–1068.

Political Identities, Emotions, and Relationships

Elaine Hatfield and Richard Rapson

1 Political Identities, Emotions, and Relationships

During Thanksgiving, many of our friends and students tell us they dread going home for a "celebratory" dinner. It isn't that their relatives disagree with their own political beliefs. It is that they insist on vehemently sharing their cockamamie ideas. Some relatives are just earnest do-gooders. "Can't you see?" they ask: carefully spelling out all the tired arguments you have heard a million times. "Trump is in line for the Nobel Peace Prize. The first to win the Nobel Peace Prize and the Prize for Literature—that is if the selection isn't rigged and if he wins the literature prize for *The Art of the Deal*." Some enjoy devilment. One student said her Fox watching uncle is an attack dog. "You are a naïve fool. How could you vote for crooked Hillary?" His kids join in, chanting "Lock her up! Lock her up."

Donald Trump Jr. even wrote a book, *Triggered,* telling Republican stalwarts how to "trigger" the sensitive spots in their liberal friends. In fact, he offered prizes for those followers who could do the best job of driving their liberal relatives crazy: an autographed copy of his tome, *Triggered* and a MAGA cap. "Just take photographs of them blowing their top," he advised and their prizes would be on the way. Trump also offered prizes for those tormenting their liberal relatives on Christmas and New Year's Eve—Trump themed Trump Christmas ornaments. "It's easy," Trump Jr. crowed: "Liberals are such haters" (Bostock, 2019). Conservatives are no slouches in that department, either.

"I just can't do it," students lamented. "Sit through another family gathering. Maybe I could volunteer at a soup kitchen."

Hatfield, E. & Rapson, R. (submitted). Political identities, emotions, and relationships. In K. Aumer *The Psychology of Extremism* (submitted). *Springer.*

E. Hatfield (✉) · R. Rapson
University of Hawaii, Manoa, Honolulu, HI, USA

A poll conducted by *Business Insider* found that politics and religion are the two most explosive topics for dinner conversations (Bostock, 2019).

What invests such disagreements with such strong emotion? How can we bring civility to the dinner table? Can we? Can we change the minds of our adversaries? Is it inevitable that we "catch" the emotions of irate celebrants—particularly their anger?

Let us begin by discussing the nature of political identities and their importance. Then we will look at Emotional Contagion and why it is so difficult to be stuck with anxious and angry people who do not share our beliefs.

1.1 Political Identities

Henri Tajfel (1982), in his Introduction to *Social Identity and Intergroup Relations,* defines social identities as:

> …that part of the individuals' self-concept which derives from their knowledge of their membership of a social group (or groups) together with the value and emotional significance attached to that membership (p. 2).

Huddy (2013) continues:

> A key concept…is political identity…. political identities refer to identification with and meaning attributed to membership in politically relevant groups, including political parties and national, ethnic, linguistic, or gender groups (p. 2).

Staerklé (2015) adds:

> Research has, for example, shown that individuals who strongly identify with their group are more likely to act on behalf of a group and related causes, to view the political environment in antagonistic terms, and to act defensively in the face of group criticism (p. 2).

The centrality of our political beliefs—especially in these intensely polarizing times—explains why such holiday debates are so explosive and why it is so difficult to devise a strategy for dealing with these powerful familial conflicts. Our political beliefs don't just stand alone. It isn't possible to say this single belief is "off-limits." We just won't talk about politics at dinner. Alas, our political beliefs are bound up with our ideas of the desirability of all-powerful rulers versus democracy, the role of government in solving social problems, the value of the economy versus public health, how much we should worry about social inequalities, the role of education in social life, and the like.

These social disagreements become especially explosive when we are confronting anxious or angry people who are eager to stir up trouble … or worry that we will.

1.2 Emotional Contagion

The great fictional detective Sherlock Holmes could detail consciously the processes of deduction that most of us carry on outside of conscious awareness (Doyle, 1917/1967). There are many clues which allow us to deduce what others really feel about us and about our beliefs, even if others try to hide it.

Holmes startled Watson that he could read his mind by looking at his furrowed eyebrows, where his glances darted, the subtle movements of his hands, and the like (pp. 193–195).

Sherlock Holmes provides tricks for figuring *what* others are feeling about our most cherished beliefs; emotional contagion provides a clue as to others' intensity of feelings.

Emotional contagion has been defined as:

The tendency to automatically mimic and synchronize facial expressions, vocalizations, postures, and movements with those of another person's and, consequently, to converge emotionally" (Hatfield, Cacioppo, & Rapson, 1994b, p. 5).

The *Emotional Contagion Scale* (Hatfield, Cacioppo, & Rapson, 1994a) was designed to assess people's susceptibility to "catching" joy and happiness, love, fear and anxiety, anger, and sadness and depression, as well as emotions in general.

2 The Emotional Contagion Scale (EC)

This is a scale that measures a variety of feelings and behaviors in various situations. There are no right or wrong answers, so try very hard to be completely honest in your answers. Results are *completely confidential*. Read each question and indicate the answer which best applies to you. Please answer each question very carefully. Thank you.

Use the following key:

4	*Always*	=	Always true for me
3	*Often*	=	Often true for me
2	*Rarely*	=	Rarely true for me
1	*Never*	=	Never true for me

1. It doesn't bother me to be around angry people	4	3	2	1
2. I find myself nodding off when I talk with someone who is depressed	4	3	2	1
3. I feel tender and gentle when I see a mother and child hugging each other affectionately	4	3	2	1
4. Being around depressed people makes me feel depressed	4	3	2	1
5. I pay attention to what other people are feeling	4	3	2	1
6. I feel alive and vibrant when I am with the one I love	4	3	2	1

7. When someone laughs hard, I laugh too	4	3	2	1
8. When people hug me affectionately, I get upset and want to back away	4	3	2	1
9. I'm very accurate in judging other's people feelings	4	3	2	1
10. When I am around people who are angry, I feel angry myself	4	3	2	1
11. I find myself clenching my fist when overhearing others quarrel	4	3	2	1
12. I wince while observing someone flinching while getting a shot	4	3	2	1
13. I'm very sensitive in picking up other's people feelings	4	3	2	1
14. I keep a straight face when those around me are laughing hard	4	3	2	1
15. Listening to the shrill screams of a terrified child in a dentist's waiting room makes me feel nervous	4	3	2	1
16. Even if someone I'm talking with begins to cry, I don't get teary-eyed	4	3	2	1
17. When someone paces back and forth, I feel nervous and anxious	4	3	2	1
18. When someone smiles warmly at me, I smile back and feel happy inside	4	3	2	1

2.1 Scoring

Items 1, 8, 14, 16 are reversed in scoring. The higher the score, the more susceptible to emotional contagion a person would be said to be.

Contagion can occur in several ways. Recently, social psychologists have assumed that primitive emotional contagion is a far more subtle, automatic, and ubiquitous process than theorists once thought. Neuroscientists, for example, have discovered that the same neurons (mirror neurons) may fire when primates merely *observe* another perform an action as when they themselves perform that same action. They propose that these brain structures may help account for emotional contagion (see Iacoboni, 2005.)

Many scientists argue that the process of emotional contagion consists of three stages: Mimicry to Feedback to Contagion. People tend: (a) to mimic the facial expressions, vocal expressions, postures, and instrumental behaviors of those around them—in the case of this chapter, those of their table companions; (b) as people mimic their companions' fleeting facial, vocal, and postural expressions, they often come to *feel* pale reflections of their companions' actual emotions; (c) by attending to this stream of tiny moment-to-moment reactions, people can and do "feel themselves into" the emotional lives of others. It is this tripartite process that accounts for the ubiquitous process of emotional contagion.

Given this view of emotion, there is really not much mystery to the observations of therapists and others that, though not *consciously* aware that their clients (say) are experiencing joy, sadness, fear, or anger, they "somehow" do sense and react to these feelings. Today, emotion researchers assume conscious awareness of only a small portion of the information we possess about ourselves and others. Not surprising then, when we are surrounded by family members behaving badly, it is very hard to retain our composure.

Given the high emotions bound to confront us at family gatherings, how can we deal with the problem. What can we do to make people more willing to go home for, say, Thanksgiving when they know they will confront a plethora of hostile family members? What can they do to make sure that in the far future, when things are less polarized, that by behaving well today they can return to the family harmony that (allegedly) once existed?

Here are a variety of suggestions psychologists and social commentators have offered for bringing peace to family gatherings. Any of them may work for some people. For some. Not for all of us. We will end by describing what has worked for some folks.

2.1.1 Solutions

Goldfarb (2019) offers several suggestions for dealing with difficult relatives.

Start out with a game plan, she advises. Identify those events that have set you off in the past and figure out how to deal with them. Make small talk. Ask people questions about themselves and their personal accomplishments. "I'm actually more interested in your new job. How is it going?" Rempala (2013) observes: Try to gain some insight into why your contentious family member is doing what he or she is doing. Are they trying to gain the upper hand? Gain status? Hurt you? This doesn't mean approving of a monster, or letting yourself get pushed around: simply that understanding helps.

There is considerable research showing that if people have to view a horrific film, they feel less upset if they view it from an anthropological perspective than if they just respond emotionally (Rempala, 2013). Think as if this were the raving of some primitive tribe. Patronizing? Yes. But, whatever works.

Goldfarb (2019) suggests that bringing a supportive friend might be helpful. If things get rough, one can always leave the table to do dishes. Beier (2018), a decided optimist, wonders how someone can expect to change the world if they can't even change their relatives' minds? She offers ten suggestions for dealing with disagreeable relatives. She observes that before one can change anyone's mind, one must think and change the way one speaks to them.

1. The first step is to try to be calm, cool, and collected. Otherwise emotional contagion might set in.
2. Make sure the other person wants to have this conversation.
3. If they do, ask how the other person feels about the issue. Let them explain their position at length. This helps establish if their beliefs are as black and white as they might appear to be.
4. Listen intently. No sighing, rolling eyes, or crossing arms.
5. Then speak. Saying what one believes—focusing on the shared values. (At the very least one can make the observation that this issue is of mutual concern. Will the relative interrupt? Maybe).

6. Next, share a personal story about how these views have impacted a close friend or relative.
7. This done, invite the person to do the same. Focus on the values they report, rather than their conclusion.
8. Offer one or two facts the other person might not know. Invite them to recipro-cate. Check in to see how the person feels about the conversation. (One might say "I still think what I thought before, but I'm glad we talked"). Keeping in mind that the facts we believe in are, of course, at the core of the problem. The "facts" offered by Fox News bear little relation to those offered by Rachel Maddow of CNN. If there is no agreement about the value of "gut feelings" versus objective evidence, reconciliation and understanding proves almost impossible to achieve.
9. Whatever the outcome, the experience of the conversation has provided a foun-dation or laid the seeds for future conversations.
10. After the conversation, one should do something restorative: walking, meditat-ing, or drawing.

2.1.2 Our Vision

When reporters call us to ask us about contagion, they inevitably end with a single question: "How, then, can people overcome the effects of contagion?" What, they are wondering, is this: How can we turn off our ability to share others' feelings so that we can deal with families in turmoil?

In this malign climate, we are less optimistic than the other authors and scholars we have reviewed here. Be aware that you are not going to change anything. If you are a parent, perhaps you can change your child's behavior, but for adults you are a fool to take responsibility when you have no power. It is the trying…again and again and again …that wears people out.

We would assume that, ideally, people would not try to alter their basic natures too much. Some people are extremely sensitive; others have to be hit over the head with a 2 × 4 before they get the point. Each nature has its advantages and disadvantages.

Sensitive people, susceptible to emotional contagion, are wonderful at under-standing and dealing with others; but after a bit, they grow quite tired. They can deal with trouble for perhaps a few hours but, soon, enough is enough: they must go back to their hotel room, be absolutely quiet, and recover.

Other, hardier (or less tuned-in) individuals are more or less oblivious to the emotional climates in which they dwell. (One of our mellow clients who, upon hear-ing a woman crying on the telephone, turned to his wife, and with a cheerful tone, said: "It's for you.") Such people might not be aware of what is going on in emotion-ally charged situations, but they can stay in them and deal with them a lot longer if they choose.

When as therapists, we sometimes offered this advice, clients would occasionally demur on the grounds of poverty or guilt. "I could never do that," they say. "My mother would be upset if I didn't stay at home. I'd end up yelling at her and she would cry and I'd feel awful about that." Or "I can't afford to get away from the fighting and stay at a pricy hotel." Guilt and poverty are often mixed. What happens if you turn down these suggestions? Think how you will feel if you get caught up in family dynamics and end up screaming at your anxious mother or lashing out at your uncle during the family get-together. Our clients who have tried our suggestion or advice have reported that their family got used to their wayward ways and admired their composure.

2.1.3 Individual Differences in Contagion

People probably do best if they accept their own temperaments and the concomitant advantages and disadvantages thereof. The very sensitive might be interpersonal experts or "angels of mercy," but only for short periods. When visiting the family, where woe and suffering and shouting and guilt inductions are the norm, they had better plan to stay in a hotel room, rest up, and meet the relatives for dinner. The money would be well spent.

Meanwhile, people who have become "turned off" to others' feelings often get overwhelmed when they begin to become more aware, feeling that they are somehow responsible for "fixing things." They do better if they remind themselves that probably the best they can do is to listen. Others should not expect them to be a miracle worker; those who demand too much attention cannot complain when the "oblivious" tune out for self-protection.

Some people love to fight. They gain energy and pleasure from their tumult. Others do not. Beware those who, through creating conflict, are self-medicating against depression. Their fighting buoys them emotionally, but it may bring you down—unless you, too, need to use conflict to rise from depression.

Several theories also suggest that how people process incoming social information can affect their ability to experience emotional contagion. For example, Byrne (1964) indicated that personality differences may affect how we respond to emotional distress. He distinguishes between "sensitizers" (i.e., individuals who are hypervigilant of their own emotions and those of others) and "repressors" (those who ignore internal and external emotional information). It would stand to reason that, among these two extremes, repressors would be less susceptible to contagion (Hatfield et al., 1994b). A similar dichotomy seems to exist based on the observer's mood state, such that happy observers are susceptible to contagion, while depressed observers are more self-focused and therefore, insulated from the mood of others (Hsee, Hatfield, Carlson, & Chemtob, 1990).

Aspects of the social situation also can affect both one's motivation to "receive" the emotions of others and one's susceptibility to emotional contagion. For example, in a dyadic interaction, the more powerful (e.g., higher status) of the pair is less affected by (and possibly less interested in) the emotions of the weaker other than vice versa (Hsee et al., 1990). Similarly, if the observer is able to generate great substantial animosity toward the target, emotional contagion is inhibited (Zillman & Cantor, 1977).

There seem to be other motivational components to one's ability to experience contagion. Extroverts, for example, are more outwardly focused, specifically toward those with whom they are interacting with or wish to interact with. It is no surprise, then, that extraverts are more susceptible to emotional contagion than introverts (Fowles, Roberts, & Nagel, 1977). Similarly, we are more susceptible to members of our in-group (Schachter & Singer, 1962; Wheeler, 1966), and the more important the relationship with the target is to the receiver, the more susceptible the receiver is (Hatfield, Cacioppo, & Rapson, 1992a; Hatfield, Cacioppo, & Rapson, 1992b).

This last point, in fact, may be key to understanding one of the most consistent findings of the empathy literature: that women are more empathic than men. Most studies that have cared to look at sex differences in empathic ability have found significant differences in this direction (Eisenberg & Lennon, 1983; Hall, 1978). However, this may be because emotional contagion is inhibited in men (Hatfield et al., 1994a; Wild, Erb, & Bartels, 2001).

Although there is no sex difference in expressiveness at birth, female infants quickly become more expressive than male infants (except for distress-related responses, which are more common in males) (Haviland & Malatesta, 1981). Social rules for emotional display are almost universally more restrictive for males than females (the lone exception being display of anger) (O'Leary & Smith, 1991; Brody, 1985; Fischer, van Rodriguez Mosquera, Vianen, & Manstead, 2004).

After all, while females showed no difference in decoding the symbolic and non-verbal messages of intimates as opposed to strangers, men were substantially better at decoding the messages of intimates than were strangers (Noller & Callan, 1960). This could be due to greater relaxation of display rules and cognitive defenses when dealing with those with whom they are familiar.

Based on the behavioral components of emotional contagion (e.g., mimicry of facial expression), if males have less freedom to express emotion, they may be less likely to feel the emotions projected by others (Wild et al., 2001). Through some of the attentional or perceptual mediators mentioned above, males may be able to inhibit the experience of emotional contagion. By extension, then, since emotional contagion is a vital component to empathy, the emotions are less likely to reach the conscious awareness of males, and the process is interrupted.

Thus, there are no one-size-fits-all strategies for dealing with nasty familial conflicts over politics and religion. We idealize family gatherings, but the realities are usually more complex, vexed, and—if one is properly armed—more interesting.

References

Beier, E. (2018, December 23). 10 steps to take when talking politics with someone you disagree with this holiday season. Before we can change anyone's mind, we first must change the way we talk to one another. *The Lily*. Retrieved from https://www.thelily.com/10-steps-to-take-when-talking-politics-with-someone-you-disagree-with-this-holiday-season/

Bostock, B. (2019, November 28). Donald Trump Jr. challenged his supporters to 'trigger' liberal relatives over thanksgiving dinner. *Business Insider*. Retrieved from https://www.businessinsider.com/don-jr-film-triggered-liberals-thanksgiving-win-maga-prizes-2019-11

Brody, L. R. (1985). Gender differences in emotional development: A review of theories and research. *Journal of Personality, 53*(2), 102–149. https://doi.org/10.1111/j.1467-6494.1985.tb00361.x

Byrne, D. (1964). Repression–sensitization as a dimension of personality. In B. A. Maher (Ed.), *Progress in experimental personality research* (pp. 169–220). New York: Academic Press.

Doyle, A. C. (1917/1967). The adventure of the cardboard box. In W. S. Baring-Gould (Ed.), *The annotated Sherlock Holmes* (Vol. 2, pp. 193–208). New York: Clarkson N. Potter.

Eisenberg, N., & Lennon, R. (1983). Sex differences in empathy and related capacities. *Psychological Bulletin, 94*(1), 100. https://doi.org/10.1037/0033-2909.94.1.100

Fischer, A. H., van Rodriguez Mosquera, P. M., Vianen, A. E., & Manstead, A. S. (2004). Gender and culture differences in emotion. *Emotion, 4*(1), 87–94.

Fowles, D. C., Roberts, R., & Nagel, K. (1977). The influence of introversion/extraversion on the skin conductance responses to stress and stimulus intensity. *Journal of Research in Personality, 11*(2), 129–146.

Goldfarb, A. (2019, November 20). How to defuse tension at the dinner table during the holidays. *The New York Times*. Retrieved from https://www.nytimes.com/2019/1120/smarter-living/how-to-defuse-tension-during-theholidays.html?fallback=false&recld=77236743&locked=1&geoContinent=N…

Hall, J. A. (1978). Gender effects in decoding nonverbal cues. *Psychological Bulletin, 85*(4), 845–857.

Hatfield, E., Cacioppo, J. T., & Rapson, R. L. (1992a). Emotional contagion. In M. S. Clark (Ed.), *Review of personality and social psychology. Vol. 14: Emotion and social behavior* (pp. 151–177). Newbury Park, CA: Sage.

Hatfield, E., Cacioppo, J. T., & Rapson, R. L. (1992b). Primitive emotional contagion. *Review of Personality and Social Psychology, 14*, 151–177.

Hatfield, E., Cacioppo, J. T., & Rapson, R. L. (1994a). *Emotional contagion*. New York: Cambridge University Press.

Hatfield, E., Cacioppo, J. T., & Rapson, R. L. (1994b). *Mechanisms of emotional contagion: I. Emotional mimicry/synchrony*. New York: Cambridge University Press.

Haviland, J. M., & Malatesta, C. Z. (1981). The development of sex differences in nonverbal signals: Fallacies, facts, and fantasies. In C. Mayo & N. M. Henley (Eds.), *Gender and nonverbal behavior* (pp. 183–208). New York: Springer–Verlag.

Hsee, C. K., Hatfield, E., Carlson, J. G., & Chemtob, C. (1990). The effect of power on susceptibility to emotional contagion. *Cognition and Emotion, 4*, 327–340.

Huddy, L. (2013). From group identity to political cohesion and commitment. In *The Oxford handbook of political psychology* (2nd ed.). Oxford: Oxford University Press.

Iacoboni, M. (2005). Understanding others: Imitation, language, and empathy. In S. Hurley & N. Chater (Eds.), *Perspectives on imitation: From neuroscience to social science. Vol. 1: Mechanisms of imitation and imitation in animals* (pp. 77–101). Cambridge, MA: MIT Press.

Noller, P., & Callan, V. J. (1960). Adolescent and parent perceptions of family cohesion and adaptability. *Journal of Adolescence, 9*, 97–106.

O'Leary, K. D., & Smith, D. A. (1991). Marital interactions. *Annual Review of Psychology, 42*, 191–212.

Rempala, D. M. (2013). Cognitive strategies for controlling emotional contagion. *Journal of Applied Social Psychology, 43*(7), 1528–1537.

Schachter, S., & Singer, J. (1962). Cognitive, social, and physiological determinants of emotional state. *Psychological Review, 69,* 379–399.

Staerklé, C. (2015). *International encyclopedia of the social & behavioral sciences* (2nd ed.). Amsterdam: Elsevier. Retrieved from https://www.sciencedirect.com/topics/computer-science/political-identity

Tajfel, H. J. (1982). Introduction. In *Social identity and intergroup relations* (pp. 1–11). Cambridge: Cambridge University Press.

Wheeler, L. (1966). Toward a theory of behavioral contagion. *Psychological Review, 73,* 179–192.

Wild, B., Erb, M., & Bartels, M. (2001). Are emotions contagious? Evoked emotions while viewing emotionally expressive faces: Quality, quantity, time course and gender differences. *Psychiatry Research, 102,* 109–124.

Zillman, D., & Cantor, J. R. (1977). Affective responses to the emotions of a protagonist. *Journal of Experimental Social Psychology, 13,* 155–165.

Homogamy and Tribalism: How Finding a Match Can Lead to Social Disruption

Martin Fieder, Alexander Schahbasi, and Susanne Huber

Homogamy—mating along similarities—has a high prevalence in humans including various traits ranging from moderate homogamy for body height (Stulp, Simons, Grasman, & Pollet, 2017; Stulp, Verhulst, Pollet, Nettle, & Buunk, 2011) to strong homogamy for religion (reviewed in Fieder & Huber, 2016), political attitudes, and ethnicity (Blackwell & Lichter, 2004; Fu & Heaton, 2008). Religious homogamy has been the norm in some religions, as marriage rules often allow only marriages within the same denomination or impose rules of conversion, so that spouses end up having the same religion (Fieder & Huber, 2016). Hence, homogamy plays a strong role in group identification and group-cohesion. Even if there is no regulative norm for homogamy, individuals on both the political left and right prefer a partner with a similar political attitude and show a preference for a partner with the same ethnic background. For those on the political right, however, a partner of the same ethnic background is more important than for those on the political left (Anderson, Goel, Huber, Malhotra, & Watts, 2014). Together with religious homogamy, political attitude is among the strongest traits along which assortment occurs (Alford, Hatemi, Hibbing, Martin, & Eaves, 2011).

Marriages within kin networks are evidently a form of homogamy, as similarity is assured through genetic relatedness. For instance, in the case of first-order cousin marriage, spouses share about 12.5% of the genetic variance. In small populations, the share might be higher as members of a kin group may have married more frequently within the group, thus the genetic share may have increased beyond "Hamilton's rule" (Hamilton, 1964; West, El Mouden, & Gardner, 2011). According

M. Fieder (✉) · S. Huber
Departement of Evolutionary Anthropology, University of Vienna, Vienna, Austria
e-mail: martin.fieder@univie.ac.at

A. Schahbasi
Departement of Evolutionary Anthropology, University of Vienna, Vienna, Austria

Erlangen Centre for Islam and Law in Europe, Friedrich-Alexander University, Erlangen-Nürnberg, Germany

© Springer Nature Switzerland AG 2020
K. V. Aumer (ed.), *The Psychology of Extremism*,
https://doi.org/10.1007/978-3-030-59698-9_6

to Hamilton (1964) kinship goes beyond social ties as it is deeply rooted in our genetic share among individuals and over generations. Within a family, individuals share a certain proportion of genetic variance according to their kinship: a mother or a father shares roughly 50% of her/his genetic variance with his/her sons and/or daughters. Siblings share 50% of their genetic variance with each other and 25% of the genetic variance with their nephews and nieces. Grandparents share 25% of their genetic variance with their grandchildren and 12.5% of the genetic variance are shared by great-grandparents and great-grandchildren, etc.... This rule of the share of inheritance explains cooperation and prosocial behaviour among kin in animals and humans and has been described in the theory of inclusive fitness. Moreover, in prehistoric small-scale human groups, usually all individuals were genetically related to some extent, thus overall genetic relatedness would have exceeded Hamilton's rule (West et al., 2011). Hence, marriage within kin-groups is an extreme form of homogamy: someone who marries his/her cousin can expect similar phenotypic traits due to genetic similarities. This may include physical traits, attitudes and behaviour, because according to the first law of behavioural genetics, "all human traits are heritable" to some extent (Turkheimer, 2000). Although the extent of heritability differs according to the trait, the fact that each trait is to some extent heritable ensures that marriage among kin leads to a stronger genotypic and phenotypic homogamy compared to non-kin marriages. Considering the small groups in which the human species evolved, frequent cousin marriages may have been the norm (Fox, 2015), but at the same time there may have been efforts to foster more heterogamous marriages.

One of the advantages of marriages among kin is the positive correlation between kin-marriage and the number of progeny. This has been demonstrated on the basis of data from Iceland: the mean number of offspring decreased with decreasing genetic relatedness from second-order cousins on, hence reproductive output was at a maximum in the case of moderate inbreeding by marrying second-order cousins (Helgason, Pálsson, Guðbjartsson, & Stefánsson, 2008). Furthermore, accumulating and keeping wealth within kinship networks (Helgason et al., 2008) is an obvious advantage of kin marriages. A further, although less obvious, benefit of kin marriages may be the avoidance of outbreeding depression (i.e., reduction in fitness due to genetic distance). Outbreeding depression has mostly been demonstrated in studies on animals. For instance, Ibex populations from Turkey and Sinai were introduced into Czechoslovakia (Templeton, 1986) to help the small and decreasing population. Although the outbred offspring were fertile, they calved too early. Outbreeding depression has also been shown for the Arabian oryx (Marshall & Spalton, 2000) and for avian species (Marr et al., 2002). However, the effects of genetic outbreeding depression (via chromosomal differences) are far less well understood than those of inbreeding depression which occurs frequently in close kin-marriages (Edmands, 2007). Therefore, albeit kin marriages—and thus inbreeding—may confer short-term reproductive benefits for the individual and keep wealth within families, inbreeding also comes with serious drawbacks, affecting long-term fitness, including increased risk of stillbirth and infant death, birth defects, and a lower post-reproductive health (Bittles, 2012).

Genetically, the main effect of inbreeding is the accumulation of homozygous segments, which may have detrimental consequences for the progeny. Thus the smaller a population, the more bottlenecks a population faced in the past, the less admixture a population was exposed to, and the more frequently kin marriage occurred, the higher are the frequency and the length of homozygous segments in the genome (Ceballos, Joshi, Clark, Ramsay, & Wilson, 2018; Clark et al., 2019). A study on 354,224 individuals of 102 cohorts showed a significant association between the total length of homozygous segments and complex traits: increased homozygosity (equivalent to first-order cousins) was correlated with lower body height, lower education, lower cognitive ability, and forced expiratory lung volume (Joshi et al., 2015). Furthermore, it has recently been demonstrated on the basis of genetic data of 1.4 million individuals, that the number and length of homozygous segments are associated with deleterious changes in 32 out of 100 investigated traits (Clark et al., 2019). Particularly interesting are the striking effects of inbreeding on fertility by decreasing the odds of having at least one child (Clark et al., 2019).

Thus, although there was a tendency towards marriage within kin-networks during our evolution, also the avoidance of in-breeding seems to have been of importance. Demonstrated on the basis of Palaeolithic data from western Russia, hunter gatherer mating networks (Sikora et al., 2017) may have existed, that may have helped to overcome inbreeding by female "marriage migration" between groups. Particularly young women are supposed to have left their natal group to live with their husband's family (Towner, 2002; Sterck, 1998; Seielstad, Minch, & Cavalli-Sforza, 1998), leading to genetic exchange and helping to avoid increased inbreeding. Along with genetic exchange, also a cultural exchange may have been a beneficial consequence of such inter-group marriage networks.

Nonetheless, in some regions of the world a high prevalence of inbreeding still exists (Bittles & Black, 2015). However, it is far less common today, whereas homogamy for certain traits occurs much more frequently, e.g. for body height, ethnicity, religious affiliation, political attitude and many other traits. Because of the high prevalence of homogamy for some traits, it has been suggested that a sort of ethnic nepotism towards genetically more similar, but not related individuals may exist (Salter, 2018; Salter & Harpending, 2013). Accordingly, it is suggested that humans may prefer individuals in whom they detect a genetic similarity on one or more traits and that such a behaviour may overall enhance fitness (Rushton, 1989).

As is the case for inbreeding, also homogamy on certain traits can enhance fertility: worldwide census data from 3,658,650 women aged 46–60 years from 32 countries reveal, for instance, that religious homogamy leads to an increase in the average number of children and a decrease in childlessness in most of the analysed countries and religions (Fieder & Huber, 2016). Furthermore, religious homogamy may compensate in reproductive terms for ethnic heterogamy and vice-versa (Huber & Fieder, 2018).

A consequence of the reproductive advantage of homogamous couples may be an increased frequency of the alleles that are associated with the trait for which a couple is homogamous in a given population. Although homogamy per se does not lead to a shift in allele frequencies, it may provide a source selection to act on

(Relethford, 2012). For instance, if religious homogamy is the norm in a population and homogamy brings fitness benefits in terms of less childlessness and a higher average number of children, homogamy definitively offers selective advantages (Fieder & Huber, 2016). On the other hand, in the case of inbreeding, individuals practicing homogamy may increase the number of offspring but concomitantly may increase homozygosity for some traits in their offspring with potentially detrimental consequences. Albeit there is a strong tendency to mate homogamously for several traits, the individually inherited predisposition of homogamy is quite low (Zietsch, Verweij, Heath, & Martin, 2011).

Notwithstanding the genetic consequences, homogamy on certain traits may also have social and cultural consequences, particularly regarding the separation of groups. If individuals within a group only marry on the basis of the similarity of some traits, as a result, a group will be divided genetically as well as socially and culturally. In addition, the emergence of new groups out of a former "unified group" due to homogamous marriage may in turn provide a strong force for a genetic cultural co-evolution: a cultural trait emerges, and due to homogamy, this cultural trait leads to a genetic separation between groups and the genetic separation, in turn, amplifies a distinct cultural evolution. Homogamy thus represents an impressive example of a genetic–cultural co-evolution (Richerson, Boyd, & Henrich, 2010). From an ultimate evolutionary perspective, these processes are of special interest for the evolution of groups and cultures. But from a social point of view, the separation of groups often is associated with conflicts between groups and extremism emphasizing aspects that differentiate groups from each other.

Modern societies are currently witnessing a process of cultural and genetic group separation on a large scale—a process that might lead to conflicts in the future: religious and ethnic assortative mating has been replaced by a high prevalence of educational homogamy. We assume that eventually educational homogamy may lead to a strong social and, via homogamy, possibly also to a genetic diversification of groups in modern societies. Although educational homogamy is not associated with a higher average number of children, it leads to a decrease in childlessness (Huber & Fieder, 2011; Van Bavel, 2012). Particularly highly educated women face nearly a doubling of the risk of childlessness if they are marrying a husband of lower education. There is no overall agreement on the underlying mechanisms, but maybe more similar marriages are more harmonious and thus childlessness could be less frequent (Huber & Fieder, 2011; Huber & Fieder, 2016).

Generally, data show that educational homogamy is particularly important for the higher educated strata of a society (Blackwell & Lichter, 2004; Huber & Fieder, 2011; Van Bavel, 2012). Female choice might be a driver of this kind of "educational tribalism". Although men are supposed to be willing to marry also a less-educated spouse (so-called "*marrying down*"), women usually search for a partner of the same or higher education (indicating an equal or higher status). Possibly this is the evolutionary relict of a search for a partner that presumably offers more resources for them and their offspring, a fundamental evolutionary principle demonstrated in tribal, traditional and even in modern societies (Fieder et al., 2005; Fieder & Huber, 2007; Hopcroft, 2006). Accordingly, as more educated women are on the "mating market", the tendency of men to marry "*down*" decreases, as more men marry homogamously. Due to educational homogamy, however, groups of similar educational attainment emerge. Moreover, as education is associated with social status, as a result, the social stratification of modern societies becomes more rigid and less permeable. So, educational groups start to "inbreed" and separate from each other and at the same time social openness decreases as particularly inter-marriage is thought to be both a cause and indicator of social openness (Birkelund & Heldal, 2003), fostering more equal distribution of status and wealth within soci-ety. Educational homogamy will thus become a major source of social inequality (Smits, 2003). As educational homogamy has such a high prevalence in modern societies, a dramatic reduction of the permeability (reduced upwards and down-wards mobility due to marriage) will emerge. This may also lead to an "intergenera-tional effect" as higher educated parents on average have also more educated children compared to lower educated couples. Hence educational homogamy will create in the long run a more diversified, but less equal society.

Education does not define political orientation per se, but generally, more edu-cated groups define themselves as ideologically to be more on the political left and more liberal versus those leaning towards the political right are attributed to the less educated. It is of course by far not that simple and the educated vs. the less educated represents more of a "group myth" to separate against the *others*, but the emergence of educational groups defined by marriage may lead to an increase in mutual incom-prehension. As educational groups are increasingly defined in some sort of "tribal" manner, we would anticipate more conflicts on the fault lines of educational strata than before, diversifying our societies in "new tribes".

Education is a rather recent item of group separation by homogamy, whereas homogamy by ethnicity and religions are much older group generating mechanisms. We know, for instance, that inter-ethnic marriages lead to a decrease in the repro-ductive output (Huber & Fieder, 2018), although religious homogamy compensates reproductively for ethnic heterogamy. During our more recent evolution in the early Stone Age in the Levant but also in East Asia, we began to settle in larger agglom-erations. It is to be assumed that people who gathered in these first larger settle-ments came from different tribal, cultural and religious backgrounds into these first "cities". To ensure genetic (intermarriage) and social cooperation between individu-als of different ancestry in those places, it was necessary to establish a common set of beliefs and values and an instance ensuring cooperative behaviour between peo-ple of different groups. This led to the birth of the so-called Big Gods (Norenzayan et al., 2016): a god who sees everything and punishes those who violate the rules. Presumably, marriage among individuals of different ethnicity may have led to a lower reproductive output, but religious homogamy may have overcome this repro-ductive loss and, thus, a common religion and religious homogamy may have brought fitness and hence selective benefits (Huber & Fieder, 2018). Concurrent with the advent of agriculture and the increase in food supplies for a larger number of people, this may have led to the spread of the newly emerging religions by the increasing number of progeny (Blume, 2009).

Religious homogamy is a very efficient cultural process of "genetic, social and cultural group building". Hence homogamy is a very strong means to form to some extent genetically related groups and in many but not all religions, a means to overcome ethnic and cultural boundaries, hence an impressive example of a cultural genetic co-evolution. The consequence of this strong tendency towards homogamy can be estimated simply with one number: the very high overall prevalence of religious homogamy of over 90% worldwide (Fieder & Huber, 2016).

To conclude, if ties within a group are strengthened, a logical consequence is to establish stronger boundaries towards outsiders in the context of "us" and "them". Historically, this separation has often been associated with some kind of hostile interactions. Someone may choose to demonstrate his or her group affiliation through an antipathy against out-group members and other groups, which might lead to violence in extreme cases. This extreme behaviour could be best interpreted with the concept of handicap theory and costly signalling (Zahavi, 1975; Gintis et al., 2001): showing solidarity and group affiliation at a high cost. These costs may consist of intensive rituals or even risking and/or sacrificing one's life for a religion or ideology and thus gaining social status within the group (Kiper & Sosis, 2016; Sosis & Alcorta, 2003). Accordingly, homogamy leads to cultural and genetic separation between groups and might also foster extreme characteristics of group differentiation.

Furthermore, in line with Hamilton (1964), the affiliation to someone's own group will be stronger if not only social ties but also ties of kinship are in place. Hence, on a social and cultural level, homogamy is the force that leads to ties beyond social relationships. These social ties are among the forces that differentiate humans from animals, as humans create biological niches with certain selection pressures through culture, which, enforced through homogamy, create a mutual feedback between culture and genetics.

References

Alford, J. R., Hatemi, P. K., Hibbing, J. R., Martin, N. G., & Eaves, L. J. (2011). The politics of mate choice. *The Journal of Politics, 73*(2), 362–379.

Anderson, A., Goel, S., Huber, G., Malhotra, N., & Watts, D. J. (2014). Political ideology and racial preferences in online dating. *Sociological Science, 1*, 28.

Birkelund, G. E., & Heldal, J. (2003). Who marries whom? Educational homogamy in Norway. *Demographic Research, 8*, 1–30. https://doi.org/10.4054/DemRes.2003.8.1

Bittles, A. H. (2012). *Consanguinity in context* (Vol. 63). Cambridge: Cambridge University Press.

Bittles, A. H., & Black, M. L. (2015). *Global patterns & tables of consanguinity*. Retrieved from http://consang.net

Blackwell, D. L., & Lichter, D. T. (2004). Homogamy among dating, cohabiting, and married couples. *The Sociological Quarterly, 45*(4), 719–737.

Blume, M. (2009). The reproductive benefits of religious affiliation. In *The biological evolution of religious mind and behavior* (pp. 117–126). Berlin, Heidelberg: Springer.

Ceballos, F. C., Joshi, P. K., Clark, D. W., Ramsay, M., & Wilson, J. F. (2018). Runs of homozygosity: Windows into population history and trait architecture. *Nature Reviews Genetics, 19*(4), 220.

Clark, D. W., Okada, Y., Moore, K. H., Mason, D., Pirastu, N., Gandin, I., ... Deelen, P. (2019). Associations of autozygosity with a broad range of human phenotypes. *Nature Communications, 10*, 1), 1–1),17.

Edmands, S. (2007). Between a rock and a hard place: Evaluating the relative risks of inbreeding and outbreeding for conservation and management. *Molecular Ecology, 16*, 463–475.

Fieder, M., & Huber, S. (2007). The effects of sex and childlessness on the association between status and reproductive output in modern society. *Evolution and Human Behavior, 28*(6), 392–398.

Fieder, M., & Huber, S. (2016). The association between religious homogamy and reproduction. *Proceedings of the Royal Society B: Biological Sciences, 283*(1834), 20160294.

Fieder, M., Huber, S., Bookstein, F. L., Iber, K., Schäfer, K., Winckler, G., & Wallner, B. (2005). Status and reproduction in humans: New evidence for the validity of evolutionary explanations on basis of a university sample. *Ethology, 111*(10), 940–950.

Fox, R. (2015). Marry in or die out. Optimal inbreeding and the meaning of mediogamy. In A. Turner, J. H. Machalek, & R. Maryanskipp (Eds.), *Handbook on evolution and society* (pp. 350–380). London: Routledge.

Fu, X., & Heaton, T. B. (2008). Racial and educational homogamy: 1980 to 2000. *Sociological Perspectives, 51*(4), 735–758.

Gintis, H., Smith, E. A., & Bowles, S. (2001). Costly signaling and cooperation. *Journal of theoretical biology, 213*(1), 103–119.

Hamilton, W. D. (1964). The genetical evolution of social behaviour. II. *Journal of Theoretical Biology, 7*(1), 17–52.

Helgason, A., Pálsson, S., Guðbjartsson, D. F., & Stefánsson, K. (2008). An association between the kinship and fertility of human couples. *Science, 319*(5864), 813–816.

Hopcroft, R. L. (2006). Sex, status, and reproductive success in the contemporary United States. *Evolution and Human Behavior, 27*(2), 104–120.

Huber, S., & Fieder, M. (2011). Educational homogamy lowers the odds of reproductive failure. *PLoS One, 6*(7), e22330.

Huber, S., & Fieder, M. (2016). Worldwide census data reveal prevalence of educational homogamy and its effect on childlessness. *Frontiers in Sociology, 1*, 10.

Huber, S., & Fieder, M. (2018). Mutual compensation of the effects of religious and ethnic homogamy on reproduction. *American Journal of Human Biology, 30*(1), e23064.

Joshi, P. K., Esko, T., Mattsson, H., Eklund, N., Gandin, I., Nutile, T., ... Okada, Y. (2015). Directional dominance on stature and cognition in diverse human populations. *Nature, 523*(7561), 459–462.

Kiper, J., & Sosis, R. (2016). The roots of intergroup conflict and the co-optation of the religious system. In J. R. Liddle & T. K. Shackelford (Eds.), *The Oxford handbook of evolutionary psychology and religion*. Oxford: Oxford University Press.

Marr, A. B., Keller, L. F., & Arcese, P. (2002). Heterosis and outbreeding depression in descendants of natural immigrants to an inbred population of song sparrows (Melospiza melodia). *Evolution, 56*(1), 131–142.

Marshall, T. C., & Spalton, J. A. (2000). Simultaneous inbreeding and outbreeding depression in reintroduced Arabian oryx. *Animal Conservation Forum, 3*, 241–248.

Norenzayan, A., Shariff, A. F., Gervais, W. M., Willard, A. K., McNamara, R. A., Slingerland, E., & Henrich, J. (2016). The cultural evolution of prosocial religions. *Behavioral and Brain Sciences, 39*, e29.

Relethford, J. H. (2012). *Human population genetics*. Hoboken, NJ: Wiley-Blackwell.

Richerson, P. J., Boyd, R., & Henrich, J. (2010). Gene-culture coevolution in the age of genomics. *Proceedings of the National Academy of Sciences, 107*(Supplement 2), 8985–8992. https://doi.org/10.1073/pnas.0914631107

Rushton, J. P. (1989). Genetic similarity, human altruism, and group selection. *Behavioral and Brain Sciences, 12*(3), 503–518.

Salter, F. (2018). The biosocial study of ethnicity. In R. Hopcroft (Ed.), *Oxford handbook of evolution, biology, and society* (pp. 543–568) ISBN-10: 0190299320.

Salter, F., & Harpending, H. (2013). JP Rushton's theory of ethnic nepotism. *Personality and Individual Differences, 55*(3), 256–260.

Seielstad, M. T., Minch, E., & Cavalli-Sforza, L. L. (1998). Genetic evidence for a higher female migration rate in humans. *Nature Genetics, 20*(3), 278.

Sikora, M., Seguin-Orlando, A., Sousa, V. C., Albrechtsen, A., Korneliussen, T., Ko, A., ... Renaud, G. (2017). Ancient genomes show social and reproductive behavior of early Upper Paleolithic foragers. *Science, 358*(6363), 659–662.

Smits, J. (2003). Social closure among the higher educated: Trends in educational homogamy in 55 countries. *Social Science Research, 32*, 251–277. https://doi.org/10.1016/S0049-089X(02)00049-2

Sosis, R., & Alcorta, C. (2003). Signaling, solidarity, and the sacred: The evolution of religious behavior. *Evolutionary Anthropology: Issues, News, and Reviews: Issues, News, and Reviews, 12*(6), 264–274.

Sterck, E. H. (1998). Female dispersal, social organization, and infanticide in langurs: are they linked to human disturbance?. *American Journal of Primatology, 44*(4), 235–254.

Stulp, G., Simons, M. J., Grasman, S., & Pollet, T. V. (2017). Assortative mating for human height: A meta-analysis. *American Journal of Human Biology, 29*(1), e22917.

Stulp, G., Verhulst, S., Pollet, T. V., Nettle, D., & Buunk, A. P. (2011). Parental height differences predict the need for an emergency caesarean section. *PLoS One, 6*(6), e20497.

Templeton, A. R. (1986). Coadaptation and outbreeding depression. In E. M. Soul (Ed.), *Conservation biology: The science of scar-city and diversity* (pp. 105–116). Sunderland, MA: Sinauer Association.

Towner, M. C. (2002). Linking dispersal and marriage in humans: Life history data from Oakham, Massachusetts, USA (1750–1850). *Evolution and Human Behavior, 23*(5), 337–357.

Turkheimer, E. (2000). Three laws of behavior genetics and what they mean. *Current Directions in Psychological Science, 9*(5), 160–164.

Van Bavel, J. (2012). The reversal of gender inequality in education, union formation and fertility in Europe. In *Vienna yearbook of population research* (pp. 127–154).

West, S. A., El Mouden, C., & Gardner, A. (2011). Sixteen common misconceptions about the evolution of cooperation in humans. *Evolution and Human Behavior, 32*(4), 231–262.

Zahavi, A. (1975). Mate selection—A selection for a handicap. *Journal of Theoretical Biology, 53*(1), 205–214.

Zietsch, B. P., Verweij, K. J., Heath, A. C., & Martin, N. G. (2011). Variation in human mate choice: Simultaneously investigating heritability, parental influence, sexual imprinting, and assortative mating. *The American Naturalist, 177*(5), 605–616.

Index

© Springer Nature Switzerland AG 2020
K. V. Aumer (ed.), *The Psychology of Extremism*,
https://doi.org/10.1007/978-3-030-59698-9